THE MAVERICK WAR: CHENNAULT AND THE FLYING TIGERS

ALSO BY DUANE SCHULTZ

Wake Island: The Heroic, Gallant Fight
Hero of Bataan: The Story of General Jonathan M. Wainwright
The Last Battle Station: The Story of the USS Houston

THE MAVERICK WAR: CHENNAULT AND THE FLYING TIGERS

DUANE SCHULTZ

ST. MARTIN'S PRESS
NEW YORK, N.Y.

THE MAVERICK WAR: CHENNAULT AND THE FLYING TIGERS.
Copyright © 1987 by Duane Schultz. All rights reserved.
Printed in the United States of America. No part of this
book may be used or reproduced in any manner whatsoever
without written permission except in the case of brief
quotations embodied in critical articles or reviews. For
information, address St. Martin's Press, 175 Fifth Avenue,
New York, N.Y. 10010.

Design by Kingsley Parker

Library of Congress Cataloging in Publication Data

Schultz, Duane P.
   The maverick war.
   1. United States. Army Air Forces. Air Force,
   14th—History. 2. Chennault, Claire Lee, 1890–1958.
   3. World War, 1939–1945—Aerial operations, American.
   I. Title
   DZ90.S338   1987   940.54′4973   87–4460
   ISBN 0-312-00618-7

First Edition

10 9 8 7 6 5 4 3 2 1

CONTENTS

Photographs follow page *182*
Map: China–Burma Theater on pages *x–xi*

In time of war the rebel against accepted doctrine who wins is decorated, promoted, and hailed as a great military captain, but in time of peace the nonconformist is looked upon as a troublemaker. He is seldom marked for promotion to higher rank and is generally retired or induced to resign.

Gen. George C. Kenney, USAF

Marshall and Arnold had made it quite plain that the Army held no future for me in China and that I would be barred from any significant participation in the victory. It was clearly time to go.

Gen. Claire Lee Chennault, USAF

THE MAVERICK WAR: CHENNAULT AND THE FLYING TIGERS

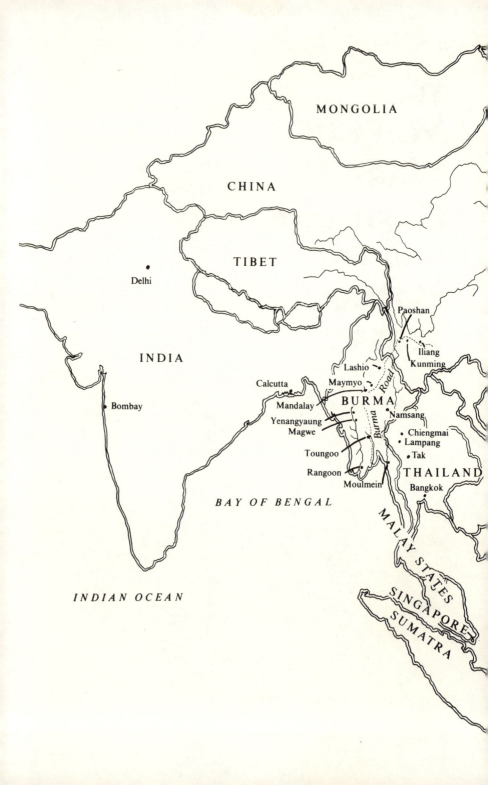

A CONSOLATION PRIZE AIR FORCE

Claire Chennault wanted to bomb Japan. He planned to burn out the industrial centers of the Japanese empire using incendiaries and create terror and chaos among the populace. On the face of it, there was nothing unusual about Chennault's plan. Every American air force general in the Pacific theater during World War II wanted to bomb Japan and bring the war home to the Japanese people.

Chennault, however, was not an air force general when he made his proposal. He wasn't even *in* the air force. He had been forced to retire from the service three years before, having made a shambles of his career as a result of his short temper, his insubordination, and his unorthodox ideas. He was now a civilian in the pay of a foreign power, a $15,000-a-year consultant to China with the rank of colonel in the Chinese air force. Furthermore, America was not yet at war with Japan. This was October 1940, more than a year before the attack on Pearl Harbor.

Chennault was proposing a preemptive strike, a covert operation against a country with which we had peaceful diplomatic relations. The bombing missions were to be carried out by American mercenaries, men released from the army and navy and paid by the United States government through a private corporation. They were to fly American planes painted with Chinese insignia. What made the plan all the more bizarre was that the highest officials in the government, including President Franklin Delano Roosevelt, approved of it. On July 23, 1941, some five months before Pearl Harbor, Roosevelt formally authorized the strikes. They were to begin the following November.

Chennault had been sent to Washington in October 1940 by his employer, Generalissimo Chiang Kai-shek, to carry out the most important mission he had ever undertaken, nothing less than the saving of China by American air power. As soon as he arrived in Washington, Chennault reported to a mansion on fashionable Woodley Road in the northwest section of the city, the home of Tse-ven Soong, one of the richest men in the world. Soong, the shrewd, rotund, Harvard-educated financial backer of his brother-in-law the Generalissimo, was well established in influential Washington circles.

Soong took Chennault to dinner with two reporters, Edgar Ansel Mowrer of the Chicago *Daily News* and Joseph Alsop, Jr., of the New York *Herald Tribune*. Alsop, a distant cousin of Roosevelt's, would later serve Chennault as a trusted aide in China and a conduit to the president. Chennault described his program for obtaining pilots and airplanes for China, but both reporters were pessimistic about his chances of getting them. Alsop was blunt. Given the needs of the Army Air Corps itself for planes, as well as the demands of the British, there would be nothing left over for China. At this Chennault became "rather cross," Alsop recalled. The fifty-year-old flyer had never been a good loser and was not about to take no for an answer. Nor was T. V. Soong.

Chennault was rebuffed again when he contacted his former colleagues in the Army Air Corps at their offices in Washington's Munitions Building. Their focus was on the war in Europe. They had no interest in China and no planes or men for her defense. And they certainly had nothing for Chennault, who, throughout his career had been too much of a maverick for them to take seriously.

In October 1940 their opinion of him was even worse. He was

considered a mercenary and a troublemaker. Neither Gen. Henry H. "Hap" Arnold, the air corps chief, nor Gen. George C. Marshall, the army chief of staff, had any use for this adventurer who had risen no higher than captain in 20 years of service and who now had the nerve to call himself a "Colonel" in the by-God Chinese air force!

But Chennault had powerful friends and allies, and they were being taken more seriously. The China Lobby was a force to be reckoned with. It reached into the Cabinet and into the White House itself.

On November 30, 1940, T. V. Soong presented Chennault's ideas to Henry Morgenthau, the secretary of the treasury, who had just approved—at Roosevelt's insistence—a $100-million loan to the Chinese government. Soong told Morgenthau that Chennault's proposed Special Air Unit, to consist of 500 planes paid for, piloted, and maintained by the United States, could defeat the Japanese army in China, neutralize the Japanese navy, and destroy Tokyo and other Japanese cities. (Historian Barbara Tuchman noted a "quality of fantasy" about Chennault's proposals.)

To Morgenthau, the plan did not seem the least fantastic. He had long been the administration's leading supporter of aid to China. He realized, as did Roosevelt, that the United States needed to help China in some fashion, if only for its own self-interest. War was coming, probably a global war, to be fought against both the Germans and the Japanese. Military and political planning dictated a Germany-first policy, with the major effort devoted to the European theater. Japan would have to come second.

China had been at war with Japan for three years. Its vast territory required Japan to commit huge armies, totaling some one million men, to its conquest. If China surrendered, those troops would be free to fight the Americans and the British throughout the Pacific. It was imperative that the United States assist China and keep her in the war. Equipment and supplies must be provided, but problems of getting that materiel there were becoming acute. Many Chinese ports had been captured by the invading Japanese, and the only land route left into the country was the tortuous Burma Road. Even that lifeline was now within range of Japanese aircraft. What remained of the Chinese air force was helpless. The only way to keep the road open and China fighting was with American air power.

Morgenthau liked Chennault's plan. Here was a way to boost Chinese morale, to damage Japanese forces, and, perhaps, to deter Japanese leaders from risking war with the United States. It was a small investment for such potentially large gains. Further, by attacking Japan in this indirect manner, in planes bearing Chinese markings, the United States would have no formal involvement. This in turn would lessen the chances of provoking a war before American naval, land, and air forces in the Pacific were ready.

Apparently, Morgenthau had no qualms about the morality of launching an attack, however indirectly, on another sovereign nation or about the possible consequences if Japan retaliated. Nor did he seem to be concerned about world opinion or the reaction of the American public. Indeed, few people in the administration, including the president, expressed such concerns.

Three days later Morgenthau consulted with Lord Lothian, the British ambassador to the United States. He knew that the only way to provide enough planes for Chennault would be to divert some of the aircraft already allocated to England. Lord Lothian later described the plan as "impracticable," but his initial reaction was enthusiastic. "It might change everything," he told Morgenthau.

On December 8, almost exactly one year before Japan's surprise attack on Pearl Harbor, Morgenthau talked with President Roosevelt over lunch and later met with T. V. Soong.

"Asking for five hundred planes is like asking for five hundred stars," Morgenthau told Soong, but then he asked Soong what he thought about getting some bombers for China, with the understanding that they would be used to attack Japanese cities. "To say [Soong] was enthusiastic is putting it mildly," recorded Morgenthau in his diary.

Morgenthau cautioned Soong that he had not yet talked to the president, but he intimated that Roosevelt favored the bombing of Japan. He was stretching the facts but not by much. Roosevelt had remarked to him in passing that it would be "a nice thing if the Chinese would bomb Japan."

On December 10, Morgenthau called on Cordell Hull, the secretary of state, to try to persuade him to support Chennault's plan. Morgenthau recalled that before he could begin, Hull said, "What we have got to do, Henry, is to get five hundred American planes to start from the Aleutian Islands and fly over Japan just once. . . . That will teach them a lesson. . . . If we could only find some way to have them drop some bombs on Tokyo." Obviously the China Lobby had done Morgenthau's work for him.

The next step was to present the idea formally to the president and his Cabinet, which Morgenthau did on December 19. "Wonderful!" Roosevelt exclaimed. After the meeting the president asked Morgenthau, Hull, Secretary of War Henry Stimson, and Secretary of the Navy Frank Knox to stay and begin work on the plans. The men assembled around a map that Soong had prepared showing the locations of the airfields that Chennault had constructed for the long-range bombers he hoped to get. The bases were only 650 miles from Japan.

"Should we work it out and come back?" Morgenthau asked. But Roosevelt wanted the job done now. "The four of you work out a program," he repeated.

The following day a delighted Soong brought Chennault and Morgenthau together to discuss the details including the number of planes the Chinese would need and the best type of aircraft for the mission. Chennault argued for the four-engine B-17 bomber instead of the twin-engine Lockheed Hudson the British were using. With the longer-range B-17s, Chennault said, they could reach not only Tokyo but also Osaka, Kobe, and Nagasaki. Chennault also wanted 200 fighter planes to protect the Chinese airfields.

Chennault and Morgenthau agreed that the bomber crews would be American personnel. Morgenthau proposed that the planes be flown from the West Coast to Clark Field in the Philippines and from there to the bases in China. He believed that the army would release the bomber crews from active duty, and he suggested that the men be paid $1000 per month.

Morgenthau seemed keen on knowing the details of Chennault's plan. He was enthusiastic about the proposed use of incendiary bombs, "inasmuch as the Japanese cities were all made of just wood and paper. . . . Chennault said that a lot of damage could be done using this method," Morgenthau wrote, "and that, even if the Chinese lost some of the bombers, it would be well justified."

By now the bombing plan had gained so much support and momentum in high government circles that it seemed nothing could stop it, but one man in Roosevelt's Cabinet was less enthusiastic: Secretary of War Stimson. He invited Morgenthau, Knox, and Marshall to his home on Sunday afternoon, December 22, for an informal discussion of the project.

"As usual," Stimson later wrote in his notes on that meeting, "the demand boils down to land planes—planes for our army—and threatens to deplete us more. The proposition as it was made to us the other day was rather half-baked. It hadn't been thought out. It was the product of Chinese strategists rather than well-thought-out American strategy and I called this meeting to try to get some mature brains into it, before we got committed to it."

The mature brains belonged to General Marshall, and he had opposed the project from the beginning. He called the plan "impractical." The United States had neither the bombers nor the trained crews to spare. Any planes given to China would be at the expense of England and of American preparedness. In addition, Marshall voiced the concern no one else had, that the bombing of Japan by American planes with American crews would provoke a Japanese counterattack against the United States at a time when we were woefully unprepared to go to war. Marshall also opposed any operation outside of the normal army chain of command and, thus, not subject to military control. In short, he said, Chennault's plan was too costly, too dangerous, and too unorthodox.

General Marshall was highly respected, and his arguments persuaded Morgenthau to change his mind. Morgenthau reported Marshall's views to the president, and the plan was dropped. However, everyone involved, including Marshall, knew that some assistance would have to be provided for China. The Burma Road had to be protected, and there was still the need to keep Japan involved militarily in China.

And so, as solace for the Chinese, as consolation for Chennault, the government committed 100 fighter planes to China. They could be used only for defensive purposes because they lacked the range to reach Japan. The British agreed to waive delivery of 100 P-40Bs in exchange for 100 later models of the same plane.

Chennault now had his air force. The P-40B was not the fastest or the best fighter available, but it was an improvement over what he had been working with in China for the past three years.

If Chennault was disappointed about not getting bombers, he did not show it. He was, after all, a fighter pilot. In his last years in the Army Air Corps he had become their leading expert on fighter tactics, although few people in the service had paid any attention. Like the man himself, Chennault's views were too controversial, and he had fought a losing battle to get them accepted, ruining his health and his career in the process.

He expected to prove the worth of his ideas in the skies over China. He had just been handed a private air force of 100 fighters—the American Volunteer Group (AVG). He now had his own independent operation and his own war. Claire Chennault was a happy man with his consolation prize air force. He would show them all that only *he* knew how to wage war in the air.

Chennault was not the only person for whom the 100 P-40s of the AVG represented an opportunity. For him, the planes were a fighting machine and a chance for the vindication of his ideas. For others, they represented a financial windfall. An enormous amount of money was involved, and for a time this almost scuttled the project. The fighter planes themselves cost $4.5 million. There were supplies to be purchased, maintenance costs, and salaries for the pilots, ground crew, and staff. The AVG formed only a small part of the overall aid package to China. Profit could be made by the intermediaries and the corporations that were established to facilitate the flow of goods and services.

Soong organized a company called China Defense Supplies

(CDS) to handle all American aid to China. Into its offices at 1601 V Street, Northwest, in Washington, came some of the best-connected men in Washington. They had been carefully cultivated by Soong to give him access to every important executive agency.

Among the most prominent of those to be employed by CDS was Tommy "the Cork" Corcoran, an affable attorney who served as legal counsel. During Roosevelt's first two terms as president, Corcoran had been his speech writer, confidant, and architect of much New Deal legislation. He left the government—but not Roosevelt's inner circle—to become a lobbyist, and he soon acquired a reputation as "a high-priced lawyer peddling inside government information to big business." A controversial figure, often the target of allegations of impropriety (none of which was ever proven), Corcoran was to remain associated with Chennault long after the war. Corcoran later wrote, "Chennault and I were in this China racket. . . . It was the great adventure of my life."

At first, Corcoran had not been impressed with Chennault, looking upon him as a fanatic. Later he developed a deep respect for the man. Chennault, Corcoran said, "explained enough in an hour to make me believe I was dealing with something original, whether it was genius or madness." He also remarked that he would hate to be Chennault's boss, that the ex-pilot would no doubt be a difficult subordinate. Corcoran was absolutely correct on that point.

Corcoran's brother David was named president of China Defense Supplies. One of the directors was Frederic Delano, the president's uncle. The corporate secretary was Whiting Willauer, who later became a partner in Chennault's postwar airline in China. The bonds forged between Chennault and these men were deep and long-lasting, and beneficial to them all. Chennault, too, was on the payroll of China Defense Supplies.

Another organization was established to recruit and pay the men of the American Volunteer Group. This was the Central Aircraft Manufacturing Corporation (CAMCO), jointly owned by H. H. Kung, who was Madame Chiang's brother-in-law and China's finance minister, and William Pawley, an aviation entrepreneur who for years had been selling American aircraft to the

Chinese government. Pawley also worked for CDS, which pro-vided all of CAMCO's operating funds. CAMCO would be the nominal employer of the AVG personnel. Chennault would be carried on its books as a "supervisor."

It was Pawley's financial dealings that almost grounded the AVG in the beginning. He held a long-term contract with the Curtiss-Wright Company, builder of the P-40 fighter plane, which granted him a 10 percent commission on all planes sold to China. Pawley demanded his $450,000 commission on the 100 P-40s, even though he had not been involved in their sale. He threatened to seek a court injunction prohibiting shipment of the planes to China until he received his commission.

Curtiss-Wright refused to pay, and for three months negotia-tions proved futile. The company prepared to resell the planes to England. Finally, on April 1, 1941, Morgenthau arranged a show-down meeting that lasted the entire day. The Chinese were desper-ate. They had already lost too much valuable time while Japanese forces were continuing their advance. They offered to pay Pawley's commission themselves, but Morgenthau objected to anyone's paying Pawley for a sale he had not arranged. Mor-genthau tried to intimidate Pawley by threatening to take over his Curtiss-Wright contract as a war emergency measure, but Pawley refused to back down.

Late in the day, out of weariness, frustration, and anger, a com-promise was reached. Pawley would be paid $250,000, and his company, CAMCO, would receive a contract to assemble, test, and service the P-40s at their assembly plant in Loiwing, China, located near the border with Burma. Under this arrangement, Pawley stood to make a good deal more money from the activities of the AVG.

The impasse had been broken, but there would be other deal-ings with Pawley that would leave Chennault with a bitterness that smoldered until well after the war.

At the end of April 1941, the P-40s were loaded aboard a slow Norwegian freighter in New York harbor, the only transport avail-able. As one plane was being hoisted, a cargo sling broke and dropped the fuselage into the water. Everyone hoped it wasn't an omen. Now there were only 99 planes.

President Roosevelt had made it legal for U.S. citizens to take up arms for another country. On April 15, 1941, he signed a secret executive order that permitted men on active duty with the army and navy to sign contracts with CAMCO for one year of service in China, after which they could rejoin the military with no loss of rank. Only a few years earlier, the State Department had seized the passports of those Americans who tried to fight for the Republicans in the Spanish Civil War. Now, instead of confiscating passports, the State Department was agreeing to falsify them for the men on their way to fight for China.

With reluctance, but recognizing his powerlessness in the face of Roosevelt's executive order, air corps chief Hap Arnold and Rear Adm. Jack Tower of the navy's Bureau of Aeronautics agreed to release men to fight with Chennault. Recruiters from CAMCO, former military pilots, were allowed to visit army and navy airfields to make their appeals. When Chennault asked Arnold for trained staff officers, however, Arnold refused. Chennault pleaded, reducing his request to six, then to three, and finally to one, but Arnold remained adamant. Chennault himself had had no staff training and was ill-equipped to fight his kind of war without staff support and planning, but there was nothing he could do. He was forced to improvise, and he would later be criticized for sloppy staff work. "I had to use whatever American adventurers I could find knocking about in the Orient," he wrote.

While his P-40s were on their way to China, Chennault was deskbound in the Washington offices of CDS. His air force had to be equipped from scratch with everything it would need. Chennault had no assistance and no precedents on which to base his efforts. He was able to arrange with a Chinese agency, the War Area Service Corps, to feed and house his men for $1 per day per man. The agency was run by Jerry Huang—"a huge jolly Santa Claus of a man," Chennault wrote—who had a Ph.D. from Columbia University and a flare for making foreigners feel at home in China.

Chennault had to estimate the amount of food his pilots and crew would eat, the monthly order of steaks, chops, eggs, and chickens. He designed their quarters, which he called "hostels," deciding on room sizes, hot water consumption, and the required number of latrines. He quickly learned that getting his force airborne required a knowledge of more than fighter tactics. He would need much more than gasoline and bullets, and if he failed to arrange for all the necessary equipment from his desk in V Street, the AVG might have to do without it. They would find little of what they would require in China.

"I had to prepare requisitions for every piece of equipment we needed—how many rounds of ammunition, how many pounds of oxygen, flying suits, paper clips, six-ton trucks, machine-gun barrels, ink, candy, sun goggles, shaving cream, razor blades, medical supplies, carbon paper, typewriters, and all the other strange gear with which an air war was fought. Dr. Soong gave me *carte blanche* on supplies. 'Buy what you need and send me the bills,' were his only orders."

While Chennault was equipping his air force, his plan to bomb Japan, dropped abruptly the previous December, was being revived. The person responsible was Dr. Lauchlin Currie, an economist who had served as a White House aide. In the spring of 1941, Currie was appointed a special envoy to China. As a result, the center of policymaking with regard to China shifted from Morgenthau and the Treasury Department to Currie and the White House. Currie allied himself with the Chinese cause and pressed for increases in aid. Morgenthau once complained to his staff, "the trouble with Mr. Currie is, I don't know half the time whether he is working for the president or T. V. Soong."

President Roosevelt now listened more to Currie than to Morgenthau, and Currie was listening to Chiang Kai-shek, to T. V. Soong, and to Claire Chennault. He was attentive to their suggestions to revive Chennault's bombing plan. On May 28, he developed a formal proposal to provide Chennault with an initial force of 66 twin-engine Lockheed Hudsons and Douglas DB-7s (the export version of the A-24 bomber), along with pilots, bombardiers, and crew, for the purpose of bombing Japan. More planes and crew would be sent as soon as they became available. B-17s, Chennault's preference, were out of the question; they were too scarce and too valuable to risk losing. Currie urged that the plan be made operational within five months, by October 31, 1941.

The first bombing raids on Japan would be scheduled for the month of November.

Currie believed that the bombing would inhibit Japanese aggression against Singapore, the Dutch East Indies, and the Philippines and would provide valuable combat experience for the American crews. The bomber force would serve as a constant threat to the Japanese and, when it reached its full strength of 150 planes, could cripple Japanese production of munitions and other war materiel. All of this could be achieved without the direct involvement of the United States government and its military services.

Currie submitted his proposal to the Joint Army-Navy Board of the War Department. It was labeled JB Paper 355. The timing was fortuitous for Currie and Chennault. While the project was being considered, the situation in the Far East was rapidly deteriorating. In June, Germany invaded the Soviet Union, freeing Japan of any concern about being attacked by her old adversary. Japan no longer needed to look warily to the north and west. She could focus her military might on the south and the rich oil and rubber resources of the British and Dutch colonies.

On July 4, American intelligence agencies learned of Japanese intentions in the Pacific. The Japanese diplomatic code had been broken, so the United States knew that Japan's first step would be the occupation of French Indochina, which action took place on July 21. Japan would then advance on the British and Dutch possessions, committed to further conquest.

Throughout July, debate raged in the White House over the best response to the Japanese aggression. An embargo on the sale of oil to Japan was proposed, but military leaders opposed it. They believed it would leave Japan with no choice but to go to war with the United States because Japan had no oil of her own. A navy report warned the president that such an embargo "would probably result in a fairly early attack by Japan on Malaya and the Netherlands East Indies, and possibly involve the United States in early war in the Pacific." For a time, Roosevelt agreed. He told Undersecretary of State Sumner Welles on July 18 that the imposition of an oil embargo on Japan "would mean war in the Pacific."

The message was plain. Yet shortly, that was precisely what Roosevelt did. Perhaps he recalled a recent letter from Secretary of the Interior Harold Ickes, who had written, "There might develop from the embargoing of oil to Japan such a situation as would make it not only possible but easy to get into this war in an effective way. And if we should thus indirectly be brought in, we should avoid the criticism that we had gone in as an ally of communistic Russia." Whether to prevent war or to get into it in an effective way, the president announced an embargo on trade with Japan on July 26.

The cessation of trade left Japan with no more than a 12-month stockpile of oil to run her economy and war machine. The only way Japan could obtain more oil would be by force from the Dutch East Indies or by agreeing to American demands to get out of China, which the Japanese could not do. The loss of face would be intolerable.

Public opinion polls in the United States revealed that the majority of the American people approved of the trade sanctions. Americans were distressed by Japan's aggression, and public sentiment was growing for direct action. Cordell Hull commented that nothing would stop the Japanese "except force."

Newspapers, magazines, and radio gave the trade embargo considerable publicity. The people were not told, however, that three days earlier, Roosevelt had approved Chennault's plan for a preemptive strike against Japan. The idea was to hit Japan before Japan could attack the United States, but only indirectly, using civilian pilots in aircraft with Chinese markings. Soong and Pawley immediately initiated plans to purchase and ship the bombers to China and to hire the pilots and crew for this Second American Volunteer Group.

Chennault was traveling during most of July. On July 7, he was staying at the Mark Hopkins Hotel in San Francisco, where he met with the first of three contingents of the volunteers for his new air force. "Nobody who saw that odd assortment of young men," he wrote, "looking slightly ill at ease and uncertain in their new civilian clothes, could have possibly imagined that in a few months' time they would be making history."

The operation was supposed to be a secret, complete with false passports and warnings to the men to reveal nothing about their destination, but the country knew all about it before the first ship sailed. The June 23, 1941, issue of *Time* magazine informed its readers that 100 P-40s had reached Burma, where they would be flown by "crack U.S. Army Air Corps pilots" who had been allowed to resign their commissions to fly air patrols over the Burma Road. "Tall, bronzed American airmen have been quietly slipping away from east- and west-coast ports making their way to Asia."

Chennault caught the Pan American Clipper in San Francisco on July 8, traveling on a passport that identified him as a farmer. After stopping in Hawaii and Manila, he arrived in Rangoon on July 23. To his dismay, most of his P-40s were sitting on the dock, still in their crates. A telegram marked "secret" from Lauchlin Currie brought better news:

> I AM HAPPY TO BE ABLE TO REPORT THAT TODAY THE PRESIDENT DIRECTED THAT SIXTY-SIX BOMBERS BE MADE AVAILABLE TO CHINA THIS YEAR WITH TWENTY-FOUR TO BE DELIVERED IMMEDIATELY.

Through the rest of the summer of 1941 and into the fall, as Chennault organized and trained the First American Volunteer Group—his fighter group—he planned for the arrival of the Second. Telegrams raced between Burma, where Chennault was training his pilots, and Washington, D.C., full of news about his preparations for the bombing missions. Chennault was energetic and eager, calculating the number and types of personnel the bombers would need and how they could best be flown to China. He favored the Pan American Clipper route via Honolulu, Wake Island, Guam, and Manila. "From Manila these bombers could be flown away at night so as to arrive at any designated airdrome in China just before dawn." He recommended a bonus payment for all bomber crews who completed their mission successfully, an extra payment of five cents per mile.

There were to be no bonus payments. There were no preemptive incendiary raids on Japan. Production and shipping bottlenecks delayed the arrival of Chennault's bombers. On November

22, Currie informed Roosevelt that he hoped the planes and crews would reach Chennault by the end of the year. On November 21, 49 ground crewmen for the bombers had embarked from California on the long voyage to China. They were still at sea on December 7 when their ship was diverted to Australia. Also on December 7, 18 twin-engine Hudsons were sitting on Lockheed's airfield in Burbank, California, waiting for cargo space. That was as close as they ever got to China.

All Chennault had on the day the Japanese attacked Pearl Harbor was his consolation prize air force of 99 outdated P-40s. His men had not yet seen combat, nor would they for two more weeks. When they finally did fight, they became the legend the world knew as the Flying Tigers. Chennault became a hero to everyone except the top brass of the air force. To Hap Arnold and the others he remained the maverick, an outspoken misfit who flouted regulations and disregarded the chain of command, who insisted on fighting his war in his own fashion. Those traits were the source of Chennault's greatness and the seeds of his eventual and inevitable downfall.

T W O

YOU WILL NEVER MAKE A SOLDIER

Chennault's face betrayed his character, as though he wanted there to be no question about it. He looked exactly like what he was—belligerent, aggressive, combative. This was easy to see in his jutting jaw, his lips pressed into a tight thin line, his fierce black eyes that stared out from half-closed eyelids. Gen. Albert C. Wedemeyer remarked that Chennault's "protruding chin . . . announced grit and extreme determination." He looked as though he had been "chiseled out of granite."

"What an extraordinary face Chennault had," wrote Eve Curie, journalist and daughter of French chemists Marie and Pierre Curie. "What a wonderful face! His features were sharp-cut, his hair and eyes were very black. The lean, heavily lined cheeks and forehead, tanned, sunburned, speckled, seemed to be made of wornout leather. His could have been the face of a buccaneer, of a great *condottiere* [adventurer] of centuries past."

Chennault was a fighter, which he proclaimed in the title of his autobiography, *Way of a Fighter*. Those who knew him did not have to be told that. They described him as "a rough, tough, ready-to-go guy," someone who had the "look and manner of a brave about to go on the warpath." They saw him as a man who loved nothing better than battling against the odds, whose fierceness and determined manner showed in everything he did.

He hated to lose, to come in second, or to compromise. He had to win, whether at a game of softball or at war. "I had an insatiable urge to win," he wrote of himself as a child. "I constantly strove to be the first in anything I undertook. I simply had to run faster, jump farther, swim faster, dive deeper, catch the longest string of fish, shoot better, make the best grades in all of my classes, do the most work on the farm, and read more books than any of my contemporaries."

He was the same at age fifty out in China. Gen. Bruce Holloway, who flew for Chennault, recalled that Chennault was "about the poorest loser that I have ever seen. We would play softball and he was the pitcher on my ball team. He was a pretty good pitcher except he would get tired after about the third or fourth inning. We would always be ahead then and we would always lose the game. Couldn't get him out of there. So he would sort of sulk off. That dispirited him.

"Then we would go home and that night—we had a badminton net out there and he would want to play badminton. Any one of us could beat him at badminton. Then he would want to play Ping-Pong. Any one of us could beat him at Ping-Pong. Then he would get lower and lower as this would go on, and if we had any whiskey, we would drink that. He would sometimes end up wanting to wrestle somebody, and he would usually challenge Casey Vincent, who was the biggest guy. Casey would stave him off usually until he went off to bed. But once in awhile he would grab Casey and would end up getting thrown over in the corner. He was just a terribly poor loser."

Chennault had to win in the world of ideas, too, particularly when dealing with his superiors. To compromise was to lose. "He couldn't get along with anybody above him unless they absolutely agreed with him," Holloway said. "If they didn't get along with him, they were just categorically wrong and he was right. He didn't know the meaning of the word 'compromise.' He didn't understand it, didn't do it; that's why he got fired in the first place and shipped off to China where nobody would have ever heard of him." Another old friend said that to Chennault, "there were only two kinds of people—those who agreed with him and those who didn't." As a result, even in his younger days in the air corps, while many people admired his skill at flying and his dedication to his beliefs about air warfare, they found him abrasive and contentious.

Chennault became defensive when he had to explain or justify his decisions and actions to his superiors. He believed he worked best when left alone. Even as a child, he had not been able to reveal his innermost thoughts and feelings to anyone who was older or in a position of authority. The war in China, his war, was made to order for him. He answered to no one. He was in full control, at least until U.S. army officers with briefcases began to appear in China in the months following Pearl Harbor. Then he began having to take orders again, to explain his decisions, and to deal with superiors who did not always, or even often, agree with him.

He was overly sensitive to criticism from superior officers. He often felt slighted and persecuted even when there was no basis for such feelings. He was quickly offended and roused to anger by real or imagined slurs. He saw insults where none was intended. If a superior disagreed with him, Chennault believed it was a personal attack. Thus, dealing with superiors was extremely difficult for him. Not only was it hard for him to justify his actions to them, and not only was he easily offended by any implied or actual criticism, but he also lacked the ability to present his viewpoint well. While he could be a master of persuasion with friends and subordinates, he was usually not articulate or effective in putting forth his ideas to his superiors.

It is perhaps easy to understand why Chennault had little success in the 1930s in persuading air corps leaders to accept his unorthodox ideas about how air warfare should be conducted. Belligerence and defensiveness are not the characteristics that make for success in any endeavor. If we add to those the social problems Chennault faced in the prewar army air corps, it is not hard to see why he rose no higher than the rank of captain in peacetime.

His long-time aide, Joseph Alsop, said, "Nothing was more

snobbish than those prewar army bases, and Chennault had no social graces himself." His sometimes rough, sometimes coarse demeanor did not always fit well with the more polished bearing of many officers of that time, particularly those in the cavalry, the leading and most socially conscious branch of the army.

In addition, there was the matter of Chennault's education compared with that of the majority of his peers and superiors. He was not a graduate of the Military Academy at West Point. Indeed, he was not even a college graduate. He had attended a Louisiana state normal school and had taught school and held a series of odd jobs before joining the army. Also, although he knew as much as anyone in the country about fighter tactics, he had little interest in anything else. His training, credentials, and background could not compare favorably with those of most of his superiors, and that alone may well have caused them to feel justified in rejecting his views.

Chennault's education within the army was also limited. He was never given the opportunity to attend the Command and General Staff School or any of the other higher-level schools designed to prepare officers for the responsibilities of high command. He had received no training in logistics, supply, personnel, strategic matters, or any other aspect of fighting a broad-scale war. As a result, even his admirers had to admit that while he was a tactical genius, he was a poor strategist who had little understanding of the role of ground forces. War correspondent Eric Sevareid said that Chennault "had developed the arts of combat tactics almost to perfection. But he was a limited technician—not, I thought, a man of expansive imagination, capable of handling the immense strategic and political problems which American officers were contending with in all parts of the world."

Before the formation of the Flying Tigers, and long before World War II, General Arnold and the top brass of the air corps had viewed Chennault with suspicion. Once he became active— and famous—in China, they were even more skeptical. They saw him as a mercenary, fighting for economic gain as well as personal glory. Gen. Laurence Kuter recalled that, to Arnold, "Chennault was an anathema, and he could see no good in him at all." Whispered allegations circulated in Washington that Chennault was involved in the black market and that he had love affairs with Chinese women. "How can you trust such a dissolute man?" said General Marshall.

Marshall conceded that Chennault might be a tactical genius, but he considered him unfit for command. He "despised Chennault's machinations and told him to his face that he did not trust him." Chennault was aware of Marshall's feelings. "I was *persona non grata* with Marshall," he wrote.

In light of all this official disdain for Chennault and his ideas, it is remarkable that he remained in the military as long as he did. He fought in China—first with his consolation prize air force of civilians and later as a major general commanding the Fourteenth Air Force—from 1941 to a few weeks before the Japanese surrender, when Marshall and Arnold were able to get rid of him. He lasted so long, despite his faults and the animosity toward him, in part because he was so good at his job. He was indeed a tactical genius in air warfare. His ideas had been proved correct time after time. General Holloway recalled, "I always listened to Chennault. He was always right as far as I was concerned on anything that involved tactics."

But there was more. Chennault was also a genius in leading and inspiring his men to give their best. He had an "intoxicating spirit," wrote Eve Curie, "enough will power and enthusiasm to lift the world." He was not a good follower, he was a terrible subordinate, but he could lead others as few could. In a tribute to his former commander, Gen. John Alison wrote, "In wartime military men possessing unusual talents largely unrecognized in a peaceful world suddenly appear at the top. They are the heroes who unify a nation at war behind its fighting men. They are men of high professional aptitude . . . and in most cases men with personalities that set them apart from their peers. Above all, they have a charisma that causes bold men to dedicate their lives to their leadership. Chennault was certainly one of these."

Chennault was an impressive figure of a man. He knew it and took pride in it. He stood five feet, ten inches tall, had a stocky build, and seemed to radiate an intense natural magnetism. He enjoyed making an impression, posing and posturing in dramatic outfits. Paul Frillman, the AVG chaplain, remembered the first time he saw Chennault, at a Fourth of July celebration in Hankow, China, in 1938. Chennault looked "very much the soldier of fortune . . . with a silk aviator's neck scarf, and other accessories."

Three years later, when Frillman and a contingent of AVG members arrived by ship at Rangoon, Burma, he saw Chennault again. "That day on the docks he was wearing some slapdash adventurous costume as usual—mosquito boots, officer's shirt with Chinese insignia, beat-up Air Force cap—which emphasized his gamecock look. Watching him for only a few minutes, anyone would get the impression of informality and lack of military pomp, plus a quick, sure air of decisive authority. I don't think any of the men on our ship had ever seen him before, and as I looked down the rail where they were lined up, staring silently at him, I could see that for the time being anyway, Chennault had them all in his hip pocket."

For formal occasions with the AVG Chennault wore a U.S. Army Air Corps uniform that he had customized. The buttons displayed the 12-pointed Chinese star, and Chinese wings were pinned above the left breast pocket. The shoulder straps sported two wide blue stripes with a bright red stripe in between.

Everyone who knew Chennault remarked on the leathery look of his face, that of a man who had flown for many years in open-cockpit planes, in sun, wind, and rain. His skin was the color of mahogany, so wrinkled and etched with lines that it reminded some of the bark of an oak tree. Tangled crow's feet cut deeply into the skin around the corners of his eyes.

The years of open-cockpit flying had also impaired his hearing. Some said he was "deaf as a post," but others, such as Greg Boyington, noticed that "the old man could hear everything he wasn't supposed to hear."

Chennault's accent was memorable, too, and it changed in different situations from a straightforward Southern drawl to a thick Louisiana delta dialect that could be almost incomprehensible. A chronic bronchial condition caused him to have to clear his throat before he spoke, and when he got angry he would suck in his teeth and make a kind of clicking sound.

He was vain about his appearance and proud of his physique, which he kept in shape through vigorous exercise. He was also, in the idiom of the day, "a ladies' man." Women were attracted to him, and a friend noted bluntly that Chennault was "a damn fool about women." The wife of one of his oldest friends noted that he had "rugged, even ugly, features, but when he walked in a room, even a crowded one, every woman knew he was there." Olga Greenlaw, the wife of the AVG chief of staff, whose own job was to maintain the outfit's war diary, said that Chennault liked the "feminine things about women—pretty clothes, flowers, and fragrant scents." She later added ". . . he can be as charming and gallant as only a southerner can."

Chennault also liked to have a good time. He was rarely without a Camel cigarette stuck in the corner of his mouth, looking as though it had been glued there. His eyes would narrow to keep the smoke out and he could carry on a lively conversation with the cigarette in place, leaving a trail of ashes in his wake.

In his younger days, he had the reputation of being a hard drinker, and he liked to tell the story of how whiskey had once saved his life. In 1919, the year of the influenza pandemic that took countless thousands of lives, Chennault, then a young lieutenant at Langley Field, Virginia, was stricken with the disease. Barely conscious, he overheard the doctor say he would be dead before morning. He was left in a shed next to the morgue where a friend found him. The man brought Chennault a quart of bourbon, which had been confiscated from rum runners during those days of Prohibition, and ordered him to drink it all. A few days later, Chennault was well.

Chennault took his bourbon straight, but by the time he was in China he never took more than two drinks during an evening. But he did not moderate his love of hot, spicy foods. He ate heartily of the fiery Chinese pepper sauces that reminded him of Louisiana cooking. Madame Chiang Kai-shek and her two sisters (Madame Sun Yat-sen and Madame H. H. Kung)* kept Chennault well sup-

---

*The three women were sisters of T. V. Soong. Ai-ling Soong, married to H. H. Kung, China's finance minister, was known for her financial shrewdness. May-ling Soong, married to Generalissimo Chiang Kai-shek, was believed to be

plied. Friends from the States and from Mexico sent him chiles pequeños and jalapeños, which he ate like candy. The ladies of Chungking competed with one another to provide him with fermented bean curd. He would cover it with a sauce of pounded red peppers and pepper oil and spread it all on toast.

When Chennault relaxed with a few close friends after a long day of training or combat, he was full of humor and fun to be around. He liked to tell stories about the stunts he had pulled— some in an airplane and some at a desk—and to complain about the brass. His jaw would jut out as he recalled some slight. "Christ from Vicksburg!" he'd shout. "Quite a fellow, that Claire Chennault," said Larry Kuter.

Chennault had come a long way from the day he saw his first airplane. He was twenty years old, and it was a sight he never forgot. In the summer of 1910 at the Shreveport, Louisiana, state fair, a flimsy Curtiss pusher biplane wobbled noisily overhead. To Chennault, the plane appeared to be both a miracle and a way out of his dull existence. "I was looking for bright new worlds to conquer." He was feeling as though he had been born too late, at a time when all the frontiers had been tamed. The West was settled, the Indians were no longer on the warpath, and the country had been at peace for a decade. What was he to do with his life? On that stifling summer day as he watched the airplane, he knew he had found the answer. There was one more frontier—aviation. He was going to be a pilot.

But nothing came easily for Chennault. It would be eight more years before he could climb into the cockpit of an airplane. He had to fight the odds and finally defy the orders of his superiors to learn how to fly. He was used to fighting for what he wanted, though. Perhaps it was in his genes. His forebears had been fighters and pioneers, Huguenots who had left France and fought

the power behind the throne. Ching-ling Soong, married to Sun Yat-sen, the founder of the Chinese republic, remained true to his revolutionary ideals. Sterling Seagrave, the biographer of the Soong family, records a famous Chinese saying about the sisters: "One loved money, one loved power, one loved China."

in the American Revolution. On his father's side Chennault was related to Sam Houston and on his mother's to Robert E. Lee.

His father, John Stonewall Chennault, was a cotton planter and sometime sheriff of Franklin Parish in northeastern Louisiana. A kindly man, he was a major influence on his son. Claire's mother died when he was five, and his father gave the boy almost complete freedom to roam the woods and swamps of the countryside. By the age of eight he was hunting with a Winchester rifle. The game he killed was for the dinner table. The boy developed considerable self-reliance and self-confidence and a strong desire to be independent.

His life changed drastically when he was ten. That year his father married a schoolteacher, a woman of whom Claire was fond. She encouraged his free-ranging life in the woods, but she also fired his ambition. She continually prodded him to excel, not only in hunting and fishing but also in his schoolwork. Claire developed a strong attachment to his stepmother and described her as his best—and often his only—companion. This idyllic relationship was shattered five years later by her death. "I was alone again," Chennault wrote, "and really never found another companion whom I could so completely admire, respect, and love."

He was never popular with the older boys at school because he always resisted following their orders. Even at the age of fifteen he was showing that he was not a good subordinate. He was, however, an outstanding organizer and leader. He was eager to assist the younger children and he became a popular figure among them. He continued to enjoy sports and hunting and became an excellent trapper, earning money from the pelts of raccoons and skunks.

He developed another love while still in grade school, a passion for military history, and he read every book he could find on the great generals, the likes of Napoleon, Lee, and Jackson. In his grandfather's library he came across books on the Peloponnesian and Punic wars and became fascinated by the ancient battles of Thermopylae and Salamis. "Although I had no idea where Greece, Carthage, and Rome were," he wrote, "I was enthralled by the charging elephants, armored warriors, and burning ships."

In 1908 Chennault entered Louisiana State University, downstate in Baton Rouge. He enrolled in the school of agriculture. This was not what he wanted to study, but he had little choice. His ten grades of a back-country public school education did not qualify him for any other program of study. He also received his first exposure to the military, becoming a cadet in the student corps.

The following year he applied both to the Military Academy at West Point and to the Naval Academy at Annapolis. He never explained in his memoirs why he did so. He traveled north to Annapolis to take the navy entrance exams but left after two days without completing them. "Sight of the grim gray walls on the Severn chilled my enthusiasm to become an admiral." He also found out that midshipmen were not allowed off the campus for their first two years. For Chennault, the thought of being imprisoned behind walls for so long a time was just too hard to accept. He told his father that he had failed the exam and returned to LSU, wondering if the military life was for him after all. Even LSU was becoming too restricting (it interfered with the fishing season).

Back home, the best fishing was in early summer. The problem was that the academic year was not over by then, and students were expected to remain in Baton Rouge. Chennault soon found a way around that when he discovered that if he carefully timed his demerits in the corps and accumulated just enough to lead to his expulsion, he could get home in time to go after the fish. Of course there was some difficulty being readmitted the following fall, but Chennault managed to do it.

At the end of his second year he was still three demerits short of the number needed to set him free. Showing up at the next cadet review with his trousers rolled up solved that. He was called before the assembled corps of cadets by the army officer in charge. "Chennault," the man roared, "you will never make a soldier."

Chennault was enjoying himself but he wasn't getting anywhere. And he certainly was no closer to becoming a pilot. Perhaps he thought that the army officer was correct. Maybe he didn't have the temperament to become a soldier. He was too used to being on his own. At any rate, he decided that he needed to get some kind of training to enable him to earn a living. He had shown that he had a knack for communicating with young people and he enjoyed being in charge. Teaching school was something he could do. It would also permit him to have his summers free.

He transferred from LSU to the Louisiana State Normal School, the teachers college at Natchitoches, and the following year took his first job in a one-room school in Athens, Louisiana. The boys at the school were rough country types, and most of them were bigger than Chennault. No teacher had yet lasted longer than one term, but this time the teacher was tougher and he did not hesitate to prove it with his fists. Chennault joked that his major qualification for the job was that he "was still a minor and could legally commit assault and battery on the unruly students. . . . It took a few stiff sessions with bare knuckles behind the schoolhouse to clinch that job." After settling the matter of who was in charge, he channeled his students' aggressive energy into his favorite sport of baseball and soon produced a winning team.

Chennault liked his job and might never have left Athens had he not met Nellie Thompson, who delivered the valedictory address at a high school where his uncle was the principal. Six months later, on Christmas day of 1911, Claire and Nellie were married. By the time two of their eventual eight children arrived, Chennault realized that he needed to find another line of work, one that would pay more.

Over the next few years he drifted from one job to another in search of more money. He taught English at a business college in Biloxi, Mississippi, and physical culture at YMCA establishments in Kentucky, Tennessee, and Ohio. He did not remain at any job for very long. None of them paid enough, and they got boring after a while.

In 1916 he took a factory job making automobile tires for the British and the French, who were then at war with the Germans. A year later, when the United States entered the war, he saw a chance to learn to fly. Surely the country would need large numbers of young men to carry on the fight in the air. But Chennault was no longer so young—he was twenty-seven and the father of three.

His first application for flight training was rejected. "Applicant does not possess necessary qualifications for a successful aviator," the army decided. But if he was too old to fly, he might at least get into the army. There was a war to be fought and he was not considered too old for Officers Training School. Three months later, in November 1917, Chennault became one of the 90-day wonders with a commission as a first lieutenant in the infantry. He was not slated to go to France. Instead, he was sent to Fort Travis at San Antonio, Texas.

Chennault thought at first that he was destined for dull stateside duty, but San Antonio turned out to be an exciting place to be stationed. Not far from Fort Travis a cotton plantation had been leveled to make a new army base. It was named Kelly Field and it was the country's only pilot training facility. It did not take long for Lieutenant Chennault to arrange to be stationed there and to find some friendly flight instructors who were willing, unofficially, to teach him to fly the Curtiss JN-4, affectionately known as the "Jenny." He would never get his wings that way, never officially be credited as an aviator, but at least he could fly. Eventually he accumulated some 80 hours in the air.

Chennault pestered the army with frequent applications to be formally admitted to the aviation cadet program and finally his persistence paid off. Shortly after the armistice of November 11, 1918, he began his formal flight training. In a matter of weeks he almost washed out. It was his obstinacy that nearly did him in. He had developed a number of bad flying habits from his earlier unorthodox training, and didn't like the way his instructor was teaching him. The man never explained what Chennault was doing wrong. Instead, he would yank the controls away whenever Chennault made a mistake.

Chennault once warned him that the next time he did that, he would refuse to take back the controls. A few days later, while they were practicing forced landings, gliding toward a cornfield with the engine off, the instructor jerked the controls away. Chennault just sat there, refusing to take back the stick, and the plane headed toward the ground with no one in control. At the last second before disaster the instructor took over and brought the plane back to base. Chennault was finished as a cadet as far as he was concerned.

Fortunately, the Washout Board routinely gave cadets another chance with a different instructor. The new one recognized and made allowances for his student's fiery temper and introduced him to aerial acrobatics. Chennault was thrilled by the intricate, violent maneuvers and found that he had an aptitude for this kind of flying. He graduated with his wings and the rating of fighter pilot. He had found his niche—his place in the world was at the controls of a single-seater pursuit ship—hunting, alone and free.

But it was peacetime and the government thought it did not need all those fighter pilots. The war to end wars had been won. Chennault was discharged on April 16, 1920, and returned to Louisiana to buy a small farm, disappointed after having fought so long and hard to earn his wings. When his crops turned out poorly, his future again seemed bleak.

All he wanted to do was fly. "I have tasted of the air," he wrote to his father, "and I cannot get it out of my craw." He saw a chance to get back in the air when the army established the Air Service, removing aviation from the Signal Corps of which it had been a part. They were offering regular—not reserve—commissions. Chennault applied, and on July 1, 1920, became a fighter pilot once more.

He went to Ellington Field in Texas, where he was assigned to the army's first course in fighter tactics. The instructors were aces from the war, men like Carl Spaatz and Frank Hunter, who later assumed important commands in World War II. The tactics they taught were those they had used themselves, individual dogfighting in which planes chased each other around the sky using acrobatic maneuvers. It was great sport. Chennault was superb at it, but he came to believe that it was not the best way to fight a war.

He set himself the task of improving on these fighter tactics, and the results were disastrous. Putting his ideas into practice caused a midair collision when two pilots attempted to perform his complicated maneuvers. One plane landed but the other fell to earth with pieces of it falling off. No one wore parachutes then and the pilot, Joe Cannon, had no choice but to ride it down. Chennault in his plane circled over the wreckage, convinced no one could survive such a crash, but Cannon did survive and went on to command the Twelfth Air Force in Italy during World War II. They did not try Chennault's tricky maneuvers again.

In 1923, Chennault received his first command, the Nineteenth Fighter Squadron stationed at Luke Field at Pearl Harbor, Hawaii. Known as the Fighting Cock squadron, it was equipped with MB-3 biplanes, made by the Thomas-Morse Aircraft Company, the first American-built fighter planes. This proved to be a glorious time for Chennault. A first command is like a first love, he said, something never to be forgotten. He was in peak physical condition, tanned and lean, sporting a big black mustache with waxed tips. His family was with him—six children then, and all boys, to his delight.

He flew almost every day and, with his own squadron, was free to experiment with new tactics. He drove himself and his men hard and was rewarded when his outfit was rated the army's best fighter squadron. On the playing fields it was the best, too. Chennault's baseball and other athletic teams beat virtually all challengers, particularly when a barrel of beer was the prize. And the fishing was great as well.

He found two adversaries in Hawaii—the artillery and the navy—and took great pleasure in baiting them. Artillery officers boasted that their antiaircraft guns could shoot down anything that flew. They claimed that airplanes were obsolete as weapons and would never be able to get close enough to a target on the ground to attack it. Their skill in gunnery exercises seemed to prove them right.

Chennault believed that the gunnery exercises were rigged in favor of the gunners. Because aviation was a new service, gunnery officers outranked pilots and were thus able to set up the conditions under which the tests would be conducted. Bombers towing targets were forced to fly at a speed, course, and altitude determined for them by the gunnery officers. No evasive action was permitted, nor were fighter aircraft allowed to simulate strafing runs on the artillery.

Chennault hated to play against a stacked deck and one day he saw an opportunity to even the odds. He was leading his squadron over the gunnery range and saw the guns lined up in a neat row on the beach, firing away at a slow-moving target. "I decided to inject a note of realism into this nonsense and give the flak gunners a taste of what they might expect in a real war." He led his squadron in a high-speed dive and pulled out at 100 feet. His planes raced back and forth over the beach in a simulated strafing attack, sending the gunners scurrying in panic. They had never seen anything like that before and they certainly did not like it. The artillery colonel in charge of the range complained loud and strong about "that damned Frenchman with the big black mustache," and Chennault was confined to base for a week. He considered it a small price to pay for the chance to practice a technique he would use almost twenty years later in China.

Chennault remained opposed to individual dogfighting as the officially endorsed fighter tactic. He believed that fighters should attack in formation so their firepower would be more concentrated. After the collision he had witnessed in Texas, however, he was more careful about testing his theories. He selected only the most experienced pilots to practice acrobatics in formation. Such actions were dangerous enough when performed individually. No one but Chennault believed they could be done as a group, with the planes almost within touching distance of one another.

With his expert teaching and patient guidance, he soon had the squadron performing in unison loops and rolls and Immelmanns (a half loop followed by a half turn), and he used their new skill against the navy during the 1925 maneuvers, in which the air corps was to defend Pearl Harbor against carrier-based navy planes. Chennault spotted a squadron of navy dive bombers streaking toward land. His outfit was flying far below the navy planes, too low, the navy thought, to attack. Chennault led the squadron in perfect formation in an Immelmann, which brought them behind the navy planes. At full throttle, his pilots maintained formation and flew right through the navy squadron. The navy pilots were so surprised that one of them spun out of control.

Chennault had proved his point. Planes could maneuver and attack in formation. The Flying Tigers would later survive and prosper, and the nature of air warfare would eventually change, because of Chennault's ideas. He was leaving his imprint on the future of aviation.

Another far-reaching innovation he introduced was an aircraft early-warning system. Radar was years away and the army had not developed any other air-raid warning technique to provide information to defending fighters. Without such warning, pursuit planes would not be able to take off in time to intercept incoming bombers before they reached their target.

Chennault's method was crude but effective, and it foreshadowed the system he would use with deadly efficiency in China. He placed two men of his squadron atop the base water tower and equipped them with high-powered binoculars. From that vantage point, they could spot approaching planes as far away as six miles. That warning time was sufficient for Chennault's fighters to get airborne and intercept the incoming planes.

Toward the end of the 1925 maneuvers his spotters reported one navy plane coming in from the sea. Chennault took off by himself, roared up to a position above and behind the plane, and dove in for the attack. Acting on his belief that exercises should be as realistic as possible, Chennault came so close to the tail of the "enemy" aircraft that it appeared as though he might ram it. The observer in the rear seat of the navy plane was stunned. Chennault said, "I will never forget the look of horror flashing across that sailor's face when he turned and saw [my] propeller flashing within an ace of his tail."

The pilot dove in an effort to escape, but Chennault stayed on his tail as though the two planes were joined. They dropped faster and faster, and Chennault began to worry when the navy pilot did not pull out at 2000 feet. He maneuvered alongside and waved, but the navy flyer seemed frozen at the controls. Chennault pulled out, but the other plane did not. It crashed into the sea.

Although the pilot survived, the navy was embarrassed over the outcome of the incident. The pilot was supposed to have landed at Luke Field and surrendered. Then the observer was to have filed a navy press release with the local newspapers, dated the following day, announcing that the navy had won the exercises. That announcement did not make the papers.

In 1926 Chennault's tour of duty in Hawaii ended. He recalled it as the happiest time of his twenty-year prewar air corps career. Life would never be so carefree again. There were good times to come but they would be overshadowed by controversy and by his growing obsession with the tactics of air warfare, an obsession that ended his career and almost consumed him.

Chennault's next assignment was as a flight instructor at Brooks Field in Texas. He was thirty-six years old, approaching the age limit for fighter pilots, but he kept himself in peak physical condition. Although he was by now partially deaf, he had been granted a waiver the previous year so he could keep flying. He flew every day, usually in trainers, and managed to get off by himself as often as he could, crisscrossing the Southwest and stopping wherever he wanted to do some hunting and fishing.

One weekend found him in Arizona, where he accumulated a heavy load of fresh game and fish. The airfield, which was ringed by mountains, had a short runway. Chennault calculated that if he left his mechanic behind, the plane could gain just enough altitude to clear the mountains, given the extra weight it was carrying. He was wrong. The plane slammed into the mountainside but Chennault emerged from the rubble with only a sprained ankle. It was his only serious accident in a lifetime of flying.

As a flight instructor, Chennault was tough. He expected the best from his students and was more interested in quality than quantity. He believed the air corps needed a small number of excellent pilots rather than a larger number of average ones. He continued to adhere to this belief in China, where he would dismiss pilots who did not measure up to his exacting standards. "You had to be pretty good to get by Pop Chennault," his students at Brooks Field recalled.

Teaching others to fly was rewarding for Chennault, but he was not content to do only that. His mind seethed with ideas for improving air warfare and for increasing the value of aviation. He became acquainted with Sgt. William Nichols, one of the first men to complete a parachute jump from an airplane, and began to consider the possibility of dropping combat-ready infantry units from planes. The idea had been suggested earlier by Billy Mitchell but had never been tested.

Chennault did not envision parachute drops by whole armies but by small, well-armed teams that could be landed behind enemy lines to create chaos. To test this idea, he borrowed four airplanes and enlisted some friends to help him. Three De Havilland two-seaters, each carrying a paratrooper in the rear seat, flew over the drop zone in a V formation. In the center of the V, Chennault piloted a Ford Trimotor carrying machine guns, trench mortars, ammunition, and food and water. When the three paratroopers bailed out, Chennault's crew tossed out the supplies, which floated down on parachutes. After considerable practice, the paratroopers were able to collect and rig their equipment, and to open fire, less than a minute after they hit the ground.

Chennault was excited about this achievement and proud of what he and his men had been able to accomplish. He arranged a demonstration during a visit by Maj. Gen. Charles Summerall, the army chief of staff. Summerall had been the army commander in Hawaii when Chennault was stationed there, and Chennault was convinced that Summerall did not know anything about aviation. The chief of staff had once stated that the air corps did not need gasoline for training. When inspecting Chennault's squadron at Luke Field, he walked along the line of single-seater fighters. A pilot and a mechanic stood at attention by each ship. Summerall was outraged to discover only one parachute per plane, being unaware that the fighters carried only one person.

Despite Summerall's ignorance about airplanes, Chennault thought the general would be impressed with his way of penetrating infantry (Summerall's branch of the service) behind enemy lines. Chennault had his planes rendezvous overhead. The chutes opened and drifted toward the field. Summerall took one look, muttered, "Some more of this damned aviation nonsense," and walked away before the men and equipment landed.

A few weeks later, however, Chennault was ordered to mount another demonstration for a visiting military mission from the Soviet Union, which was traveling under the auspices of the War Department. The Russians were seeking the latest in tactics and equipment to build up their army and air forces. They were enthusiastic about the parachute drop and bestowed gifts of vodka and caviar on Chennault. They asked him if he would come to the Soviet Union to train their airborne forces. Chennault declined the invitation but the Russians persisted, telling him to name his own terms.

Chennault considered the offer for a few weeks and thought seriously about his own future in the Army Air Corps. After eleven years of service he was still a first lieutenant earning $225 a month. He had compiled an excellent record and believed that his future held promise. Surely better things were in store for him. On a whim, however, he proposed to the Russians what he thought were ridiculous terms. He requested a five-year contract at $1000 per month plus expenses. In addition, he wanted the rank of colonel in the Soviet air force and the right to fly any plane they had. He never thought he would hear from them again, but a telegram arrived asking when he could start. He stalled for several months but they did not give up. Finally he returned their letters unopened.

Shortly thereafter Chennault's situation improved. On April 12, 1929, he was appointed director of flying at Brooks Field and promoted to captain. The best news was his next assignment—the Air Corps Tactical School. There was no better place for someone who held such strong views about air tactics.

Chennault remained at the school for almost seven years, as a student, an instructor, and chief of the pursuit section. It was where his troubles began in earnest and from where, in 1937, his first career in the air corps ended ignominiously.

WHO IS THIS DAMNED FELLOW, CHENNAULT?

As soon as Chennault arrived at the Air Corps Tactical School he found himself on the losing side of a debate that would rage for the better part of a decade. The odds were clearly against him. The majority of his fellow students and instructors—indeed, the majority of the entire air corps—believed there was no future for fighter planes. The next war would be won by bombers alone. Fighter aircraft were obsolete, worthless. Claire Chennault, the zealous, dogmatic apostle of the fighter plane, had a battle on his hands. It was one he could not possibly win, although he tried hard for the next seven years.

Larry Kuter was also involved in the fight. He was part of the group that opposed his good friend, Chennault. "Well," he recalled years later, "there was strong competition at that time between the fighters and the bombers, and Claire was head of the fighters. Claire was not articulate. . . . Opposed to him was a very articulate group. We just overpowered him; we just whipped him."

Another member of the opposition was Clayton Bissell, who had been a World War I fighter ace and one of Chennault's instructors at the Tactical School. He taught the tactics of that war, individual dogfighting. That alone was sufficient to rile Chennault, but Bissell also taught that fighters could offer no defense against large, heavily armed bombers. Chennault was not the kind of man to remain silent in the face of what he considered a ridiculous notion, and he and Bissell must have had some heated arguments. If so, Bissell exacted his revenge in 1942 when the two men met again in China.

After World War I, fighter planes emerged as the most romantic and dominant weapon of the air. Fighter pilots got the glory and many books and movies were produced about them, adding to their heroic image. By comparison, bombers received little glory or publicity. The future of air warfare surely seemed to belong to the fighters. As early as the summer of 1921, however, the balance began to change. Billy Mitchell, in several spectacular and highly publicized demonstrations, led his bombers in successful attacks on captured German battleships off the Virginia coast. With this vivid display of the power of heavy aerial bombardment to sink warships, the emphasis shifted to bombers, where it was to remain for the next twenty years. Not until the Battle of Britain and the success of the Flying Tigers did anyone—other than Chennault and his handful of supporters—believe fighters could shoot down bombers.

The Germans demonstrated this when they started shooting down large numbers of B-17s and B-24s when those bombers were sent over Germany in 1943 and 1944 without fighter escort. Some of those officers who had advocated the development of bombers over fighters at the Tactical School in the 1930s were later killed leading those bombing raids. General Kuter was asked after the war about the failure to use fighters to escort bombers and whether the bomber people had ever recognized the need for fighters. "I wish I could say yes," he reported, "but I can't. We just closed our minds to it; we couldn't be stopped; the bomber was invincible."

During the early 1930s, bombers did indeed seem invincible, and large numbers of fighter pilots switched over to bombers where they saw more of a future. As a result, technical advances in aircraft design focused on bombers, and by 1933, fighters could no longer fly as fast.

It was in that year that the most dazzling plane yet designed and built in the United States became operational. It had a range of 1400 miles, greater than that of any other aircraft, a speed of 235 miles per hour, and it was a bomber. The earlier bomber model, the clumsy Keystone, a fabric-covered biplane, had a maximum speed of only 90 miles per hour. The new plane, the Martin B-10, boasted two Wright Cyclone engines, all-metal construction, retractable landing gear, and an enclosed cockpit. It carried a crew of four. The hottest air corps fighter at that time, the first monoplane ever built, was the P-26, affectionately known as the Pea Shooter. It had an open cockpit, fixed landing gear, and a top speed of 225 miles per hour. In addition, the P-26 was armed with only two machine guns. The B-10 carried four.

Given the speed of the new generation of bombers, combined with their heavy defensive firepower, which was increased by having the bombers fly in formation, they were soon seen as invulnerable. And the next generation, already on the drawing board, would have four engines, greater speed, and even more firepower. They promised to be as impregnable as a fortress, and when the first B-17s were flown only two years later, they were called Flying Fortresses.

In 1933, Brig. Gen. Oscar Westover, assistant chief of the air corps, concluded that bombers, along with observation planes, "will suffice for the adequate defense of this country." He went on to state, "no known human agency can frustrate the accomplishment of a bombardment mission." There was no need for fighter aircraft. "Since new bombardment aircraft possesses speed above 200 miles per hour, any intercepting or supporting aircraft must possess greater speed characteristics if they are to perform their mission. In the case of pursuit aviation, this increase of speed must be so great as to make it doubtful whether pursuit aircraft can be efficiently or safely operated either individually or in mass."

The striking technical advances in bomber design in the 1930s were paralleled by changes in strategic thinking first in Europe, then in the United States. Italian aviator Gen. Giulio Douhet published a book entitled *The War of 194–*, in which he described how that war would be won by great armadas of heavily armed bombers flying unmolested across vast distances to destroy enemy cities. Douhet's work was brought to the attention of U.S. Air Corps leaders in the May 1933 issue of *U.S. Air Service* magazine. Coinciding with the development of the B-10 bomber, Douhet's ideas profoundly influenced American air strategy into the early years of World War II.

Chennault vehemently disagreed with the claim that bombers were invincible, but he was not so closed-minded as the bomber advocates were. He did believe in the importance of bombers as weapons of war. "It is certain," he wrote, "that in the next war bombardment will constitute a most dangerous threat." Indeed, it was because of that threat, he argued, that fighter aircraft were so important. They were vital to help prevent bombing attacks. For all his obsession with fighters, however, Chennault did not claim that they alone could accomplish that. Antiaircraft and other defensive measures would also have to be developed.

Chennault believed that fighters could effectively attack bombers, even though they were not as fast, if their offensive firepower were increased and their tactics improved. For years he argued these points, urging that fighters be equipped with .50-caliber machine guns, whose greater range would enable fighters to strike at bombers while staying beyond the range of the bombers' .30-caliber guns.

He also wanted to arm fighters with four guns in the nose, synchronized to fire through the propeller, instead of the two guns that had been standard since 1916. Air corps engineers at Wright Field in Ohio, the air corps' engineering and development center, told Chennault it would be impossible to synchronize four guns. Yet a few years later the Russians were using four-gun planes with deadly effectiveness in the Spanish Civil War, and their German and Italian adversaries were forced to do the same. By then, U.S. fighters were being equipped with six guns, two in the nose and four in the wings, but the wing-mounted guns remained the lighter and shorter-range .30-caliber type.

One of Chennault's ideas on fighter design opposed a technical advance. He was against closed cockpits for fighter planes. Kuter recalled that Chennault had said that "in lieu of a closed cockpit, he would rather have carpet tacks scattered through the flying suits of his fighter pilots. He wanted them to be uncomfortable and alert. He didn't want them to be comfortable and quiet and indoor pilots. They had to be out fighting, and they had to be mad about it."

As the decade of the 1930s wore on, air corps leaders were less concerned with how many and what type of fighters they should have than with whether they should have fighters at all. The arguments between Chennault and the bomber advocates became more acrimonious as the cost of the ever-larger and more complex bombers increased. They were competing for the small amount of money the military had been allocated in the 1930s. Air corps funds had been cut so much that there was barely enough gas for pilots to fly the four hours per month required to qualify for flight pay. If fighter planes were of no value, why waste precious funds to acquire more of them?

Although money for fighters was never eliminated from the air corps budget, it was greatly reduced. Each year the faculty at the Tactical School considered dropping the fighter courses from the program, and finally they did so. Chennault was recalled to teach fighter tactics on a part-time basis, but the bomber people were winning the war.

Chennault worked long hours to marshal his arguments for improved tactical use of fighters so that they could effectively operate against bombers. He developed his ideas in the classroom in spirited discussions, on blackboards, and in the air. He spent his evenings studying and writing articles for the service magazines, and he became recognized throughout the world for his advocacy of the fighter plane. Maj. Gen. John Curry, commanding officer at the Tactical School, said that Chennault was "a fearless pilot, an able air leader, and one of the outstanding authorities on pursuit aviation." In 1933, Chennault wrote a mimeographed text entitled "The Role of Defensive Pursuit," which was used in China years later but ignored in the United States at the time it was written.

One of his basic criticisms of existing air corps policy related to the lack of an early-warning system that would provide a continuous flow of information to fighters about the location of the approaching bombers. That, Chennault argued, was the major reason why fighters were not more effective against bombers in maneuvers. They didn't know where the bombers were! During maneuvers in 1931, for example, one fighter group never spotted any attacking bombers in the entire two-week period.

Chennault studied English and German air-warning systems and made his own improvements. He believed fighters could easily intercept bombers if spotters would provide precise information on the bombers' speed, direction, distance, and altitude. In one set of exercises Chennault established mobile field radios manned by trained spotters and arranged them so there were no gaps or blind spots through which bombers might slip undetected. Using the information supplied by the spotters, the fighter pilots were able to intercept the bombers every time they approached. Chennault's system worked well, as the Japanese would learn to their regret in China in 1942.

Chennault continued to insist that fighters were most efficient when they operated in teams instead of individually. He proved this to his own satisfaction in the formation acrobatic flying he had taught his squadron in Hawaii, and he found confirmation of his views in his study of the fighter tactics used by the Germans in World War I. He discovered that Oswald von Boelcke, an early ace, had demonstrated that two planes could fight as a team and could function much more effectively than three or four planes flying separately.

Von Boelcke had taken advantage of an old military axiom that the difference in firepower between opposing forces is not simply the difference in the number of guns on each side, but rather is the square of the difference when those guns are concentrated. Thus, two planes attacking together offer the same firepower as four planes attacking individually.

Although he was killed in a collision in 1916, von Boelcke had taught his approach to a pilot named Richtofen, who used it with terrifying accuracy. His Flying Circus squadron was never defeated in combat until after he was killed. His flamboyant successor preferred the glamor of the individual dogfight, and under his leadership the squadron of aces was almost destroyed. His name was Hermann Goering.

Chennault learned from these examples and urged the adoption of the two-plane element with a lead plane and a wingman, always operating as a team. He later trained his Flying Tigers to fight that way, but the army and navy did not adopt his approach until after their disasters in the early months of the war.

Chennault never hesitated to criticize what he saw as the ineffective use of air power. It did not matter to him who was the target of his criticism or how high his rank; to Chennault, his adversaries had to be proven wrong. The future of air power depended on it. He was particularly incensed about the 1932 Pacific coast maneuvers led by Lt. Col. Hap Arnold.

Arnold sent B-10 bombers to attack March Field. The defending fighters took off as ordered. Following the prevailing orthodoxy, they circled the field until all were airborne, and they remained there until the various squadrons formed up and the group commander had taken off to lead them. Only then did they start toward the bombers, which, in the meantime, had attacked and were returning to their base!

The only fighters able to intercept the bombers were a few from an outlying field. These planes had scrambled the instant they received word of the approaching bombers. They had not waited to form up according to regulations. Arnold, however, concluded that fighters could offer no defense against a bombing attack, and his report on the maneuvers was circulated at the Tactical School. Chennault wrote a critical eight-page rebuttal. When Arnold received his assessment, he contacted the school. "Who is this damned fellow, Chennault?" he asked.

Chennault got into greater trouble after the large-scale ground and air maneuvers of 1934 conducted by Gen. C. E. Kilbourne of the War Department's general staff. Air corps officers were irate over the restrictions Kilbourne had placed on the use of aircraft. The maneuvers involved an amphibious landing on the New Jersey coastline. Under Kilbourne's orders, the defending army would not oppose the landings on the beach. Instead, they were to dig in some 30 miles from the beach. Thus, the invading army was able to land all its troops and equipment without interruption. They marched in orderly fashion up to the line of the defending army, whereupon both sides settled down to the kind of static trench warfare by which World War I had been fought.

The situation was ideal for the defending air force to bomb and strafe the invaders when they were approaching the beaches, their most vulnerable time. The 30-mile supply route from the beach to the trenches was also a perfect target for air attacks. Kilbourne, however, did not allow the aircraft to attack until the two armies had met, and he would not permit them to hit the supply line at any time.

Bomber and fighter advocates were united in their opposition to Kilbourne's restrictions, and six air corps officers—five bomber people plus Chennault—volunteered to testify before a government commission established to investigate the use of air power. The Howell Commission, headed by Clark Howell, a publisher, was not investigating the Kilbourne maneuvers but was concerned with the larger issues of the theory and practice of strategic air warfare. The timing was coincidental.

The commission was scheduled to meet in executive session so that the airmen could feel free to express their views without fear of harming their careers. When the six arrived at the hearing room, however, they found General Kilbourne there, along with two secretaries, prepared to record their words. "We could feel the official noose tightening around our necks," Chennault said, "but we had gone too far to turn back."

The five bomber people had spent the weekend coordinating their testimony, and they presented their views clearly and concisely, refuting in detail the War Department policy involving the air corps. When they finished, they expected to be roundly lambasted, but to their surprise, Kilbourne congratulated them on their testimony. He said he had learned a great deal that had not been clear to him before. It was a magnanimous and open-minded gesture on the part of a man whose policies had just been criticized, however politely, by five junior officers.

Then it was Chennault's turn. He did not deal with broad matters of policy, nor was he especially polite. He charged ahead in his bullheaded fashion to attack Kilbourne for his conduct of the

New Jersey maneuvers. He detailed the restrictions on the use of air power in the exercise as an example of the inept thinking of the general staff and of Kilbourne himself.

The general was visibly upset when he rose to reply. He did not thank the hot-tempered captain for his testimony. He pounded the table and shook his finger at Chennault as he defended his tactics in the New Jersey maneuvers, which he described as the only possible way to have handled the situation.

"General," Chennault said, "if that is the best you can do in the way of planning for future wars, perhaps it is time for the Air Corps to take over." Chennault later claimed that because of this confrontation, his name was permanently removed from the list of candidates for the Command and General Staff School.

Chennault did not spend all his time at the Air Corps Tactical School studying, writing papers, and provoking generals. He managed to do a lot of flying, and some of it was the most fun he ever had in the air. In 1932, his CO, General Curry, had witnessed a performance of the Hell Divers, the navy's three-plane acrobatic team. They were generating considerable favorable publicity for the navy in appearances throughout the United States. Curry wanted the air corps to have its own acrobatic team, and he called on the best flyer he knew to start one.

Chennault was delighted. Not only would this give him the opportunity to do more flying, but he could also test the team fighter tactics he had been developing. He would be in command of the outfit and would fly the world's fastest and most nimble fighter plane, the Boeing P-12E. With its 500-horsepower Wasp radial engine, the plane could reach a top speed of 200 miles per hour. It was the last of the military biplanes and the standard fighter for both the army and the navy. The navy version was known as the F4B-3.

Chennault used a simple but effective procedure for choosing the other members of his team. He selected only those who could stay close on his wing during his acrobatic maneuvers. Only three pilots met his standards. One was Lt. Haywood "Possum" Hansell, who remained with the team for a year and later became a wing commander in the Eighth Air Force in Europe during World

War II. The third member of the original trio was a sergeant pilot, John H. "Luke" Williamson, who had been a student of Chennault's at Brooks Field. When Hansell left he was replaced by another sergeant pilot, Billy McDonald. Both Williamson and McDonald later went to China and were instrumental in bringing Chennault there.

They called themselves "The Three Men on the Flying Trapeze," a name that came to them one night in a bar in Macon, Mississippi, while singing "The Daring Young Man on the Flying Trapeze." For the next four years, Chennault's acrobatic team was a familiar sight at state fairs, air shows, and national air races, thrilling audiences with their death-defying routines. "We did every acrobatic maneuver in the book," Chennault said, "and some that weren't, all in perfect formation. We did loops, spins, wingovers, chandelles, Immelmanns, snap and slow rolls, double rolls, and a squirrel-cage effect in which each plane rolled around the other while doing an individual barrel roll. We did 3-turn tail spins in close formation and came out in formation although all three planes were out of control during the spin."

One favorite of the crowd involved tying the wingtips of the planes together with 20-foot ropes, then taking off abreast, performing several loops, and landing still tied together. Chennault liked to claim that their stunts appeared more dangerous than they really were and that the planes never came closer than three feet, a distance most pilots would not find comfortable.

He never took unnecessary chances with his team. He was not the daredevil he appeared to be from the ground. Before he attempted any maneuver, Chennault calculated the stresses the various movements would put on the aircraft. Only when he was satisfied that the planes would perform properly would he attempt the maneuver in the air. Months of practice were required before he would perform a new stunt in public. Alcohol was forbidden and the men drank only modest amounts of coffee. Before every flight, whether performance or rehearsal, the men did a rigorous set of exercises.

Still, the flying was dangerous and it required precise eye-hand coordination, split-second timing, superb physical conditioning, and steady nerves. Chennault was forty-two years old when he formed the group and forty-five when they stopped flying. Only a few men could compete in professional sports at that age, and even fewer could fly a plane so well.

In hundreds of performances he had only one close call, and it occurred over his own house on the old Selma Road, ten miles outside of Montgomery, Alabama. The only witness was his wife. A sudden gust of wind forced Hansell's wing into the tail of Chennault's plane, where it jammed the elevator and froze the control stick. No one had had any training in flying a plane without the use of ailerons and elevators, but Chennault managed to land using the throttle alone.

The Three Men on the Flying Trapeze won commendations from the air corps and trophies from many civilian groups. They became famous throughout the country and were in great demand. This kind of flying provided great excitement for Chennault, of course, but there was a serious side to it that had little to do with improved public relations for the air corps. Those acrobatic performances were like a laboratory in which Chennault worked to prove that he and von Boelcke had been correct, that fighter planes could stay in formation through the most difficult maneuvers. In the years to come, Chennault would teach this to a new generation of pilots in the skies over China.

The acrobatic team flew its final performance in 1936. What destroyed them was not an accident but a personnel decision made by air corps brass that embittered Chennault. The enlistments of Williamson and McDonald were due to expire in 1935. Although they were sergeants, the air corps allowed them to wear the single gold bar of their reserve commissions as second lieutenants when they performed publicly, so that the service would not be represented by enlisted men. Between performances, however, they served as sergeants and got the flying assignments the officers did not want. Williamson and McDonald knew that their future in the air corps was limited if they remained sergeants, so they applied for regular commissions, competing with more than 400 applicants for 52 slots. They led all the others in ratings of their flying ability and stood third in hours of flying time. Their years of acrobatics as part of Chennault's team had provided ample demonstration of their flying skills.

Despite these obvious qualifications they were rejected because they did not have more than two years of college. Chennault responded with an angry letter to the Montgomery *Advertiser,* a newspaper read by everyone at nearby Maxwell Field. He described Williamson and McDonald as outstanding pilots and decried what the air corps had done to them. "If I was going to war," he wrote, "and I were ordered to the front, I would choose these two men to accompany me into combat, and that is the highest compliment a combat-formation leader can pay."

The team gave one last performance in January 1936, at the Pan-American Air Show in Miami, Florida, and it was destined to change Chennault's life. In the audience was Gen. Mow Pang Tsu of the Chinese Air Force, and he was extremely impressed with the trio. Later that day the three pilots were invited out on William Pawley's yacht so that General Mow could meet them. He asked them to come to China to serve as flight instructors. Roy Holbrook, another former air corps friend of Chennault's, was already there. Chennault advised Williamson and McDonald to go, and he held out the possibility that he might join them before too long.

Chennault's health and morale declined during 1936. Things were going badly for him and he admitted that his "heart was no longer in the fight." He told an old friend that he felt he had outlived his usefulness to the service. He believed that everyone had turned against him. Perhaps he was experiencing what one historian described as a "sense of persecution that afflicts men with a mission when they are not listened to."

The hectic pace of the last five years had caught up with him. He had never taken a day of leave and had worked late many evenings to write his articles for the military journals, battling the bomber advocates. Every morning he had flown practice sessions with Williamson and McDonald, and afternoons were spent teaching or in meetings and debates about the future of air power.

He lost yet another battle for his fighter aircraft. The air corps proposed to build a multipurpose, multiple-seater plane that would serve as bomber, reconnaissance plane, and fighter. It would be cheaper, they argued, to have one plane perform all these functions instead of three separate planes. Chennault was irate. He knew such a plane would be useless as a combat fighter.

As head of the pursuit design board, he was required to travel to Wright Field to argue with the air corps engineers about the futility of the design decision. He was in such poor health that the Maxwell Field flight surgeon had ordered him to bed for two weeks, with a diet of raw liver, before he would clear him for the trip.

The exhausting meetings at Wright Field lasted five days. The air corps, unconvinced by Chennault's arguments, spent $2 million on a multiseater fighter to be called the Bell Aircuda. Only 13 were ever built, and they were finally put to use to train student mechanics. They were of no value for anything else. Chennault flew home from the meetings tired and depressed.

The flight surgeon reexamined him and restricted his flying to trainers, and then only with another pilot in the forward cockpit. Not long after, Chennault was permanently grounded because of low blood pressure, chronic bronchitis, and deafness. The only way he was permitted to fly was as a passenger. Then came a transfer from the Tactical School to Barksdale Field in Louisiana as executive officer of a fighter group. Although he was promoted to acting major, it provided little solace for all that he had lost.

"It was obvious that I was going around and around and getting nowhere," he wrote. His deteriorating health caused him to be sent to a hospital at Hot Springs, Arkansas, where he stayed through the winter of 1936 and into the spring of 1937, brooding about his failed career. He couldn't fly, and his removal from the Tactical School meant that he had no chance to influence air corps policy decisions. The best he could hope for, if he regained his strength, was a series of unimportant desk jobs until retirement.

He had been receiving letters from Billy McDonald keeping him informed about developments in China, but he could no longer consider going there as a flight instructor because of his poor health. Then his fortunes changed dramatically. The Chinese Air Force had hired Col. George E. A. Reinburg, who had retired from the Army Air Corps after serving as military attaché in Berlin, to serve as its chief air advisor. Reinburg died suddenly of a heart attack, and Madame Chiang asked McDonald and Williamson if they could suggest a replacement.

They could, indeed, and in the spring of 1937 a letter arrived from the Chinese government asking if Chennault would be interested in conducting a three-month survey of the status of the Chinese Air Force. The pay would be $1000 per month, plus travel and other expenses, and he would be supplied with a car, driver, and interpreter. He would also be allowed to fly any of their planes.

Chennault's health improved remarkably. On April 30, 1937, he retired from the U.S. Army Air Corps at the permanent rank of captain. The following day he embarked on a journey that took him halfway around the world. He planned to go for three months. He stayed eight years.

FOUR

I NEVER RUN FROM A FIGHT

Chennault stopped in Japan on his way to China to see his future enemy in person. As did many other American military officers of the time, he believed that we would one day be at war with Japan. He saw the present hostilities between Japan and China as a prelude to the larger-scale war that would rage throughout the Pacific. Japan's aggression could be stopped only by war with the United States, and Chennault meant to be ready for that war with a list of Japanese targets to attack.

He began his preparations for war on May 31, 1937, when his ship, the SS *President Garfield,* docked at Kobe, Japan. He had been at sea for a month. Among the crowd of people meeting the ship was Billy McDonald, Chennault's former partner in the acrobatic team. The ex-sergeant, now a flight instructor for the Chinese Air Force, was traveling in the guise of the assistant manager of a troupe of Chinese acrobats on tour in Japan. The Japanese would never have allowed McDonald into the country had his passport listed his real occupation.

Chennault and McDonald hired a car and set off on a month-long tour of Japan. They kept their cameras hidden as much as possible because they were looking at the sights not as tourists but as flyers, judging the worth of potential targets. They traveled to Kobe, Kyoto, and Osaka, taking pictures and making notes on shipping routes, manufacturing centers, war industries, and the flimsy wooden construction that characterized Japanese cities.

Chennault would learn later that as meager as his notebook and snapshot file was, it contained more information on Japanese targets than the entire U.S. army and navy intelligence files at the time of Pearl Harbor.

The two men boarded a ship at Osaka and sailed down the Inland Sea, surreptitiously taking pictures, making notes, and storing up impressions for the future. From there they sailed for China.

China had already been at war with Japan intermittently for six years. The Japanese had invaded Manchuria in 1931 and occupied it quickly. It was a rich prize with its heavy industry, raw materials, and cheap labor. The occupation of Manchuria provoked a flood of Chinese nationalism and anti-Japanese sentiment. The Chinese people boycotted Japanese goods and began harassing the Japanese who lived in other parts of China.

In 1932, Japan manufactured an incident in the city of Shanghai. Two Japanese monks were killed and two others injured, allegedly by Chinese hooligans. Using the attack as a pretext, Japan landed troops in the city and bombed the Chinese quarter, killing several thousand people. To their surprise, the Chinese army held them in place, and three months later, the Japanese agreed to a truce and removed their 100,000 troops from Shanghai.

The Chinese victory was short-lived. A few weeks later, Japanese troops advanced from Manchuria into the neighboring Chinese provinces. By late January of 1933 they had reached China's Great Wall. World opinion was aroused and coalesced solidly against the Japanese aggression. The next month the League of Nations voted to condemn Japan for her actions. The response of the Japanese government was to withdraw from the league and to continue the advance into the north of China. By May, the Chinese signed a truce, formally ceding all of the occupied territory to Japan.

But the Japanese wanted more. Indeed, they wanted all of China. A year later, in April 1934, Japan boldly announced that China was henceforth its client state. No other nation could deal with China without Japanese approval. Although other nations again condemned Japanese aggression, none was willing to take steps to curb it. Several more Chinese provinces fell into Japanese hands. For the next two years the situation was relatively quiet as Japan consolidated the gains made in China.

By 1936, Japan's armies were on the march again, to occupy more northern provinces and establish a puppet government in Mongolia. As before, the Chinese sued for peace, the Japanese continued to provoke the Chinese, and anti-Japanese incidents occurred in Nankow and Shanghai. Japanese marines moved into the cities, triggering additional riots and attacks on Japanese troops and civilians. This, in turn, gave Japan an excuse for further incursions until there seemed to be no way to stop the escalating violence. On January 7, 1937, Japanese troops buried six Chinese leaders alive. The following day the Chinese retaliated by burying 16 Japanese alive on the same spot.

In March 1937, 70 Japanese warships conducted maneuvers at the port of Tsingtao in the north of China. In April, at the time when Chennault retired from the U.S. Air Corps, Japan had sent much of its fleet to the Chinese port of Swatow. As Chennault sailed from Japan to China, all signs pointed to an early and major escalation of the war.

Chennault arrived in Shanghai in early June. He was dismayed to find that the large foreign colony there was more concerned with business than with the prospect of war. The "disturbances," as they called them, were interfering with profits, and economics was the overriding concern of the wealthy, high-living community ensconced in their protected settlements. Few people seemed to believe that the Chinese were capable of fighting a major war with Japan, and more than one foreign businessman expressed the hope that the Japanese would bring some semblance of order to the country so that normal business activities could resume.

Like most Westerners, Chennault at first found the ways of the Orient bewildering. He was befriended by an Australian journalist, William H. Donald, a man often compared to Lawrence of Arabia for his understanding of and acceptance by the local population. Over the years Donald had served as personal consultant to some of the most powerful warlords in China and eventually to Chiang Kai-shek himself.

Three years later Donald would be banished because of his overzealous efforts to eliminate corruption in high government circles. He found himself in Manila when war came and, unable to escape after the Japanese invaded the Philippines, was imprisoned at Los Baños internment camp. Although the Japanese had put a price on his head, he remained undetected as their prisoner for the duration of the war. When he met Chennault in 1937, however, he was still held in high regard by Chiang, and he arranged for Chennault to meet the power brokers in the government. Chennault said that had it not been for Donald's instructions on how to deal with these people, he would not have been able to accomplish anything. He would have probably left China in disgust soon after he arrived.

Another person helped immensely during these early days in China, a woman who left a deep and lasting impression on him. Officially, Chennault was to be an employee of the Bank of China, which was headed by T. V. Soong. This was done to avoid the appearance of violating American neutrality laws. In reality, Chennault reported to the National Secretary of Aviation, who had recently been appointed to root out graft and corruption in the Chinese air force. The person who held this important post was Madame Chiang Kai-shek, and Chennault was enchanted by her. Their first meeting was, he wrote, "an encounter from which I never recovered. To this day I remain completely captivated. That night I wrote in my diary, 'She will always be a princess to me.'" He never wavered in his opinion of Madame as one of the world's most brilliant and determined women. She looked twenty years younger than he expected and was vivacious and brimming with energy. She spoke English with a lovely Southern drawl, a product of her early years spent in Georgia.

"I reckon you and I will get along all right in building up your air force," Chennault told her.

"I reckon so," she said.

Chennault was not the only American to be captivated by Madame Chiang. Even Vinegar Joe Stilwell, who was not impressed by many people, found her "charming, highly intelligent and sincere." "She is all right," he added. That tough, no-nonsense old soldier sent her flowers after their first meeting. Their mutual admiration for Madame Chiang might have been the only thing on which Stilwell and Chennault ever agreed.

She was also a favorite of the publisher Henry Luce and his wife Clare Booth Luce. It was primarily through their efforts in generating so much favorable publicity for her that Madame Chiang was regarded by Americans for decades as one of the world's ten most admired women. To journalist Theodore White she was "a beautiful, tart and brittle woman, more American than Chinese, and mistress of every level of the American language from the verses of the hymnal to the most sophisticated bitchery. Madame Chiang, always stunning in her silk gowns, could be as coy and kittenish as a college coed, or as commanding and petty as a dormitory house mother. She swished briskly into any room like a queen."

Her legendary charm was much in evidence when she met Chennault for the first time, and so was her great sense of discipline and determination in tackling her new job as head of the air force. She told Chennault that she wanted an honest evaluation of the status of that force. He would have three months to undertake his survey and report back to her.

At Madame's orders, he was to begin in Nanking, at that time China's capital. He picked up Billy McDonald, Col. P. Y. Hsu (who would be his interpreter for the next eight years), and Sebie Biggs Smith. Smith was a highly skilled mechanic who had served with Chennault at Maxwell Field before coming to China with Williamson and McDonald the year before. Chennault and his party flew in two BT-2 training planes, with Smith doing most of the flying for Chennault. Still, it was a pleasure for Chennault to be back in the air again, with his old friend McDonald on his wing.

Unlike complacent Shanghai, which had seemed oblivious to the prospect of war, Nanking was tense and teeming with anti-Japanese demonstrations, reports of Japanese atrocities, and the imminence of war. Chennault also found the reason for Madame's concern about the state of her air force. It was a terrible mess. It was here that Chennault got what he described as his first taste of the monumental corruption and inefficiency that permeated virtually all aspects of Chinese aviation.

There had been no national air force in China until the Japanese attack on Manchuria in 1931. Prior to that time, the only military planes in the country were owned by warlords who hired Western adventurers to fly them in their frequent battles against their neighbors. The person responsible for the development of the Chinese Air Force was T. V. Soong, who recognized that the Japanese navy had the ability to blockade all Chinese ports. Soong knew it was impossible for China to build a navy of sufficient size to defend the coastline, but it was possible to build an air force that might be able to neutralize the Japanese naval threat.

Soong turned to the United States for help after his first choice, Britain, turned him down. The British were afraid of offending the Japanese. American authorities had the same concern, but they agreed to send an unofficial mission to China in 1932. The group was led by Col. John H. Jouett, who had recently retired from the air corps. Jouett had played football at West Point and had been in the famous 1913 game in which he played end against Knute Rockne of Notre Dame. He went on to become a pioneer in military aviation. He brought with him to China some two dozen air corps reserve officers including Christy Mathewson, Jr. (son of the New York Giants pitcher), Harvey Greenlaw (who would become Chennault's executive officer in the Flying Tigers), and Roy Holbrook.

They found an assortment of old British and Soviet aircraft that looked more dangerous to their pilots than to the enemy. The planes would not have been out of place in a museum. At Hangchow Field near Shanghai they established the Central Chinese Aviation Academy, a flight school modeled after those of the U.S. Army Air Corps, which held students to strict American standards. Several hundred Chinese pilots were trained, and the country became a new and valued customer for the American aviation industry. Over the next two years, China purchased more than

$9 million worth of equipment and gasoline and a large number of training and combat airplanes. American aircraft salesmen soon learned, however, that the graft and corruption that were a way of life in China ran rampant within the new aviation industry. It was impossible to sell anything without resorting to bribery and kickbacks.

The Jouett mission lasted for two years, but its prestige and influence dropped sharply when Jouett refused to help the government suppress a rebellion in one of the provinces. He argued that the Americans had been sent there to train and to advise, not to fight. General Mow Pang Tsu (who later witnessed the final performance of the Flying Trapeze team in Miami) led a flight of six old, flimsy bombers against the rebel stronghold. Using 500-pound bombs, he smashed holes in the otherwise impregnable stout walls, allowing infantry to rush through and crush the rebellion. This demonstration of the successful use of airpower greatly impressed Chiang Kai-shek.

China's finance minister, H. H. Kung, Soong's rival for power, was in Europe at the time looking for weapons to purchase. Coincidentally, Benito Mussolini in Italy was having trouble financing the expansion of his air force. Soong, who had backed Jouett's refusal to help fight the rebels, was now out of favor with Chiang. Kung and the Italians arrived to fill the vacuum. Jouett and most of his pilots left and an Italian aviation mission headed by Count Ciano, Mussolini's son-in-law, came with 100 engineers and mechanics to set up an Italian aircraft factory at Nanchang and with pilots to man a flying school at Loyang.

The Chinese bought millions of dollars worth of Italian aircraft, virtually all of which were obsolete or of poor design and thus worthless for combat. The Italians padded the roster of the air force's planes by the unique practice of never removing a plane from the list, even if it had crashed and was a total loss or had been cannibalized for spare parts. On paper, then, China had an impressive air force. In reality, it had gotten very little for its money.

This was true for the Italian-trained pilots as well. In their flight training program, every Chinese student-pilot who survived was graduated as qualified, regardless of his actual level of performance. The Jouett mission, by contrast, had graduated only the best and most skilled pilots, washing out those of mediocre or average ability. Chiang preferred the Italian approach for social reasons. When the Americans were in charge he had received numerous complaints from the families of the failed aviation trainees because they all had lost face. Under the Italian system everyone was happy, and China appeared to have not only a huge air force but also a large number of pilots.

This was the nature of the Chinese Air Force Chennault encountered, for the Italians were still in charge in 1937. Chennault set up an office at the Nanking Country Club, within sight of the tomb of Sun Yat-sen, the founder of the Chinese republic. One of his first activities was to inspect the Italian flying school at Loyang, and he was there on July 7, 1937, the day the war began in earnest at the Marco Polo Bridge. The Chinese called it the "war of resistance."

The Marco Polo Bridge, 211 meters long, is a footbridge located eight miles southwest of Peking. It is decorated with 300 marble lions that look down on the Yungting River. While holding maneuvers close to the bridge, Japanese troops were fired on by Chinese forces and one soldier was reported missing. The Japanese asked permission to enter the old walled village of Wanping at the end of the bridge to search for the missing man. The Chinese commander refused. The bridge was in a strategic location, adjacent to the only remaining railroad line connecting Peking with the south of China. The river itself was a natural barrier. Beyond it lay 300 miles of open country stretching to the Yellow River and Hankow, a major industrial center. The Chinese could not afford to let the enemy cross the bridge.

The Japanese responded by shelling the Chinese troops in place on the other side of the bridge. The next day, a truce was arranged and both sides agreed to pull back. The Chinese troops began to withdraw but the Japanese did not. Fighting flared up again and the Chinese managed to hold the Japanese in place. Chiang rushed three divisions up to reinforce the crossing.

On July 17 Chiang made a major speech. "Now is the time to act," he declared. China had been pushed too far, he added. Although they were not yet prepared for a war with Japan, they no longer had any choice. They could not give up any more territory.

Chennault's reaction on learning that China had committed herself to war with Japan was to send a telegram to Chiang offering his services. After twenty years of military training, he finally found himself in a war that would give him the chance to try out his theories on air tactics. "I wanted a chance to give them an acid test in combat." Also, he saw the war in China as an opportunity to serve the United States as well. By fighting the Japanese in China, he could learn a great deal about their equipment and their tactics, information he thought would be valuable to America when it came time for her to go to war with Japan. Finally, he wanted to be fighting for a personal reason. It suited his natural belligerence. "I never run from a fight," he said.

Two days later, Chennault was informed that his offer had been accepted. He was ordered to report to Nanchang to take charge of the combat training of several squadrons of fighters and bombers. The experience turned out to be a nightmare. The weather was abysmal—he felt like a "steamed clam" most of the time—and the food at the hotel where he lived was the worst he had ever eaten. The planes, however, were not so bad. There were some Curtiss Hawk biplanes that the Chinese used for dive bombing, and some P-26s and B-10 bombers, all purchased during the Jouett mission, as well as some Italian fighters. Chennault's friend General Mow was in command, and the only pleasant times Chennault recalled of his stay there were evenings spent with the general eating iced watermelon and drinking cold beer.

It was the pilots who made the experience so terrible. Most were products of the Italian flight training. These supposedly combat-ready fighter pilots routinely crashed while flying basic trainers, sometimes as many as five crash landings every day. Furthermore, these Italian-trained Chinese pilots looked upon practice missions as losing face. After all, they were, of course, superior pilots, and flyers of their caliber surely did not need to practice. To do so was a sign of weakness and cast doubt on their abilities. Although Chennault and Mow scheduled practice flights day after day for the B-10 bomber squadron, no pilots ever appeared at the appointed times.

In desperation Mow obtained orders from Chiang himself mandating the squadron practice. In a fit of pique, the squadron leader took off, circled the field a few times, and deliberately crash-landed his plane. He walked away unhurt and approached Chennault and Mow with a look of utter contempt on his face. "That is what comes of practice," he said. Chennault wrote in his diary that he did not think the Chinese Air Force was ready for war.

On the other side of Poyang Lake from the city of Nanchang, Chiang Kai-shek sat in the cool mountains at Kuling, the summer capital, wondering if the nation as a whole was ready for war. He had no navy worthy of the name, although it boasted the highest-ranking admiral in the world. His army, with the exception of one German-trained unit of 80,000 troops, was ill-equipped to face a million highly-trained Japanese troops. The only salvation might lie with the air force. He needed to know right away how well prepared it was for war, so he sent for Mow and Chennault.

As they were carried up the steep slopes of the mountain in sedan chairs, Chennault noticed that Mow was sweating, even though the air was cool. The general had good reason to sweat. He knew what to expect when one was summoned by Chiang. He could be shot before the day was out.

Even as a child Chiang had been prone to violent outbursts, fits of temper and rage. As he got older, he channeled his anger into robberies and gang murders and lived a dissolute life. At the best of times he was difficult to get along with. A biographer wrote that "Chiang is by nature obdurate. Not infrequently he would fly into storms of temper before which few human beings could stand. . . . No one could endure him, and by degrees he became more and more disagreeable to his associates."

He was intensely ambitious and cunning, with a yearning for power and a genius for manipulation and intrigue. He was fascinated by Adolf Hitler and modeled his secret police after the Gestapo. He also formed a Blue Shirts unit along the lines of Hitler's Brown Shirts. His youngest son was sent to Germany for military training. The young man became a lieutenant in the *Wehrmacht* and participated in the occupation of Austria before returning home.

During his years in China, Chennault developed what he described as respect and appreciation for the Generalissimo and was impressed with his determination to fight. To Stilwell, however, who was blunt in his characterizations of those he neither liked nor respected, Chiang was a "peanut" who was more concerned with protecting his position from the Communists than with fighting the Japanese. Stilwell's appraisal turned out to be correct.

Chennault remained loyal to Madame and the Generalissimo throughout his life and was understandably grateful for all they had done for him. They gave him position and power as well as the opportunity to try out his ideas, a chance his own country had consistently refused him. They offered him a new life when he was at his lowest point. Because of them he was no longer a farmer in Louisiana but was to become a heroic figure known throughout the world and, eventually, a three-star general officer in the army that had let him go as a captain. With respect to Chiang and Madame, Chennault was, perhaps for the only time in his life, a good subordinate.

He met Chiang that day in Kuling on the screened porch of a one-story bungalow. Madame Chiang acted as translator because her husband spoke no English. Chiang shook hands with Chennault and began to talk rapidly through his ill-fitting false teeth to General Mow. He asked him how many air force planes were ready for combat. Mow told him there were 91.

Chennault and Madame stood off to one side while she quietly translated the conversation. Chennault watched closely and later described what occurred.

"Chiang turned turkey red, and I thought he was going to explode. He strode up and down the terrace, loosing long strings of sibilant Chinese that seemed to hiss, coil, and strike like a snake. Madame stopped translating. Color drained from Mow's face as he stood stiffly at attention, his eyes fixed straight ahead."

Madame leaned closer to Chennault and said that her husband had threatened General Mow with execution because according to Chiang's information, the air force had 500 combat-ready planes. The Italian accounting system had come back to haunt Mow.

A moment later the Generalissimo turned to Chennault and asked him the same question. How many planes were ready for war? Chennault corroborated Mow's figures. At Madame's urging to tell Chiang the whole truth, Chennault spoke for twenty minutes describing the abysmal condition of both aircraft and pilots. He gave Chiang an honest, straightforward appraisal, holding nothing back, not attempting to sweeten the bad news in any way. By doing so, Chennault established the reputation for frankness and honesty, of reporting the facts no matter how disagreeable they were, that gave Chiang such confidence in him for the rest of the war. Chennault was one of the few people who could always be trusted to tell him the truth.

Chiang was not the only person to overestimate the size of the Chinese Air Force. By August, the Japanese were fighting in Shanghai and they were worried about the safety of their troops there. Their intelligence reports showed that the Chinese had 300 warplanes in the Shanghai area alone. In addition, the Japanese may have overestimated the ability of the Chinese Air Force. They received an indication of its weakness, however, on August 14, a day that came to be called Black Saturday.

Japanese ships in Shanghai harbor were shelling Chinese positions in and around the city, causing many casualties. Madame asked Chennault if the air force could help. He recommended bombing the Japanese heavy cruiser *Idzumo,* which contained the naval headquarters, as well as other light cruisers in the harbor. Chennault and Billy McDonald stayed up most of the night planning the attack. After twenty years of practice, exercises, and maneuvers, Chennault was, at last, planning the real thing, but it was ironic that his first combat mission should involve bombers, not fighters.

Chennault's preparations for the attack could not be faulted, but the Chinese pilots did not follow his instructions. The *Idzumo* was to be hit by Northrop light bombers flying at a fixed air speed at an altitude of 7500 feet. The pilots were told to approach the ship from a direction that would not take them over the crowded International Settlement. The bomber pilots found that they could not see the ship because of a heavy cloud cover. Rather than abort the mission and lose face, they dove to 1500 feet where they had the target in sight. They did not, however, compensate for their changed speed, altitude, and angle of attack and their bombs fell into the International Settlement. One bomb exploded on Nanking Road, probably the most densely populated street in the world. The death toll was 950 and more than 1100 other people were wounded. Although the *Idzumo* was not touched by so much as a single piece of shrapnel, the U.S. cruiser *Augusta* had much of its glass broken by the shock waves. And on that same day, Japanese bombers destroyed the Hangchow Flying School outside of Shanghai.

The following day Chennault was flying from Nanking to Shanghai when he spotted six Chinese dive bombers attacking a warship in the Yangtze River. Chennault flew lower in an effort to identify the ship. Bullet holes appeared in his wings as he got close enough to see the ship's flag. It was the Union Jack. The Chinese had been firing on a British cruiser.

The Japanese shifted their air attacks to Nanking and warned foreign diplomats to evacuate the city. The U.S. State Department ordered all Americans to leave China's combat zones, but Chennault stayed where he was to plan his defense of Nanking. This time he would be working with an elite group of Chinese fighter pilots trained to attack bombers. The men had been trained by the old Flying Trapeze team—Chennault, Billy McDonald, and Luke Williamson.

Before he could go on the offensive, however, Chennault and Sebie Smith were caught in an air raid. It was "a hot soggy summer day with a low ceiling," Smith recalled, "and all of a sudden, it seemed like all hell had turned loose. The Japanese formation dipped down from under the clouds with their machine guns firing away and all the antiaircraft in Nanking firing away and everything bursting in the sky. Bombs started to fall on the airport and I saw Chennault run for the first time to a dugout and I was behind, running and trying to get a picture of him. All the other times, it seemed that Chennault would just dare anything to happen. He seemed to take unnecessary chances."

When the all-clear sounded, Chennault and Smith drove out to the airport as fast as they could. When they got there, the first person they saw was Madame Chiang, who was walking around a damaged plane. She had beaten them to the field.

Chennault knew that the Japanese, like the Americans, believed Douhet's preachings and had faith in the invincibility of the bomber. As a consequence, the Japanese used no fighter escorts in their bombing raids. Chennault was happy to have the chance to show them all how wrong they were. A month earlier he had established an extensive air-raid warning net, based on his old Maxwell Field approach. Thus, he knew when the enemy bombers were on their way, how many were coming, and at what altitude they were flying. His pilots were ready for them.

Chennault was determined to give his fighters every advantage. He instructed them to wait high above the bombers until after the bombing and strafing runs had been completed and the enemy planes were starting back for their bases. By then, he reasoned, the Japanese pilots would be overconfident and less alert. Also, their machine guns would be low on ammunition or out altogether. Chennault drilled his pilots on the weak spots of bomber aircraft. He taught them to fly in threes and to attack only one plane at a time. One fighter would hit the bomber from above, the second would approach from below, and the third would then zoom in for the final attack.

The Japanese made three bombing raids on Nanking over the next five days and lost 54 planes and crews. Almost half of each attack force was wiped out, by fighters that flew no faster than the bombers they challenged. After so many futile years of trying to prove the worth of his fighter tactics, Chennault had finally done so in grand style. A Japanese combat report on their losses concluded that "bombers are no match for enemy fighter planes." Japanese bombers did not appear again over China in daylight without a fighter escort. The Japanese learned their lesson well.

The Japanese did not initially have any fighter planes available because they believed in the invincibility of the bomber. Not wanting to slacken the pace of their raids, however, they switched to nighttime attacks. Instead of using massed formations, they sent only one or two bombers over the city at a time. Chennault was ready for them, with tactics he had developed at the Air

Corps Tactical School and had tried out on the old Keystone bombers.

He ordered all the Chinese searchlights placed in a grid pattern. Once a searchlight picked up a bomber, it stayed on it until the next light in the pattern could pick it up. The enemy plane would be passed along from one light to another, deprived of the protection of darkness as long as it was over the city.

The Chinese fighter pilots were taught to cruise below the bombers and to fly directly up the beam of light toward the underside of the enemy ships. This was a variation of flying out of the sun. Japanese crews were blinded by the searchlights and could not see the fighters. At Maxwell Field, Chennault had been able to close within 50 feet of the bellies of the bombers without being detected. The first night he tried this tactic in China, one fighter was in the air and the pilot shot down one bomber. On the second night the whole squadron of fighters was ready and they shot down 7 of 13 bombers. The Japanese did not try night bombing again and did not appear over Nanking at all for nearly six weeks.

While they revised their tactics for their next aerial assault against Chennault's planes, the Japanese demanded that all American pilots leave China. They included not only Chennault's group of flight instructors but also the Americans who flew for the China National Aviation Corporation (CNAC). Chennault claimed that Clarence Gauss, the U.S. consul general in Shanghai, threatened him with arrest, court-martial, and loss of citizenship if he did not leave China. Chennault reportedly told him that he would not leave until the last Japanese had left.

Gauss was acting either in ignorance or in defiance of the official State Department reaction to the Japanese demand. Although the State Department did stop issuing passports to Americans who wanted to offer their services to China, it decided to take no action against persons like Chennault who were already there, even though technically they were in violation of American neutrality laws. Nevertheless, Chennault, feeling the need to evade the U.S. sheriff that Gauss threatened to send after him, kept a low profile for several months. Officially, and with much help from Chinese officials, he disappeared from Nanking. If the sheriff was sent, he never found Chennault. As a result of his disappearance, however, nasty rumors began cropping up back home. When Chennault heard about them—particularly the rumor that he was fighting under an assumed name—he was furious. To suggest that he would not use his own name was an attack on his honor that had to be answered.

He wanted his friends—and perhaps more important, his enemies—to know the truth, so in September 1937, he wrote a letter to the newspaper in Montgomery, Alabama, where Maxwell Field was located. He began by pointing out that China was fighting for all the nations of the Pacific, including the United States. The Chinese people could not understand why Americans had deserted them when the Japanese attacked. Then he came to his main argument.

"I am curious to know why I am 'accredited' with serving under an assumed name? Was there something in my twenty years of service in the Army Air Corps or my conduct as an officer at Maxwell Field for five years that would make me adopt an assumed name? Or is it thought that I fear to reveal my hatred of war and aggression under my true name? I have no apologies to offer for my twenty years of service, nor do I hesitate to take responsibility for my feelings with regard to the imperialistic designs of the Japanese or their murderous attacks on a peaceful people. I assure you that you can always address me by my true name."

Chennault and the other Americans lived at the Nanking Country Club, where Chennault enjoyed playing Ping-Pong every evening after dinner. He teamed up with Billy McDonald against Sebie Smith and Harry Sutter, a Swiss national who worked for the Chinese Air Force. Chennault and McDonald almost always won, but they let the other two beat them occasionally, just often enough to keep them playing.

Chennault never held any formal staff meetings during that time, but every morning at breakfast he would discuss his plans for the day. It was at one of these breakfast discussions that the idea of an all-American volunteer force was first mentioned. "At that time," Smith said, "the idea was so farfetched that none of us thought it could ever come about."

On September 18, after a hiatus of some six weeks, the Japanese were back in the air over Nanking, this time with a new and frightening weapon. It was Chennault's weapon, a fighter plane, but it was superior to anything he had. The plane was the Mitsubishi A5M, Type 96, an open-cockpit monoplane that was considerably faster and more maneuverable than the P-26s, Curtiss Hawk biplanes, and Italian Fiat biplanes flown by the Chinese.

Chennault was learning that the Japanese built lightweight aircraft, sacrificing armor plating and tough airframes for greater speed and maneuverability. Their philosophy, it seemed to him, was that the planes were expendable, that it was better to replace them than to repair them when damaged. American planes were tougher and were built to protect the pilot as much as possible. They were constructed to withstand battle damage so they could be repaired and sent back into action. This crucial difference between Japanese and American airplanes would hold true four years later, when Chennault was training his Flying Tigers, and would remain true for the duration of the war.

The Mitsubishi Type 96 fighters were part of the Japanese Navy's Second Combined Air Flotilla. Their pilots were among the best in the world. On the first day of battle the Chinese lost 11 of the 16 fighters they sent aloft. Every day the Japanese fighters came over Nanking and shot down more Chinese planes. Chennault's air force was helpless against them.

Only one fighter was faster than the Type 96, and that was Chennault's personal plane, the Curtiss Hawk Special, an export version of the Army Air Corps' new all-metal monoplane, the P-36. Madame Chiang had bought it for Chennault for $55,000, and Chennault had it specially armored around the seat. Because of its superior speed, it was used for reconnaissance missions.

Much has been written about how Chennault flew combat missions himself and allegedly shot down some 40 enemy planes, making him America's first air ace in the war with Japan. In his memoirs he refers to combat missions but never indicated that he shot down any aircraft. He did note that in October 1938, he flew his last fighter mission after a full year of combat. His second wife, Anna, whom he married after the war, wrote that he was the greatest but most unheralded flying ace of World War II, having shot down at least 40 Japanese planes. Madame Chiang, however, had specifically requested that Chennault not fly combat missions.

Chennault and McDonald agreed never to discuss publicly their part in any fighting because they were civilians and their country was not then at war with Japan. McDonald kept to this agreement. "Even now," Sebie Smith wrote in 1983, "Mac indicates a very negative headshake when the question is discussed in his presence."

Smith was in an excellent position to know whether Chennault was in combat. He was present every time Chennault flew. "I looked out for his aircraft as if I were his crew chief. . . . The only bullet hole I ever discovered on his return was one hole straight up through the bottom of the fuselage." To have flown in combat for a year and to have shot down 40 planes with only a single bullet hole in return seems less than credible. Furthermore, there are the facts of Chennault's age and health, neither of which was adequate for the strain of such combat. "Frankly," Smith said, "I don't think he ever shot down any planes." Certainly there is no evidence to indicate that he did.

Using their new Type 96 fighters, the Japanese attained total air superiority over Nanking, Shanghai, and most of eastern China in fewer than two months. The Chinese planes that they did not destroy in the air, they bombed and strafed on the ground. Madame Chiang frequently visited Chennault's airfield at Nanking, despite the continuing bombing raids, because she felt a personal responsibility for her Chinese pilots. She liked to be there, with tea ready, to listen to their stories when they returned from a mission and to mourn those who did not come back.

One clear morning she joined Chennault to watch the return of 11 dive bombers. They counted the incoming planes and noted that all had survived the mission, a rare event. The planes circled over the field and prepared to land. The first pilot overshot the runway and crashed in a rice paddy beyond it. The second pilot ground-looped and his plane exploded in a fireball. The third landed safely, but the fourth crashed into the fire truck that was speeding toward the burning wreckage of the second plane. Of the 11 dive bombers, none of which had sustained battle damage, 5 crashed on landing and 4 pilots were killed.

"What can we do, what can we do?" Madame asked, tears streaming down her cheeks. "We buy them the best planes money can buy, spend so much time and money training them, and they are killing themselves before my eyes. What can we do?"

The pilots she had watched were the products—or the victims—of the Italian flight school.

Courage was not lacking among the Chinese pilots. Stories of their heroism and fortitude are plentiful. The handful who did display cowardly behavior in the face of the enemy met death by firing squad. More typical is the story of Art Chen, a fighter pilot, born in Oregon, who took on three Japanese fighters and shot one down before running out of ammunition. He deliberately rammed the second Japanese plane and then bailed out. He landed close to the wreckage of his ship and salvaged one of the machine guns, which he carried eight miles back to the airfield. Presenting the heavy gun to Chennault, Chen said, "Sir, can I have another airplane for my machine gun?"

But heroism and courage were no longer enough. The Chinese government purchased as many new fighters and bombers as they could, but the Japanese shot them down as quickly as they appeared. And pilots, particularly the good ones taught by the American flight instructors, could not be replaced as rapidly as the planes. By the end of October 1937, the Chinese Air Force had almost ceased to exist. Most of the better pilots were dead and fewer than a dozen fighter planes remained of the 91 with which they had begun the war.

For a brief time Chennault had been able to strike back at the enemy with some light bombers he had stationed in the Canton area. They remained relatively safe from air attack because the Japanese were concentrating on the Chinese fighter bases. The light bombers sank several freighters and small destroyers off the coast before the Japanese loosed their fighters on them. On their next bombing mission, only 1 of 12 returned. Several days later, as the repaired bomber took off, a Japanese fighter shot it down within sight of the field.

Without air power, Nanking and other Chinese cities on or near the coast were nearly defenseless. They no longer even received warning of impending air raids because the Japanese had overrun Chennault's air-raid warning net. Chiang decided to move the government into the interior, first to Hankow, then to Chungking, some 2000 miles from Nanking. New airfields would be established far beyond the range of the Japanese fighters so that training could be conducted without interruption.

The coastline, with its major ports, and the capital were under siege. All of Shanghai province was overrun by the middle of November. On December 7, 1937, the Japanese launched their ground offensive against Nanking.

Four days later the remaining members of the American diplomatic staff boarded a U.S. navy gunboat. With them went several crates of new Japanese aviation equipment that Chennault had salvaged from wrecked Japanese planes. A navy intelligence officer had examined the lot and recognized its value. He was shipping it back to the States the safest way possible, on the gunboat, the *Panay*. The following day, 32 miles upriver from Nanking, Japanese planes sunk the *Panay*, killing 3 people and wounding 48. The Japanese government apologized, paid an indemnity of more than $2 million, and allegedly reprimanded the pilots responsible. A regrettable accident, they said. No one knows if they were aware of Chennault's valuable cargo, so one is left to speculate on how accidental the attack really was.

Japanese troops battered their way into Nanking against fierce opposition. Chiang ordered Chennault out of the city, and he took off at the first light of dawn. Shells were exploding nearby as he sped down the runway. "As I roared over the city wall, the sun was just beginning to rise, casting a pink glow over the stricken city, which gradually changed to a prophetic bloody red."

Prophetic indeed. What the newspapers throughout the world would report as the "rape of Nanking" began as soon as the fighting ceased. Japanese troops went berserk and over the next four weeks they sacked and pillaged the city, raping, slaughtering, and mutilating as many as 300,000 men, women, and children. They killed uncounted numbers of prisoners-of-war and bayoneted or machine-gunned 20,000 young men of military age. This butchery was one of the greatest atrocities of the brutal Pacific war.

Over the next eighteen months, Chennault played only a minor role in China's air war. He became more of an observer than a participant, although he remained an advisor to Madame Chiang. He reported that every year he was paid more than had been agreed upon. His part in the war was soon overshadowed by the substantial assistance being supplied by the Soviet Union. China had pleaded for help from all the civilized nations but only the Soviets responded in any significant way. Soviet aid went only to Chiang, not to the large Chinese Communist armies that had ideological ties to the Soviet Union. They chose to help Chiang because his armies were larger and thus represented a more effective fighting force against the Japanese. In their eagerness to assist anyone who might weaken the Japanese and keep them from menacing Russia, the Soviets were willing to overlook Chiang's suppression of the Communists, and they continued to support him until 1939.

The Soviet aid began to arrive shortly before the fall of Nanking. While the United States was still selling high-octane aviation fuel and scrap iron to Japan, Russia sent four fighter squadrons and two bomber squadrons, with their best pilots and crews, to China. They sold the Chinese some 400 planes and established flying schools for Chinese pilots. The Russians kept to themselves, living in hostels built for them by the Chinese government's War Area Service Corps. They brought their own supplies, guards, and vodka. The only things they relied on the local community for were prostitutes and wristwatches.

Olga Greenlaw, wife of one of the American instructors still in China, recalled how the Russian pilots "had a passion for wristwatches and wore three or four on one wrist at a time." They were paid quite well by Russian standards and spent the money with abandon. The Russians were enthusiastic about Hollywood movie stars, and asked Olga for confidential information about Mary Pickford. They traded their best vodka for old American movie fan magazines.

While they were on duty, the Russians were highly disciplined fighters. Chennault observed that they apparently did not know the meaning of the term "combat fatigue." They could remain on alert status, sitting in their planes, for 12 hours at a time, fly into combat, and return for a night of carousing.

They were very inquisitive about American airplanes but would not let any of the American personnel examine theirs. This restriction became a challenge to Chennault when he learned that the Russians had developed a synchronizer that allowed four machine guns to fire through the propellers of their fighter planes. He was determined to get one to send to the air corps engineers at Wright Field.

As a mechanic, Sebie Smith was allowed into the Russian parts depot to exchange equipment. "It's the only thing I've ever stolen in my life," Smith recalled. He carried an old cylinder with him into the depot, walked past the armaments bench, picked up a synchronizer, concealed it inside the cylinder, and walked out. "Every step of the way from there back to the field I could just feel those Russians pouncing right down on me and in fact, for months, I'd wake up at night thinking the Russians were coming to get their synchronizer." Chennault sent the equipment to Wright Field for evaluation but never heard from them about it.

The Russians took orders from no one but their commander, General Asanov. Chiang Kai-shek had no influence over them. Occasionally, however, they would heed Chennault's advice, and one of the few times they listened to him led to a victory on April 29, 1938, Japanese Emperor Hirohito's birthday.

Chennault encouraged the Russians to team up with the Chinese fighter squadron at Hankow Field to bait a trap for the Japanese. The enemy had not bombed Hankow often because of their heavy losses to the Russian fighters. To encourage the Japanese to return to Hankow, Chennault had all the Russian and Chinese fighter planes take off one afternoon and circle the city slowly, so that all the spies could spot them as they headed in the direction of Nanchang. An hour later the planes slipped quietly back to Hankow Field from another direction. Chennault and Billy McDonald watched and listened from their vantage point in the tallest building in downtown Hankow, but neither could detect the planes returning.

The Japanese took the bait. Air-raid sirens sounded the next morning as a force of 15 bombers escorted by 24 Mitsubishi Type 96 fighters approached Hankow. The 40 Russian fighters were already in the air, waiting to attack the Japanese on their way back to their bases. Twenty Chinese pilots attacked the Japanese fighters on their approach, prepared to engage them in combat as long as possible so that the Japanese would use up much of their gasoline and ammunition.

The Chinese pilots played their parts well but at a heavy cost, losing 11 of the 20 planes. The Japanese, convinced that they had thus eliminated the defending forces, dropped their bombs and started home, flying in loose formation with the fighters well separated from the bombers. They felt no need to remain alert.

The Russians struck from out of the sun. When it was over, only three Japanese bombers escaped. Every enemy fighter had been destroyed. Russian losses totaled two fighter planes. It was the greatest air disaster of the China war for the Japanese.

Even after that victory, the Russians fought their own war in their own way, freezing Chennault out. As a result, he had little to do. When Sebie Smith left China for the States in June 1938, he found Chennault "disheartened and blue. . . . Chennault said, 'Well, I may be joining you soon.' "

By the fall of 1938 the Chinese Air Force was desperate. So few of their American-trained pilots remained that it could hardly be called an air force, and Madame Chiang still had no control over the Russians. She and Chennault wanted to revive the Chinese Air Force and Chennault knew that the only way to accomplish that was with a training program run according to his exacting standards. Such a program would take months.

Madame Chiang believed she could not wait that long to take action against the Japanese, so she approached Chennault with an idea that he had consistently opposed in the past, the formation of a flying foreign legion composed of Western mercenaries. Chennault did not like the idea because he thought it would attract undisciplined adventurers, barnstormers, and soldiers of fortune who would not necessarily make good combat pilots. This time, however, he softened his opposition. Perhaps he was enticed by the possibility of commanding a fighter unit again and getting back in the war from which the Russians had sidelined him.

Also, another opportunity presented itself. William Pawley, the aviation entrepreneur (who two years later would be instrumental in establishing—and in delaying—the Flying Tigers), had 30 bombers for sale, single-engine Vultee V11GB attack planes. With a crew of three, the Vultees could carry a heavy bomb load to a range of 2000 miles. Chennault, that most zealous of fighter plane advocates, wrote that he was "desperate for a long-range bombing outfit." He wanted to continue to bomb the enemy shipping off the coast, which his Chinese pilots had hit with their Northrop light bombers, all 150 of which had since been lost.

The International Squadron, consisting of three Americans, four Frenchmen, one Dutchman, and one German, was formed to serve as flight leaders for the Chinese pilots who would fly the rest of the 30 Vultee bombers. The group was described as a "ragged and somewhat motley mob," and their operation was a fiasco.

At first, the Chinese pilots refused to fly under the leadership of the foreigners, which they took as a criticism of their abilities, and stormed off the field in protest. Chinese bombardiers walked off in sympathy with the pilots. Not losing face was more important than striking at the enemy. The Chinese rear gunners, the third members of the bomber crews, were eager to fight and they did not seem to care who flew the planes. The problem with the gunners was that they could not shoot very well. A special training program had to be set up for them at Ichang. Chennault sent Rolfe Watson—an ex-Army Air Corps armaments specialist who had come to China with Williamson, McDonald, and Smith—to take charge of the training. When Watson arrived at Ichang, he sized up the situation and telegraphed Chennault: FIELD UNDER WATER. NO STUDENTS. WHAT SHALL I DO? Chennault wired back: STUDENTS ARRIVED FRIDAY. BAIL OUT FIELD. CARRY ON.

There were several good pilots in the International Squadron and the outfit did make a few successful raids. However, as one of the American pilots, Tommy Walker, noted, "It was the most disorganized mess you ever saw. The flying was ragged as hell and it was just plain dangerous to fly with most of the men— some of the International Squadron people were nuts who never did know how to fly, and most of the Chinese just couldn't fly. In the air, the word discipline was a hollow joke. If Chennault could have seen those formations—I use the word loosely—over target, he would have wept. Everybody flew where the hell they pleased. It was worth your life to rely in battle upon a Chinese crew member. Most of them were brave enough, but they were always being insulted by some thing or another. The crazy bastards would sulk at their guns and refuse to fire at the Japanese whenever they thought somebody had insulted them."

Discipline in the International Squadron was even worse on the ground. The men spent most of their time in the bars and brothels along Hankow's Dump Street, drinking heavily, bragging about their exploits, and talking openly about their forthcoming missions. Finally, they talked too much. An early-morning raid was planned. To be able to sleep later, the men loaded their planes with bombs and gasoline the day before. The Japanese arrived a few hours later, at sunset. One bomb exploded under the wing of a Vultee and within five seconds the entire row of planes was on fire. That was the end of the International Squadron.

Chennault was left with no combat forces to lead. He was exiled, as he put it, to the interior and the training facility he established at Kunming. So far removed from the fighting, and with the continuing difficulties of training Chinese pilots, he grew discouraged again about his future. He applied to the U.S. Army Air Corps in an attempt to return to active duty, believing that his year of experience in fighting the Japanese would be recognized as valuable in the training of American pilots. "It seemed to me," he wrote, "that this experience could be applied faster and more fruitfully in training American airmen than in trying to hatch a Chinese phoenix in the mountain-ringed hinterlands." The air corps turned him down, saying that there were no funds to pay for retired officers to return to active duty.

Chennault tried again when he returned to the United States to visit his family during Christmas of 1939 and was rejected once more. In 1940 he wrote to Hap Arnold, then the air corps chief of staff, asking for a job as an instructor in fighter tactics. Arnold offered him a position, but it was at the Coast Artillery School training antiaircraft gunners. Chennault turned it down, but he tried one more time to rejoin the air corps, in December 1940 when he was back in Washington trying to secure bombers with which to attack Japan. The coast artillery assignment was re-offered, with the promise of a promotion to major. Chennault was unable to persuade the leaders of the air corps that he had some unique experience to offer—knowledge of how to fight the Japanese.

People who accused Chennault of being nothing more than a mercenary lost sight of the fact that four times between 1938 and 1940 he was eager to give up his generous salary to work for one-fourth of that amount and wear the uniform of his country. Chennault was a patriot who wanted to serve and if he could not do so directly, then he would indirectly by helping to prepare for the inevitable war between the United States and Japan.

One way he could help was to make sure that when the Americans came to China to fight, they would have airfields in strategic locations for reaching Japan, fields that would be suitable for heavy bombers such as the B-17. Before Chennault went to work, the Chinese airfields consisted of dirt runways that turned muddy in the rain and dusty in the sun. They were useless for heavy bombers.

As early as 1937 Chennault had begun the first solid runway in China, at Nanking, constructed of brick and tiles from the Ming tombs. The Japanese captured it before it was finished. He started another one at Hankow, which was completed in two months by 120,000 coolies who had only hand tools with which to work. That runway, too, was captured, but Chennault had others built in the eastern provinces, each with a 5000-foot runway capable of handling the bombers that had not yet been built. He stocked caches of gasoline, bombs, and bullets in bombproof shelters near each field.

Another way Chennault tried to prepare his country for war was through the collection of intelligence data on the Japanese Air

Force. After his initial batch of materiel went down with the *Panay*, he proceeded to compile an encyclopedia on Japanese tactics, the caliber and training of their pilots, the technical specifications of their aircraft, and the locations of their airfields in China and on Formosa. This information would form a major part of his training manual for the Flying Tigers, but earlier, in 1939 and 1940, he wanted the U.S. Army Air Corps to have it to plan the coming war.

The air corps was not interested in Chennault's data. In 1939, on his Christmas visit, he personally delivered to air corps intelligence officers a detailed report on the engineering and performance characteristics of a new Japanese fighter plane, the Nakajima Type 97. Several months later, the air corps responded, saying that the performance characteristics he had cited were impossible to achieve, given the engineering specifications of the aircraft. Chennault knew better. He had flown the plane himself, one that had been captured by the Chinese.

On his 1940 visit to Washington Chennault asked his old friend Possum Hansell, of the Flying Trapeze team, to check on his report about the plane. It could not be found in intelligence files and apparently had been discarded.

Chennault also submitted to the U.S. Army Air Corps the first information they had seen on the new Japanese Zero, a plane that had first flown in China that summer. Despite his detailed data on the Zero's flying characteristics, American pilots in the Philippines and elsewhere in the Pacific had been told nothing about it when war began a year-and-a-half later. No American aviation publication even realized that the Zero existed before the attack on Pearl Harbor. The air corps did not take Chennault's information seriously.

The failure of the air corps to use Chennault's information worked to the advantage of the Japanese. Commander Masatake Okumiya of the Imperial Japanese Navy wrote after the war, "Our potential enemy was sadly misinformed as to the true performance capabilities of our warplanes, and American aviation magazines especially went to great lengths to deride our air forces. Clearly they dismissed as inconceivable that Japanese planes could effectively carry the war to the Americans and the British."

The September 1941 issue of the American magazine *Aviation* described Japanese pilots as infinitely inferior to the Chinese, as having the highest accident rate in the world, as lacking experience in large-scale combat operations, and as deficient in the ability to develop an effective air force. The article went on to note that "America's aviation experts can say without hesitation that the chief military airplanes of Japan are either outdated already, or are becoming outdated." This was published three months before Pearl Harbor.

Chennault tried to tell them otherwise, but no one listened.

The Russians left China at the end of summer, 1939. Japan's air force was now virtually unopposed. The Japanese began a systematic program of terror bombing of the cities of western China. The new capital at Chungking was devastated as an object lesson. Incendiary bombs set off huge firestorms that at one point burned for three days and nights. As many as 10,000 people were killed the first night alone.

Chennault was in Chungking during much of the bombing. A journalist with him recalled that "Chennault would never take shelter in an air raid, but would study the Japanese formations as they came over, as a football coach studies films of a team he expects to soon meet in the field." He watched the bombers from a hillside near the Methodist mission, taking motion pictures of them, admiring their skill, and hating them for what they were doing and for being unable himself to attack. He could take some small consolation in that the casualties would have been even greater if not for his air-raid warning system. It had never failed to alert the city to an impending raid.

When the bombers left, Chennault went into the smoldering ruins to do what he could, but there was little hope. The city was constructed primarily of wood and bamboo. Whole neighborhoods blazed like forest fires out of control. In the first six months of the attacks, the Japanese dropped 35,000 tons of bombs on the city, one third of the total tonnage that would be dropped on Japan during the entire war.

For the next year, as Chennault found himself in city after city that was being pounded into destruction, he took films of the enemy formations and filled up notebooks with his observations on their tactics.

Few fighter planes were left to challenge the Japanese. Chennault's training field at Kunming was bombed almost every day. He had no fighters there and only a few short-range antiaircraft guns for protection. Flight training was restricted to early-morning and late-afternoon hours. The rest of the time it was unsafe to be in the air. One raid destroyed Chennault's house. He found his office sliced through with shrapnel and fragments of tile.

On August 9, 1940, the Japanese introduced the Mitsubishi Zero-Sen, which had twice the speed and range of the Type 96 and was one of the most maneuverable planes ever built. The Zeros flew over Chungking every day, escorting the bombers and looking for Chinese fighters. None rose to challenge them. The fighters fled the city when the alert was posted and returned when the raid was over.

On September 13 the Zeros were waiting. Thirteen of them circled high overhead. Below, 27 outdated Russian fighter planes manned by Chinese pilots headed for their airfield. Chennault watched as the Zeros plummeted down with the sun behind them "like hawks in a chicken yard." The Zeros shot down all the planes without sustaining a single loss.

Chennault could do little but watch, take pictures, and gather intelligence data that no one in the States seemed to want. And he could try to train a capable new generation of Chinese pilots. "Days were spent in the endless grind of training," he wrote. "Cribbage, poker, and an occasional movie, old before I came to China, that was shown in the Nanping Theatre, absorbed our nights." He was as removed from active participation in the war as if he were back home in Waterproof, Louisiana. It began to appear that his twenty years of preparation had been wasted. His country would not take advantage of his experience, and without better planes and pilots China was unable to take advantage of it either.

In the middle of October 1940, Chiang Kai-shek summoned Chennault to Chungking. "You must go to the United States immediately," he told him. "Work out the plans for whatever you think you need. Do what you can to get American planes and pilots."

Chennault came to Washington with his plan to bomb Japan and left with his consolation prize air force of P-40s. It was the beginning of the Flying Tigers. Claire Chennault was getting back into the war.

F I V E

THE MOST UNDISCIPLINED OUTFIT I'VE EVER SEEN

Claire Chennault was not impressed with the pilots of his new air force. "Pilots looked far from promising as they checked in," he wrote. They were overweight, flabby, and in poor physical condition after too much eating and drinking on their long sea voyages, and they seemed to wilt in the heat and humidity of the monsoon season.

He was not impressed with their flying records either. He had wanted pilots in their twenties with at least three years of experience in flying fighter planes, pilots who had logged a minimum of 300 hours of flight time. When he told Hap Arnold of his requirements, the air corps chief of staff said, "If I were to give you 100 pilots with that kind of experience, you would fold up my entire pursuit section." Chennault replied, with his usual lack of tact, "You're wrong. If you can't spare that many pilots with that kind of experience, you don't have a pursuit section to begin with."

Of the 110 men who started with the First American Volunteer Group, only 12 met Chennault's standards. Most of the pilots had never seen a P-40, much less flown one, and more than half had never flown any kind of fighter plane. The men were bomber, patrol plane, torpedo plane, and dive-bomber pilots. Nearly half came from the navy, and they ranged in age and experience from a twenty-one-year-old army pilot who had just graduated from flying school to a forty-three-year-old navy flyer who had almost as many hours in a fighter as Chennault. They were not what he wanted, but they were all he was likely to get.

Chennault had not personally recruited the men of the AVG. That had been William Pawley's job. The men were hired by Pawley's company, CAMCO, which, as the contract the men of the AVG had signed stated, "among other things operates an aircraft manufacturing, operating and repair business in China." CAMCO's new employees agreed to "render such services and perform such duties as the Employer may direct." Nothing was put in writing about what those duties might be, but the pay was generous for 1940, ranging from $250 per month for the clerical and technical personnel to $750 per month for squadron leaders. The minimum monthly pay for pilots was $600. The contract called for one year's employment, dating from the time of arrival in China.

Pawley had assigned the recruiting to Richard Aldworth, a retired air corps pilot, who directed the operation from his hospital bed in Washington's Walter Reed Hospital, where he was being treated for a kidney ailment. Aldworth enlisted the help of a half dozen men including C. B. "Skip" Adair, an ex-army pilot who had been in China and would return as the AVG's supply officer. Another recruiter was Rutledge Irvine, a retired navy pilot. They visited every army and navy flying field in the United States, carrying with them letters from Hap Arnold and Secretary of the Navy Knox, authorizing them to talk to the pilots and ground crew.

Some of the base commanders did not like the idea that people in civilian clothes were trying to take their personnel away from them, and they called Washington for confirmation. They got it. A few commanders even tried to prevent their subordinates from joining this new outfit. At Randolph Field in Texas, the CO of 2nd Lt. Albert E. "Red" Probst was irate at the thought of losing one of his flight instructors.

"I don't know who you think you are," he told Probst. "War is imminent and it is with Germany! We're training fighter pilots and you're a fighter pilot and if you think you're going to resign you're out of your mind."

"Sir," Probst said, "I don't know anything except that I need for you just to endorse this request for resignation, approve or disapprove it—doesn't make any difference to me, sir!"

The CO disapproved the request but two days later called Probst to his office.

"I don't know who you know," he said, "but I have a telegram that you have been resigned. You are to be processed off this base and separated from the Air Corps within 24 hours."

The recruiters told the men what the contract did not: they would be flying P-40s over China to defend the Burma Road from attacks by Japanese bombers. They were also told about a rumor—and there must have been many a sly wink at this point—that the Chinese government would pay a bonus of $500 for every enemy plane destroyed. To no one's surprise, the rumor turned out to be true.

CAMCO agreed to pay the premiums on the $10,000 government life insurance policies given to all members of the U.S. military but would deduct the amount of the premium from the employee's monthly pay. The company also agreed that in the case of death or total disability, it would pay six months' salary to the employee or the employee's beneficiary. "In the event of death the employer shall defray the expenses of a decent burial of the remains."

The conditions of continued employment were spelled out on the second page of the contract. The services of the employees could be terminated for misconduct including insubordination, revealing confidential information, the habitual use of drugs, the excessive use of alcoholic beverages, illness or other disability incurred not in the line of duty and as a result of the employee's own misconduct, and malingering.

Before the AVG disbanded, at least one man would be discharged for all these causes except one: no one ever revealed confidential information.

It was not only pilots who were recruited. The AVG had to function like any self-supporting combat group and needed a full complement of personnel—mechanics, armorers, radiomen, parachute riggers, cooks and bakers, paymasters, photographers, clerks, meteorologists, doctors and nurses, a dentist, and a chaplain. Including the pilots, some 240 persons in all joined the AVG.

They volunteered for a variety of reasons, but mostly for excitement, adventure, and money. Many were like Chennault and welcomed the opportunity to escape the discipline, regimentation, and red tape of military life. A few were idealists with a desire to save China from the Japanese, and some joined to escape from some problem in their personal lives.

Charles Bond, a twenty-five-year-old air corps pilot, was bored with his job ferrying bombers from California to Canada. He heard about the AVG from a friend and called Skip Adair to see about joining up. He had several reasons for wanting to go to China. "The lure of adventure in a foreign country on the other side of the world was exciting. More important, however, was the unique and ideal manner in which this opportunity served to satisfy my dreams: a chance to get back into fighters, a chance for combat experience which might help me secure a regular commission, and a chance to earn fast money which would put me in a position to buy my parents a home."

Greg Boyington joined for the money. Divorced and heavily in debt, he was under orders from the Marine Corps to devise a plan to repay his creditors or face disciplinary action. Each month he had to account to HQ the amount he had paid on each of his many debts. Out of fear of not being selected, he did not tell the CAMCO recruiter about his financial problems. "Nor did I tell him that I was a whiz at a cocktail party." The AVG would find out soon enough that Boyington was not the only one who liked to drink.

A number of others joined for the money. "Of course we were mercenaries," Sgt. Robert M. Smith said. "We were paid well.

. . . Some were patriots and idealists, but most of us liked to make money." Smith earned $84 per month in the air corps. CAMCO would pay him $300 a month as a radioman.

Pilot Red Probst said he "didn't know anything about Chennault or anything about the AVGs until Skip Adair walked into my office. He talked to me a few hours. I was head over heels in debt, and he was going to pay me $600 a month. And, I said, 'Let's see now, I am making $210 a month now, and you are going to pay me $600. I get a free trip to China.'"

At the naval station in San Diego, Loy F. "Sy" Seamster changed into civilian clothes. His hitch as a radioman was up, but before he left the naval base he remembered that a sailor owed him $5. The money was worth a detour. As he walked to the hangar where the sailor worked, a buddy stopped him and asked if he would like to go to the Far East. "Some damn fool is hiring people for $500 a month," he said. "Going to pay all expenses and all this good stuff to go there and have a ball. Come along and let's go see about it." Seamster went along with his friend and signed up on the spot.

At the naval air station in Norfolk, Petty Officer Melvin H. Woodward got the news from a friend who was stationed on the USS *Wasp*. "You hear about some bastard in Hangar Four who's offering a chance to get out of the Navy, see the world, fight the Japs, and get good money?" In thirty-six hours, both men were out of the navy and on their way west.

Some men expressed a desire to fight for a just cause. Robert J. "Sandy" Sandell, an army pilot, was one of them. "There was a lot of fighting going on in the world for causes I believed were right and just—and I wanted to be in on it. I had been trained to fight but it didn't look then as if the United States would ever get into the war."

John Tyler Donovan, a twenty-six-year-old navy pilot, thought that service with the AVG was "the best opportunity for immediate action against the Axis." He wrote home to his mother about his belief that "war is a horrible idiocy of human beings. People who cause a war should be dealt with severely. The great tragedy in the past has been that other nations sit by and wait until it is too late."

The promise of adventure was a powerful lure for many of the men. Radioman Smith was attracted by the money, but he thought that service in China offered even more. "I have always wanted to see more of the world and experience adventure with a big 'A' ever since I read Richard Haliburton's *The Royal Road to Romance.*"

The oldest AVG pilot, forty-three-year-old Louis "Cokey" Hoffman, had a devil-may-care expression that reflected his character. "That's why I came over," he said, "to get into good fights. For the hell of it." He was one of the few men in the AVG who was married and had children. He knew his wife was worried, but he had to go anyway. "If anything happens to me, she'll know I'll go the way I want it—fighting."

John Van Kuren Newkirk, a navy pilot from Scarsdale, New York, who became known in the States as "Scarsdale Jack," said he "could not stand lack of action, and was always planning some if the situation failed to produce it naturally." He had always taken risks. In his college years he survived a dozen automobile accidents, and in the navy he had crashed his plane three times. He did not hesitate a moment to sign up with the CAMCO recruiter. "It will give me a chance to find out if I really have the guts to fly combat."

David Lee "Tex" Hill and Edward F. Rector, dive-bomber pilots serving aboard the USS *Ranger,* signed up for the AVG because of their fascination with the Orient. Hill was born in Korea, where his father had been a missionary, and he had long wanted to go to China. Rector was interested in the Far East because of his appreciation of the poems and stories of Rudyard Kipling.

Jim Howard, a Navy fighter pilot aboard the *Enterprise,* was also fascinated by the Orient as well as by the chance for adventure. He had spent his first fourteen years there; his father had been professor of ophthalmology at the Peking Union Medical College. "The chance of returning to my boyhood home in China, while defending the interests of America at the same time, was the opportunity of a lifetime. I couldn't have been in a better position at a better time. The nostalgia of going to China would be a strong incentive, but the overriding reason was my yearning for adventure and action."

Allen "Bert" Christman, a navy pilot, had a unique reason for wanting to fly with Chennault. Before he joined the navy, Christman was a comic-strip artist, working with Milton Caniff on "Terry and the Pirates." He also drew a strip of his own, "Scorchy Smith," about the adventures of a daredevil pilot. He volunteered for China because he thought he could get "lots of good material for a comic strip out there."

Samuel B. Prevo, an AVG doctor, may have joined to try to forget someone. Olga Greenlaw suspected as much and tried to draw him out. "He started to tell me about a girl nurse back in the States when he suddenly stopped and said: 'And just why should I be telling you all this?' I still suspect there is something in his past."

The AVG chaplain, Paul Frillman, joined Chennault because he was dissatisfied with his chosen career as a missionary in China, but he didn't know what else to do. He thought the call from the AVG was a godsend. Years later, he wrote, "Most men were escaping from frustrations or disappointments, as perhaps I was. They hoped an unknown future in unknown places would somehow give them a second chance."

So for some it was a second chance, but for others, it was their last chance.

Discipline was a problem in the AVG from beginning to end. With such a diverse group of people, freed from the constraints of military life and their own culture, in a strange land with a great deal of money to spend, it was not surprising that their behavior was often less than exemplary. "Disintegration always seemed close to the surface," Paul Frillman said. It is a tribute to Chennault's leadership that he was able to keep them together and mold them into a first-class combat unit. Pilot Robert M. "Buster" Keeton spoke for most of them when he said, "Colonel Chennault is the only person who could hold such a group together." They had few problems in the air, but on the ground it was a different story.

The popular image of the Flying Tigers later promoted by the newspapers, magazines, and movies depicted them as wholesome, clear-eyed, lovable American boys fighting for God and country. Clare Boothe Luce wrote in *The New York Times* that they were the "most wonderful bunch of kids that ever drew the breath of life."

The reality was something else. One U.S. Army general described them as "the most undisciplined outfit I've ever seen." The British troops stationed near an AVG base in Rangoon called them ruffians and roughnecks. The Flying Tigers liked to whistle at the British dressed in their Bermuda shorts and to challenge them to fights when they declined a drink. The AVG pilots staged rickshaw races in the streets and festooned the sedate lounges and clubs with bullet holes in the ceilings.

On one occasion a Chinese official complained to Chennault that "for the past few weeks, I have found that some of the personnel in the American Volunteer Group are always drunk in the hostel, and this is not the worst. On several occasions they were badly drunk in the city, so much so that one of them lost his head completely and caught hold of a cook's chopper intending to kill a woman with it."

"Some of the guys seem to be off their rockers," Charlie Bond wrote in his diary, recording his concern about the group's behavior. "Some of these guys are just plain prima donnas and others are just plain scared." But he also admitted his own drinking. "Several of us went on a binge tonight—we needed it!" The next morning six pilots were too hungover to show up for duty.

The drinking and brawling had started on the ships that brought the men to the Far East. "Everyone is becoming tense and irritable," wrote Bond aboard ship. He challenged another pilot to step out on the deck and settle things with fists, but the other man declined. "We're all drinking a lot," he said. A few days later two other pilots began fighting, and a third man, who tried to break it up, was hit in the mouth.

Buster Keeton also kept a diary on the voyage. "There were some mighty drunk boys in the outfit. Gunner and Greg Boyington were plastered to the gills." Keeton described how Boyington was still drunk the following day. "He fell into the swimming pool and received a few bumps and rope burns." A week later Boyington cut his hand in several places when he ran it through a plate glass window.

Things were not so different after they reached their destination. When the men weren't flying, they were raising hell. "Today the Scotch was distributed," wrote pilot Charles Mott, "and all the drunks were around and howling. One bottle per man is plenty with a capital 'P.' "

Boyington was one of the heaviest drinkers in the group. Keeton recalled how Boyington once "got to talking about how tough he was and threw his fist through the bamboo wall. I retired before the party got too rough." Boyington once wrestled a stray cow to the ground and frequently challenged people to fights. It was not a wise idea to accept the challenge, and apparently no one did while sober. Olga Greenlaw called Boyington "the bulldog," the toughest man in the AVG, and a wild man when drinking.

Years later, Boyington wrote about himself at that time. "I was an emotionally immature person of the first order, which does not help peace of mind or make happiness. Frankly, this is what makes screwballs, and I'm afraid that I was one." *

He wasn't alone. Keeton remembered one beer party during which "a couple of the pilots went hog wild in town. Running up and down the streets . . . chasing natives and scaring half the population to death—going into restaurants jerking tablecloths off tables, breaking glass and threatening to beat hell out of the door."

Charlie Bond was returning to the airfield one night when "everyone decided to get a snootfull." He heard the sound of a pistol shot and came upon one of the pilots who was obviously intoxicated and firing his pistol wildly in the air. Bond tried to get the gun away from him. At least two other pilots went on similar shooting sprees and later beat up the American representative of the Allison Company, the P-40 engine manufacturer. The men were arrested and confined to their rooms.

Not every member of the AVG presented a discipline problem. There were those who drank only in moderation, attended church

---

*Later in the war, Boyington acquired the nickname "Pappy." Stationed in the South Pacific, he commanded a fighter squadron appropriately named the "Black Sheep." He shot down 22 enemy planes, received the Medal of Honor, spent twenty months as a Japanese prisoner-of-war, and returned to the United States a hero.

services regularly, sent most of their pay home, and led quiet lives. Similarly, not every member of the AVG dabbled in the black market, but the actions of those who did—like the activities of the habitual drunkards—tarnished the reputation of the AVG among the local populace and with the American army. The black market dealings were particularly troublesome for Chennault.

There was a great deal of easy money to be made in these illicit operations, particularly after the United States entered the war and began shipping millions of dollars worth of supplies to the China–Burma–India theater. In late February 1942, when Rangoon fell to the Japanese, some pilots and ground crew loaded trucks with supplies—food, gasoline, liquor, guns, and ammunition—to take up the Burma Road into China. Much of it was for their own use, but some was intended for the black market.

Chennault had assured Chinese customs officials that all vehicles with AVG markings would be carrying goods intended only for his outfit, and the government agreed to pass all such vehicles without inspection. When Chennault learned that some of his men had smuggled goods into China and sold them, he was furious. To him the action represented a serious breakdown in morale. In addition, it would make him lose face among the Chinese after his assurance that the trucks would contain only essential supplies.

Chennault ordered the AVG provost marshal, Melvin Ceder, to search the quarters of the men accused of smuggling. Ceder was beaten severely and taken to the hospital. Sam Prevo, the doctor, reported that "he may have a concussion. If he snaps out of it he'll be damn lucky." Ceder recovered, but the beating made Chennault even angrier.

He called a meeting of pilots and ground crew and delivered an ultimatum. Men who did not turn in the looted supplies or the profits made from selling them would be dishonorably discharged. "Most of the looters made amends, but a few took the dishonorable discharge and set up flourishing black market businesses. One in particular became a leading entrepreneur in the Chinese black markets with his loot from Rangoon. After his discharge he took quarters in the largest hotel in Kunming and ran his business in style. At one time he had a series of gasoline stations along the Burma Road selling looted gas at 85¢ a gallon. He became an expert in foreign exchange, and within a few months he accumulated more money than he would have netted from personally annihilating a whole Japanese air regiment."

Most of the AVG members speculated in currency exchange and sold their clothing and other personal items to augment their income. To some it was a game, taking the place of poker and acey-deucy, an amusing and profitable way to pass the time in those boring periods between combat missions. Chennault continued to oppose these practices, but he was powerless to stop them altogether. The black market activities became even more widespread after the AVG was replaced by a larger American military presence beginning in the summer of 1942. By 1944, the army was investigating some 300 cases and estimated that the profits exceeded $4 million. By then, even Chennault, who was wearing the two stars of a major general, was under suspicion, which did not help his standing with Hap Arnold.

If the AVG was viewed as full of renegades, mavericks, and ruffians, then they also did their best to look the part. There was an official AVG uniform, modeled after a U.S. Army uniform, but it was worn only for funerals and other formal occasions. Usually the men dressed for comfort and convenience. No two outfits were alike and sometimes the men could have passed for gypsies—or pirates.

In hot weather they wore pith helmets or cowboy hats, shorts, and boots. Chennault frequently wore shorts himself and an old felt hat, but he at least put on a shirt. In cold weather sheepskin and leather flying jackets were typical, along with Russian astrakhan hats. Some of the men wore Chinese army cloth caps and overalls, with a .45 on their hip and a cartridge belt stretching across their chest. Many sported beards and bristling mustaches.

One day in November 1941, Charlie Bond, the officer of the day, decided to defy tradition. He put on starched trousers, a shiny belt buckle, a regulation flying cap, and a necktie. "I realized how slovenly I have gotten, as have all of us. The tie was uncomfortable, and I dragged it through my soup at lunch. Hell's bells!"

Considering their behavior and appearance, then, it was no wonder their critics agreed with the judgment that they wouldn't "last three weeks in combat."

Chennault knew before he met any of the members of his new air force that discipline would be a problem. The greatest danger to the group would come not from the Japanese but from within. He also knew that given the high-spirited adventure seekers who would volunteer for such an outfit, a special kind of discipline would be necessary. He could not operate like a rigid military commander. There were no military ranks, and salutes were not required, although most of the men did salute Chennault and address him as "Colonel." "For rigid discipline I tried to substitute a measure of simple American democratic principles," Chennault wrote. "Rigid discipline was confined to the air and combat matters." The problems of daily life—how late the bar should remain open or when the lights should be turned out—were resolved by majority rule. Chennault held weekly meetings where everyone with a complaint or an idea for improving living conditions had a chance to speak.

A system of fines for minor violations of the rules was spelled out in the CAMCO contract, and these were invoked only after a meeting with a board of staff officers and squadron leaders. A person accused of a violation was given the opportunity to defend himself against the charge before the board passed judgment. If guilty, he was subject to the fine and to other disciplinary action when warranted. Chennault's files were full of reports of such actions for causes ranging from failure to maintain proper physical condition to drunk and disorderly conduct and being AWOL.

Some of the punishments imposed on the AVG included the following: a mechanic fined $25 and restricted to quarters for five months for entertaining a woman in his quarters; a clerk fined $50 for trying to smuggle goods through Chinese customs for resale; a pilot fined $20 for being late to work; a line chief fined $50 for being absent without proper authority; a crew chief fined $25 for intoxication and disorderly conduct off the field; and a group of pilots fined $25 each for disturbing the peace after midnight, being boisterous and pounding and scuffing about in their rooms, ignoring warnings to be quiet.

On December 31, 1941, three weeks after the attack on Pearl Harbor, Chennault issued a memorandum on rules and regulations. "To maintain our prestige as a fighting group," he wrote, "and to be of the greatest possible service to our country, the Group Commander now calls upon each and every one of you, pilots and men in all categories, for the following: implicit obedience to orders; stricter discipline, both personal and unit; increased respect, both of self and others; suppression and punishment of malcontents; greater courtesy toward our associates [the Chinese]; and strict and immediate suppression of all individuals who attempt to arouse animosity, envy, jealousy, and ill will or to incite disrespect for other individuals, categories and units of the group."

When fines and admonitions were not sufficient, Chennault wielded his ultimate disciplinary weapon: dishonorable discharge. In the eight months of the AVG's existence, he was forced to discharge 22 pilots and 43 ground crew. Approximately one in four of the AVG members overall were discharged for disciplinary reasons.

Like Chennault, the men were good at their jobs, but they were terrible subordinates. They proved that they could improvise and fight and endure like no other air unit in history, but they could not tolerate routine, rigidity, and regimentation. Perhaps that was why they, like Chennault, were attracted to China in the first place.

The AVG assembled in separate groups in Los Angeles and San Francisco between June and September 1941. Chennault placed one man in charge of each group for the voyage to the Orient. It was a difficult job because the leaders could only try to persuade the men to behave. They could not give orders or command them to stop drinking, getting into fights, gambling away their future paychecks, and gorging themselves with food.

The leader of the first group to embark was Paul Frillman, the chaplain, but he didn't know of his appointment when he met the rest of the men. His primary concern when he checked into the Jonathan Club, a businessmen's club in Los Angeles, was that none of the 50 ground personnel find out that he was a missionary. They were a tough-looking bunch and he knew they could make his life difficult on the trip. He tried not to look like a chaplain. "I guess I overdid this," he recalled. "I got the loudest suit I ever had, a regular racetrack model with stripes and padded shoulders, plus a floppy Panama hat and some screaming neckties."

As he gave his name to the desk clerk, he drew stares. Gene Pawley, one of the five Pawley brothers now involved in CAMCO, came to meet him. "Holy smoke!" he said. "You can't be the Frillman we're expecting."

Frillman suggested that he be permitted to check in quietly, but several men followed him to the elevator to ask if he was a pilot or ground crew. He managed to evade them and rushed into the elevator. Pawley advised him not to answer questions. "This was welcome," Frillman said, "as I hoped to get to know some of the men and let them see I was human before I was tagged as the chaplain."

His secret was out before the day was over. One of the men greeted him in the lobby with a shout. "Guys! We've got a Holy Joe." "I felt about the size of a peanut," Frillman said. But by evening, as some of the men got to know him, they began to call him by his first name instead of "Holy Joe" and "Sky Pilot."

The next day the men were told they would be traveling first class, but a few days after that they found themselves jammed into two broken-down buses for the long ride to San Francisco. Their first-class meals were hamburgers and hot dogs brought aboard by the trayload from greasy roadside diners. Most of the food was thrown out of the bus windows accompanied by curses.

Anger mounted when the men saw their ship. They had expected a luxury cruise liner full of pretty girls and plush quarters. What they found was a U.S. Army troop ship carrying a load of soldiers to the Philippines. The AVG men were assigned to a lounge filled with cots. No lockers, showers, or even toilets for their private use. That was when Frillman received a telegram from Chennault appointing him leader of the group. It was an unpromising beginning to a hard, forty-nine-day voyage.

The army troop commander ran the ship like an army camp, with orders blaring over the loudspeaker and drills and inspections, the very things many had joined the AVG to escape. He was irate at having fifty civilians in his midst who refused to take orders. Confrontations erupted frequently and the growing indignation of the AVG men in their close quarters led to fights among themselves.

The situation improved after a few days ashore in Honolulu. The liquor supply was replenished and the city's bars and brothels eagerly patronized. A few men tried to smuggle women aboard ship. The diversions had a good influence on the men and they fought less among themselves. Frillman noticed that they even became more tolerant of him.

Their arrival in Manila brought more shore leave. They had tropical suits made to order and generally indulged themselves. "It amazed me," said Frillman, "how men who had no foreign languages and didn't seem resourceful outside a familiar setting could disappear into an Asian city, then weave back after dark, having found every novelty they fancied in the way of sports, drinks, or girls. As often as not, they were laden with other novelties to mail back to their dear old grandmothers—stuffed rats in hula skirts, for instance."

Also in Manila they got rid of the army. The officious colonel marched his troops off the ship. Six months later they would be dying in the malarial jungles of the peninsula they passed on their way into Manila, a peninsula called Bataan.

The now virtually empty troop ship took the AVG contingent on to Hong Kong, where a CAMCO representative distributed their first month's pay and announced that their final destination was not China but Rangoon, Burma. He put them aboard a small Dutch freighter bound for Singapore, where they spent two riotous weeks. Frillman was constantly on call to break up fights, collect money to pay for damages to shattered bars, and soothe the British establishment. He had to make several trips to the Raffles Hotel, where two young AVG mechanics had taken a room to practice their newly discovered game of golf. Their swings did considerable damage to windows, lamps, vases, and the manager's temper.

Two other AVG men placed an advertisement in the local news-paper announcing that they were Hollywood talent scouts hunting for Singapore's most beautiful young woman. Contestants were invited to come for interviews, and the winner would receive a trip to Hollywood and a screen test. Frillman was appalled, but he admired their ingenuity.

The bulk of the AVG volunteers traveled to Rangoon in greater style. On July 10, 150 men boarded the MS *Jaegersfontein,* a Dutch passenger ship of the Java Pacific Line. Pilot Sandy Sandell recalled with a grin how everybody in San Francisco seemed to know who they were and where they were going. "It was a deep, dark secret," he said. "I heard a cigarette girl tell an elevator operator, 'Yes, they're all going to China to keep the Burma Road open. They're sailing Monday on the *Jaegersfontein.*'"

The men were in a happy mood, feeling as if they were taking a holiday. The accommodations were comfortable, and they had enjoyed themselves in San Francisco. A few had regrets about leaving, however. Pilot Charlie Mott would miss his wife. "When I left my darling wife at ten," he wrote in his diary, "I was trying to be casual about it but just managed to do it without breaking down. Words can't tell of the void this parting has left in me. The remembrance of her standing waving on the pier I will never forget." But Mott's mind would soon be on other things. He had been appointed leader of the group.

Like the first group of AVG volunteers, those aboard the *Jaegersfontein* enjoyed the stop in Honolulu. Radioman Robert Smith observed that "the local 'houses' had customers lined up, just like a butcher shop." The second day out of Honolulu two warships pulled alongside, the cruisers USS *Salt Lake City* and USS *Northampton,* sent by the navy as escorts. "This would make headlines in the States," Smith said. "I guess the cargo on this ship must be valuable!" The navy ships stayed with the liner for three weeks until a Dutch gunboat took over. At night the ship was blacked out, with all doors and portholes closed.

"The boys have gotten into a real groove of living," wrote Jim Howard in his diary on July 19. "There is much poker, blackjack and just plain crapshooting going on. Some of the games last all day long, and some fall far into the night. With their shirts off, amid a cloud of cigarette smoke and the din of clinking glasses from the bar, the gamblers hammer out at each other in a most frenzied way. The money that changes hands is tremendous. The speculation is high but the winners and losers do not talk."

They reached Singapore on August 11. Neither the British authorities nor the American consul was pleased to have another group of such Americans descend on them. The earlier batch had caused so much trouble that this group was allowed off the ship for only one night while hasty arrangements were made for their transportation to Rangoon.

Singapore was the first truly Oriental city most of the men had ever seen, and their impressions were not altogether favorable. "Singapore is filled with one permeating odor that fills the streets, cafes, and theaters," recalled Robert M. Smith. "It is the result of open sewers—gutters that line the sidewalk. We crossed one canal that was so bad that we ran two blocks holding our noses to escape the worst of it. There are many other strange smells, all different, that seem to be attempting to subdue the rest.

"Mothers and husbands here bargain for their daughters and wives. One Chinese wanted 10 [Straits dollars] for her fourteen-year-old daughter or $5 American money. Several of the fellows, when they left in the morning, found the husbands sleeping on the floor or on a sofa outside the bedroom door."

Another group of about two dozen pilots and ground crew left San Francisco on July 24 aboard the Dutch passenger ship MS *Bloemfontein*. Among the eighty-five passengers was a group of missionaries who quickly irritated the men of the AVG. Pilot R. T. Smith wrote home about them. "The damn missionaries— 'Holy Joes' to us—are driving us nuts with their constant gatherings around the piano and singing hymns by the hour. So we drive them nuts by playing hot swing records on the phonograph."

Tex Hill set out to convert an attractive, unmarried, thirty-year-old missionary woman. She tried equally hard to rescue him from his sinful ways. There is no report on who won the contest, but it was noticed that they were quite friendly by the time the voyage ended.

The ship took six weeks to reach Singapore, stopping first in

Honolulu, where some of the pilots saw their first P-40s at Hickam Field. The *Bloemfontein* also called at Brisbane, Manila, and Batavia, where two of the ground crew jumped ship. The men grew irritable as the journey wore on and morale dropped. The only one who seemed to be enjoying himself was Tex Hill.

In Singapore the men stayed at the Raffles Hotel, which, to R. T. Smith, had "all the charm of a funeral parlor." On their first night they attended a dinner party hosted by the Chinese consul general and learned that Scotch whiskey and shark's-fin soup do not mix well—they had terrible hangovers the next morning to prove it. They embarked on a small, decrepit coastal steamer and reached Rangoon on September 1, more than five weeks after leaving the States.

Another AVG group, about twenty-five strong, left San Francisco on September 24 aboard the Dutch passenger ship MS *Boschfontein*. Charlie Bond spent the first evening at sea wondering if he had made "a mistake in launching out on this adventure."

Greg Boyington must have wondered the same thing when he learned that Curtis Smith, a gung-ho ex-Marine pilot, had been placed in charge of the group. Smith scheduled their time in military fashion with roll calls, watches, and disciplinary actions. "How I dreaded Smith's formations," Boyington said. "I had counted on getting away from it all when I resigned, and hoped for something better instead of something worse."

Boyington admitted that he envied Smith for his apparent refinement, a characteristic Greg knew he himself lacked, and he also gave Smith credit for making him realize that not everyone had joined the AVG for the money. "They were going to free the world for democracy," Boyington recalled, "and were willing to give their lives if necessary. And, funny as it may seem, after a lengthy session in his cabin one lonely blacked-out night at sea, [Smith] damn near had me convinced. Looking back, I think he might have convinced me at that—if he hadn't run out of whiskey."

There were only seven women aboard the ship including four missionaries and a lady from an Arab country. After nine days at sea, one of the AVG pilots thought, "I have begun noticing the dark Persian lady on board more than usual. We exchanged glances but not conversation. I wonder what that cute little photographer in Long Beach is doing these days."

Charlie Bond attended church services and thought of his mother as he sang "Rock of Ages." One reason he had volunteered was to earn some money for his parents. "God grant me the power to make the lives of her and Dad as comfortable as I can the rest of their days," he wrote in his diary. He spent much of his time on the ship reading William Shirer's *Berlin Diary,* becoming angered at the British and French appeasement of the Germans. It made him itchy to get at the Japanese.

The men drank and ate too much. "I am taking on weight like a prize hog," said pilot George Burgard. Bond gained twelve pounds in only fifteen days at sea. The men soon became irritable and fights broke out. When they crossed the Equator, they painted their faces with rouge and were smeared with a foul-smelling mixture of flour, fruit juice, and spoiled fish soup before they were tossed into the pool and held under by King Neptune and his court.

The *Boschfontein* stopped at Java and the men immediately set out for a brothel. "I kidded the gals," Bond said, "but had been forewarned about Asian VD. No soap—left." Some took a side trip to Bali, hoping to see bare-breasted women. Bond took snapshots. He thought that otherwise the folks back home would find the sights hard to believe. He also met some men who had come over with the first AVG group. "They are throwing in the towel and returning to the States. They painted a bad picture of the organization and raised doubts in my mind: what am I getting myself into?"

It was early November by the time they reached Singapore, where they met Chennault's second-in-command, Harvey Greenlaw, who had come to get supplies. He described the situation at the AVG base at Toungoo, 170 miles north of Rangoon, and it sounded better than the reports they had heard in Java. Greenlaw said something, however, that Bond found puzzling. "There are some awful flyers here in Toungoo flying for Chennault." Bond didn't know whether Greenlaw was referring to their character or to their flying ability. He would soon find out.

Boyington's experiences in Singapore were even stranger. He learned that drinking hard liquor in such a hot climate affected a man's virility. The young women who entertained him always provided the Scotch-and-soda he requested but never drank liquor themselves. He found out why before the first evening was over. Fortunately, the women knew how to refresh him with steaming towels. Most of the men regretted leaving Singapore.

On November 11, 1941, Armistice Day, the group was one day out of Rangoon and the fighting for which they had volunteered. At 11:00 A.M. they observed the traditional moment of silence to honor the dead of the last war, as they sailed closer to the next one.

Two months earlier, Harvey and Olga Greenlaw checked into a Rangoon hotel, the Minto Mansions. In the lobby they spied an extraordinary sight. "The first thing to catch my eye," Olga recalled, "was a carrot-colored head surmounting a red face powdered with freckles—above a khaki shirt, shorts, and high-heeled Texas boots! He was with three or four other scarcely less colorful young men, all wide-eyed and having themselves a time."

"They're part of our gang," Harvey said.

"Those little boys? Why, they're just children. They looked healthy and spirited, but very young."

"It's a young man's war," Harvey said.

"But not their war."

"Before it's over it'll be everybody's war."

Olga said that at least they seemed to be enjoying themselves.

"Sure," Harvey said. "They think they're on a picnic. They always do at first, but wait till the hard work and the boredom and the homesickness set in."

And the killing, too, he might have added.

S I X

THOSE MONGREL PLANES

Chennault had a difficult time in the late summer of 1940 while he was waiting for the men of the AVG to join him. His basic plan for fighting the Japanese had gone awry. He had wanted to train his group at Kunming during the dry season of spring. That way, they would be ready to fight by the beginning of the summer. As it turned out, he did not have his men or his planes in China that spring, and he himself did not return to China from his trip to the United States until July 23. Pawley's delaying tactics for getting a commission on the sale of the P-40s set Chennault back three months. It also took longer than he expected to recruit the members of the AVG.

Training in Kunming in August and September was out of the question. That was the rainy season, and because the landing strips were not hard-surfaced, they became quagmires in the daily downpours. Chennault needed a paved airfield beyond the range of Japanese planes. Through the intercession of William Pawley and General Mow, the British agreed to lease to the AVG an airfield in Burma, the Kyedaw Airdrome located seven miles from the town of Toungoo and 170 miles from Rangoon.

Although it, too, was in the monsoon belt, it had a 4000-foot asphalt runway. At least there the airplanes could take off and land between the deluges. The British did not inform Chennault about why they were willing to give up one of the few airfields in the Far East with a paved runway. Every year during the rainy season the RAF abandoned the place because they considered it unfit for human habitation, what with the awful weather and the terrible swarms of insects. As undesirable as this was, it would have to do, and Chennault knew he was fortunate to get it.

His problems were not yet over, however. The British, already engaged in their war with Germany, did not wish to provide Japan with an excuse for attacking British possessions in the Pacific. They were wary of provoking the Japanese in any way. Although they gave Chennault permission to assemble and test-fly his airplanes at Kyedaw in Burma, they initially forbade any combat training there. Eventually they were persuaded by General Mow's argument that because Japan had never officially declared war on China, the AVG could not be labeled belligerents and, therefore, their activities would not violate British neutrality. The British then agreed that combat training could take place in Burma but stipulated that no attacks be launched against the Japanese from Burmese airfields.

Having secured a base and permission to undertake combat training, Chennault now needed permission to practice strafing runs at targets in the vicinity of Toungoo. For this he went to Singapore to meet with Air Marshal Sir Robert Brooke-Popham, who gave his approval despite official British concern that the shooting would foment unrest among the natives, who were known to have no love for the British.

It seemed to Chennault that as soon as he resolved one problem, another rose in its place. Next, the British in Burma refused to allow him to place American armed guards around the airfield, nor would they permit him to hire Burmese citizens as guards. As a result Burmese natives were free for a time to wander around the AVG facility day or night. Because some of the Burmese were sympathetic to the Japanese cause, Chennault worried about sabotage and spies. After his repeated complaints, he got from the British a contingent of Gurkhas to serve as guards.

Group Captain E. R. Manning, an Australian who was the senior RAF officer in Burma, was not pleased at having the AVG—

a group of irregulars, and American ruffians at that—in his command area, and he exerted his authority every chance he got. He pestered Chennault about niggling details in enforcing RAF regulations. He refused to allow any alterations of the facilities at the Kyedaw field. Even installing a new light socket required permission from Manning's headquarters in Rangoon.

Permission was usually granted but at a high cost in time and paperwork, and Chennault was running out of time and had no patience with paperwork. He lost three months, for example, obtaining permission to build a small earthen hill for use in boresighting the P-40s' machine guns because there was no such thing in the RAF engineering and construction manuals. Furthermore, he noted, "Manning could not understand why I was so concerned over the accuracy of our guns."

Despite Chennault's obvious need for frequent contact with RAF headquarters at Rangoon and bases elsewhere, Manning would not supply him with a copy of the RAF codebook. Nor would he accept the AVG codebook. This meant that Chennault had no radio communication with the RAF. He offered to send his own radiomen and equipment to Rangoon, but Manning refused. The only way for Chennault to communicate with Rangoon was through the commercial telegraph system operated by the Burmese, which could not be considered secure.

Although Manning made daily life difficult for Chennault, Brooke-Popham in Singapore was doing his best to help the AVG become operational. He arranged to supply Chennault with aviation gasoline and oil, with .30-caliber ammunition for the British machine guns installed in the wings of the P-40s, and with an aerial camera—an item in short supply throughout the Far East. A plane equipped with this camera served as Chennault's only source of photo reconnaissance for the better part of a year. He was grateful to Brooke-Popham and wrote that without the air marshal's considerable aid, "it would have been almost impossible to get the AVG into fighting condition."

One thing Brooke-Popham could not help Chennault with was the matter of a staff. Hap Arnold had seen to it that none of the AVG pilots had any staff experience or training, forcing Chennault to scrounge for staff personnel wherever he could find them in China. There were not many Americans to choose from, but he needed to find people to handle the day-to-day operation of the air group. Even if Chennault had had the time himself, he did not have the training or experience either.

The first person he took on was Boatner Carney, who for a time was the entire AVG staff. Carney had come to China in 1938 as one of Chennault's flight instructors. For chief of staff Chennault selected Harvey Greenlaw, then forty-four years old, a graduate of West Point who had gotten his wings as a fighter pilot in 1925. Greenlaw had resigned his commission in 1931 to work for the North American Aviation Company, and in 1933, with his wife Olga, had gone to China as part of the Jouett mission. He stayed in China for three years, assembling and testing the American airplanes that were sold to the Chinese government, then returned to the United States to work in commercial aviation. From 1938 he was in China again as a flight instructor when Chennault called on him to join the AVG. Olga was hired to maintain the AVG's daily war diary.

Harvey Greenlaw was an outgoing, sociable adventurer. He and Olga lived for a time in a Presbyterian mission, hardly the best choice for them or for the mission. "Harvey did not at all times manage to conform to the mission code of conduct," Olga later wrote. "He persisted in sneaking into the church and playing honky-tonk music on the melodeon. He plays quite badly but appears to enjoy it. And then one evening he gave a dinner for all the Chinese officers at the field, in the town's largest restaurant. Mr. Greenlaw is strictly a one-bottle-of-beer man. Beyond that his behavior is unpredictable. It is the Chinese custom that the dinner host must, individually, drink with all of his guests. There were forty guests. Harvey said the trouble was the beer was warm. The missionaries said the trouble was Harvey. He also acquired a bad habit of shooting firecrackers at the compound entrance to announce his arrival for dinner. China is a paradise for a man with a penchant for firecrackers."

Olga Greenlaw was described as an exotic and sexy-looking woman. Jim Howard said she was "startlingly attractive. What with the name of Olga and with many White Russians who escaped to China [after the Russian Revolution], the rumor got around that Olga was Russian. When the word got back to her, she denied it vehemently and stated that she had been born in the Bronx and was as American as blueberry pie like the rest of us. Her tight slacks and alluring makeup gave her a provocative look that suggested she was on the make."

Chennault selected John Williams as communications officer. An ex-army radioman, Williams had known Chennault during the 1930s and came to China in 1939 as a radio instructor for the Chinese Air Force. Most members of the AVG agreed that Williams was excellent in his job and one of the few really good staff they had.

The only staff member who deliberately sought out Chennault was journalist Joseph Alsop, who had met him in Washington the previous October. Erudite and urbane, the Groton- and Harvard-educated Alsop was the antithesis of the roughhewn Chennault, yet the two men developed a mutual respect and admiration. Alsop was to serve Chennault ably until Chennault left China in 1945.

Alsop, who knew everyone of importance in the War Department, had been given a direct commission as a lieutenant (jg) in the navy and assigned to Bombay as naval observer. This was not to his liking. He discussed the problem with two close friends, Jim Forrestal, the undersecretary of the navy, and Bob Lovett, the assistant secretary of war for air. "Now what do I do?" Alsop asked them. "I've got myself in this frightful mess." "Well, there's this fellow Chennault," they said, and went on to tell him that the AVG had been launched.

Alsop arranged his journey to Bombay by way of Chungking, where he met Chennault at a garden party given by Madame Chiang. Chennault said he was having trouble assembling a competent staff, and he gladly accepted Alsop's offer to join him. All Alsop had to do was get out of the navy. As a reserve officer, he was eligible to volunteer for the AVG, so he telegraphed the secretary of the navy to announce his intention. This action was inconsistent with proper military channels, and he received an angry refusal to accept his resignation and orders to proceed to Bombay. Undaunted, Alsop dispatched a private telegram to Forrestal at his home, stating that he had "every intention of joining Chennault and that they could come and arrest me if they chose." Forrestal arranged matters, and Alsop reported to Chennault on October 29, 1941, as staff secretary, the hardest work he said he'd ever done. Alsop was to produce all the correspondence and memoranda that poured out of AVG headquarters. He was responsible for communicating the group's needs not only to China Defense Supplies in Washington and to the American government but also to the British and Chinese governments. Later in the war, through a family connection with Roosevelt, Alsop was able to provide Chennault with direct access to the president. This enraged George Marshall and Hap Arnold, but it gave Chennault a highly privileged position.

In his own way, Alsop was as unconventional as Chennault and most of the others in the AVG, operating in an independent fashion. On Christmas Day of 1941, while trying to track down spare parts for the P-40s, Alsop found himself in Hong Kong when it fell. He persuaded the Japanese that he was there only as a journalist and was repatriated to the United States. (Journalists and diplomats were routinely repatriated.) He quickly got himself appointed as a lend-lease official to China and resumed his position on Chennault's staff.

The AVG staff was subject to a great deal of criticism from American army officers, once the United States was in the war. Alsop himself was highly critical of his colleagues. "Such an excuse for a staff I've never seen in my life," he said in one of his milder comments. He was not the only member of the AVG who was critical. Greg Boyington was outspoken in his condemnation of the AVG staff and said that Chennault agreed with him. Even considering the traditional disdain of the fighting man for staff personnel, Boyington's comments are harsh.

"Most of the men in this non-flying staff Chennault was stuck with were Asiatic bums of the first order. Chennault later had to call us pilots together when he realized we wouldn't take orders from the staff . . . He said: 'I was to have a competent military staff for this group. However, everyone of staff rank is frozen in the United States. I have to do the best I can with what little staff

I've been able to pick up out here. All I can ask of you is—please understand—and bear with me.' "

Boyington also found the staff to be exceptionally large and suggested that there were so many of them because, as Chennault reportedly told him, it took ten of them to do the work of one competent staff officer.

Boyington and others were especially critical of Harvey Greenlaw. "Many of us couldn't tell just what it was he was supposed to do," Jim Howard said. "He usually dressed smartly in a khaki bush jacket and spent much of his time sucking on his pipe observing others at work."

Preparing the airfield, dealing with the local RAF command, and assembling a staff of sorts having been accomplished, Chennault realized that the AVG was still not ready to begin training or become operational. The latest problem was assembling the P-40s, which he found still in crates on the dock at Rangoon when he returned from the United States on July 23, 1941.

The man in charge of putting the planes together was Walter Pentecost. Prior to going to Burma, Pentecost had worked for North American Aviation and had spent months at the Allison Company factory learning about the intricate 12-cylinder V-type engine with its controversial glycol cooling system. One day he saw a newspaper ad calling for aviation experts to work overseas. When he went for the interview, he was treated to a slide show of exotic Burma. The recruiter was CAMCO. Pentecost, however, had no need of a travelogue. "I'd already made up my mind to go," he said. "I didn't care what they showed me. It was something different, and I was ready." He signed a contract with the Pawleys for a small salary and $100 per month in expenses, which, through his skill at poker, he parlayed into a considerable sum of money in the year he was to spend in Burma.

When Chennault met Pentecost shortly after his arrival in Rangoon in July, he expressed his utmost confidence that Pentecost would be able to do the job. But when Pentecost saw the meager facilities and tools he had to work with, he was not so optimistic. Like everything else with the AVG, assembling the planes took longer than anyone expected, and longer than it should have. Pentecost's first task, before he could even begin to uncrate the airplanes, was to find a makeshift factory in which to assemble them.

He located a brick building which—unfortunately, it being the rainy season—had no roof. He hired Burmese workers to build a roof and to pave an area adjacent to the building to serve as a hard surface on which to park the assembled planes. Chennault, increasingly impatient with the delays, persuaded the Pawleys to send several mechanics from the CAMCO factory in Loiwing.

By the end of August, only 22 planes were ready for use. At that rate—about two dozen completed per month—the entire force of 99 P-40s would not be ready until November, only weeks before Japan attacked the U.S. naval base at Pearl Harbor.

Just when Chennault believed he had everything under control, he found himself trapped for two weeks in Chungking during the worst bombing raids he had experienced in his three years in China. Chiang had summoned him to the capital for a series of strategy conferences, and during his stay there, his life was at risk several times. Once Chennault was caught aboard a Yangtze River ferry in midstream. On another occasion he was trapped in a house for seventy-two hours with no water, electricity, or telephone service, surviving on cold rice, and eventually forced to take shelter in a cave. Japanese bombers were overhead daily from dawn to dusk.

"I sat [in the cave] listening to the intermittent thunder of the bombs, more angry than ever before as I thought of the delays that had made it impossible to hurl the American volunteers into this battle and prevent what turned out to be the final ordeal of Chungking."

On August 22, Chennault had made his way to the AVG field at Kyedaw, where the first two groups of pilots and ground crew had already assembled. Not all the men were pleased with what they had found. They were "seething with griping and unrest when I arrived," Chennault noted. He was confronted with the resignations of five pilots and several ground crewmen, and many of the others were on the verge of mutiny.

Their new home in Burma had come as a shock, being so unlike the American facilities they were used to. Disillusionment had begun in Rangoon, which was hot, dirty, and humid almost beyond endurance. The sidewalks were stained red, caused by thousands of natives chewing betel nut and spitting. Disease was rampant, especially elephantiasis, and beggars clustered on every street corner. The afternoon rains fostered the growth of mildew and mold. Leather shoes turned green overnight.

Conditions at Kyedaw Field and the neighboring town of Toungoo were worse. Facilities for aircraft were satisfactory, but the accommodations for personnel were abysmal. The runway was hard-surfaced, and there was a hangar large enough for several P-40s. A few maintenance and supply buildings were scattered about, and a control tower of sorts—a small, open-sided hut—stood five feet off the ground on bamboo poles.

The barracks were new, built of teak with woven bamboo walls and corrugated tin roofs. The sides were open to allow the breeze to come through, but there were no screens. Along with the breeze came hideous and dangerous insects. It was described by Olga Greenlaw as "an entomologist's paradise . . . all the bugs God created to fly through the air or crawl on the ground, floors, walls, ceilings, into your food, down your back, up your legs, and in your hair—beetles, lice, spiders, flies and fleas, moths, mosquitoes, centipedes, bedbugs, ticks, and a lot more." One morning, one of the pilots forgot to shake out his shirt before putting it on and was stung by a scorpion. The bite left a lump the size of a cantaloupe on his back.

The heat and humidity were enervating and a further cause for depression. Radioman Robert Smith remembered lying awake on his bunk every night, bathed in sweat, unable to fall asleep before 2:00 A.M., when it cooled down a bit. Greg Boyington found the heat so fatiguing one morning that he did not have the energy to get off his bunk while the other pilots were chasing a deadly cobra—inside the barracks!

The food was terrible. It was impossible to read or write letters after dark. If a light were turned on, thousands of insects would descend. The men could turn in early and wait on their bunks until it was cool enough to sleep or go to an occasional American movie in town.

Most of the men bought bicycles and held afternoon bike races between the airfield and Toungoo. The idea of racing in that heat the few miles to Toungoo is an indication of how bored the men were, for there was little to do once they got there. The main street was jammed day and night with trucks heading north to join the Burma Road. A few shops lined one side of the street. The other side held open market stalls. Some 40 Europeans lived in the Toungoo vicinity, but there were few unattached women.

The railroad station restaurant served up a dinner of steak and french fries, and the Toungoo Theater showed old American movies. The theater was also the place to watch the cockroaches march resolutely across the floor and the bats flit through the air, casting shadows across the screen.

The men bought whatever the shops had to offer—gems, leather wallets, boots, custom-made shirts, bush jackets. Because they were so free with their money, prices zoomed to extraordinary levels, well out of range for the British and the Burmese, whose rate of pay was much lower than the AVG's. Shopkeepers soon ran out of leather and khaki, and the British became more irritated at the behavior of the ruffians in their midst. The district commissioner complained to Olga Greenlaw. "One of your men went into a bazaar, picked up a cheroot, handed the merchant a rupee and walked out. The fellow ran after him to give him his change, but instead of taking it your man pulled out another rupee and gave it to the merchant. Mrs. Greenlaw, here in Toungoo, for one rupee you can buy a *hundred* cheroots!"

Robert M. Smith wrote in his diary: "We are rowdy, rich, objectionable, but friendly. But *I* doubt that we are understood, for how could we be when we ourselves are amazed at our fellows."

By the time Chennault arrived at Kyedaw Field on August 22, the second boatload of AVG had been there for almost a week and the first group for nearly a month. The novelty of life in Burma had long worn off, replaced by boredom, anger, and discontent with the weather, the primitive conditions, and the lack of planes to fly and Japanese to fight. No wonder some greeted Chennault with resignations in hand. "Lord knows we need him and need him badly," wrote Charlie Mott in his diary the night before Chennault arrived.

Some of those who joined the AVG to escape from military discipline or from some personal problem were now just as anxious to escape from Kyedaw, and others would have resigned even if the facilities in Burma had been ideal. A few arranged to have telegrams sent to them from the United States, notifying them of family members suddenly taken ill. As it turned out, they had joined the AVG as a ruse, to get out of their military commitment so they could then accept higher-paying jobs with the airlines.

Some of the pilots were discontented because, they claimed, the conditions of service with the AVG had been misrepresented by William Pawley's recruiters. Five days after Chennault's arrival at the field, he wrote to T. V. Soong to complain about Pawley's hiring practices. Chennault told Soong that 15 percent of the pilots told him they had been misinformed about the nature of the combat they would be expected to face. Specifically, the recruiters had said the men would face only Japanese bombers, not fighters, would not engage in night flying, and would undertake only defensive missions.

Chennault accused Pawley of hiring pilots who did not meet Chennault's qualifications, especially with regard to fighter experience, only to meet employment quotas. "I am willing to give a certain amount of transition training to new pilots," Chennault wrote, "but we are not equipped to give a complete refresher course. It is too much to expect that men familiar only with four-engine flying boats can be transformed into pursuit experts overnight."

Pawley took sharp exception to Chennault's criticisms, which he called baseless. In a letter to Soong, Pawley wrote, "In all my experience I have never seen a finer aggregation of pilots and enlisted men as were dispatched overseas by this company. . . . This force is so superior, in my judgment, that even inferior leadership cannot destroy its effectiveness." Before long, Pawley would cast aspersions on Chennault's leadership abilities more directly, and the resulting bitterness between Chennault and Pawley would last for the rest of Chennault's life.

A few of the ground crewmen who resigned remained in Rangoon and established lucrative black market operations in partnership with Burmese girls. Other ground crewmen left when they learned how much work needed to be done to make the planes ready for war and how little was available in the way of tools, spare parts, and equipment. Even among those who had not chosen to resign, morale was not high. As Chennault assembled them for a meeting, he realized that the future of the AVG and the course of the war in China, as well as his own future, depended on whether he could raise their spirits.

Chennault stood before the group "with his face like a chunk of lava ready to explode," recalled Paul Frillman. He sounded as grim and as stern as he looked. He announced that combat preparations would begin the following day, and he outlined the training program. Pilots would undergo 60 hours of flight training and 72 hours of lectures, beginning at 6:00 the next morning. Because only some two dozen P-40s were available, the flight training would have to take place in batches. No additional training was scheduled for the ground personnel, but Chennault reminded them of the terms of their contract, which spelled out a system of fines and dismissals for dereliction of duty.

His words and his manner made a positive impression on most of the men. Chaplain Frillman noticed that within 24 hours, "the air of the camp freshened." The men now had a leader and a sense of direction and purpose, all of which brought them closer to their objectives—adventure, a chance to fight the Japanese, and an opportunity to make good money doing it. The sooner they got into action, the quicker they would earn their bonuses.

Not everyone was pleased, however. Some were angry at the thought of additional flight training, believing themselves to be hotshot pilots. They had spent their six weeks at sea bragging about their skill in the air. To hear them tell it, they could disembark in Rangoon, take off from the nearest airfield, and begin shooting down Japanese planes. What else was there for them to learn, especially from some "beat-up old Army captain" who had been buried in China for years.

Fortunately, few of the pilots expressed that attitude. Most were impressed enough with Chennault to believe that they could learn from him. They were ready to follow his lead. "I was genuinely impressed," Boyington recalled. "In fact, seeing Chennault, and listening to him talk, was the only thing about this deal I had seen so far that did impress me. Everyone addressed him as Colonel, I gathered right off, and with genuine respect as far as I could see. Chennault seemed to be a person who commanded respect."

"I like the Old Man," Charlie Bond wrote in his diary. "He impresses me as a commander rather than a director or manager." To pilot Tex Hill, Chennault was "a rugged-looking guy, the type you immediately felt a lot of confidence in. He exuded leadership." Pilot Charlie Mott added, "The more I see of the old boy, the better I like him and the more I admire his talents. We are indeed fortunate in having such a man as head of this project."

Jim Howard recalled the day Chennault arrived at the airfield. "As Chennault stepped from the plane and looked around at the airfield and the motley group of men standing nearby, I knew instinctively that here was a man who was going to make a go of our organization. [He] radiated a feeling of confidence that everything was going to be all right, now that he was here and in charge. . . . Here was a man who said what he believed and did not mince words with apologies or excuses. He touched all of us with his sincerity and singleness of purpose. Here was a man we could follow."

Chennault had won them over; now he had to teach them how to fight the Japanese. The next morning he began what he called "the kindergarten," designed to teach multi-engine pilots—those from the navy who had flown big patrol planes and those from the army who had flown B-17s and other bombers—how to fly a single-engine fighter. The pilots were used to long, slow takeoffs and landings and to flying lumbering planes that were not very maneuverable compared with the nimble P-40. The adjustment was difficult for some, being unused to the high speeds, the instantaneous response from the controls, and the high G-forces that almost knocked them out when they turned sharply or pulled out of a dive.

Landing was particularly difficult. Joe Alsop recalled how "former navy pilots of flying boats had a sad tendency to try and land P-40s twenty feet above the runway, which is not a wise idea." They stalled and dropped so hard that they ruined tires and landing gear mechanisms. Others approached too fast and ran out of runway before their wheels touched down. And some made six-point landings, bouncing hard on the runway until they ground-looped, bent a propeller blade, or skidded off the runway into the mud. Chennault was not pleased.

He was even less pleased one day in November when the AVG lost more aircraft to accidents in a single day than it would ever lose in combat. As he watched each crash he was reminded of the Chinese pilots who had been trained by the Italians. None of the pilots was hurt on what came to be called "circus day," and all the planes could be repaired, but Chennault judged it a fiasco. Five planes crashed while landing too high or too low, too fast or too slow. Two other planes ran into each other while mechanics were taxiing them along the runway.

That was enough for Chennault. Even though there were two remaining hours of flying time that day, he canceled all flights. While he was doing so, a mechanic riding a bicycle, his attention distracted by one of the wrecks, collided with a parked P-40 and damaged its aileron. "Kindergarten," Chennault wrote, "got a long lecture on landings that afternoon." To reinforce the lesson, he had a white line chalked across the runway one-third of the way down its length. Any pilot who touched down beyond that point was fined $50.

Few of the pilots repeated their mistakes, and most of the former multi-engine pilots compiled combat records equal to those of the pilots who had flown fighter planes before coming to Burma. But not all, despite Chennault's rigorous training, could meet his standards. Seven months later, in March 1942, there were still eighteen pilots whom he considered not ready for combat. Despite his desperate need for pilots and the lack of reinforcements from the States, he would not let these eighteen men fly combat missions. "I refused to throw a pilot into the fray until

I was personally satisfied that he was properly trained." The AVG became a superb combat unit, losing only four pilots to enemy air action in six months of fighting. Those who survived Chennault's training program were ready for anything the Japanese could throw at them.

Chennault's style of leadership and his methods of training helped to raise the morale of his men. The weather helped, too. In September, the monsoon rains were ending, and the mud that filled every unpaved surface was drying up. Chennault hired some Chinese cooks from a Rangoon nightclub, and complaints about the food stopped. He ordered daily calisthenics, led by the chaplain, and the men began to feel healthier and more vigorous. To increase fitness, he made sure that the AVG's few cars and trucks were not available for jaunts into Toungoo. Bicycling the seven miles there and back was better for the men than sitting in a car. Spirited baseball games were held most afternoons, usually with Chennault pitching and playing as if each game were the crucial one in a pennant race back home.

Each morning at six, Chennault was back in the classroom, teaching, doing what he had always been good at. Pilot Jim Howard recalled that Chennault "had the knack of embellishing and dramatizing his speech." Chennault once said that of all the teaching he had done, from a one-room schoolhouse in the Louisiana backwoods to the Air Corps Tactical School, he was at his best in a shack made of teak in Burma.

His course for the AVG pilots began with a geography lesson and the history of China's war with Japan. He taught them how the all-important air-raid warning net worked, and he described in detail their enemy—the Japanese pilots. Here Chennault drew on his experiences of the last three years and all the notebooks he had filled with his observations of Japanese character and tactics. These became his textbooks, along with captured Japanese flying and staff manuals that he had had translated into English.

"You will face Japanese pilots superbly trained in mechanical flying," he told his men. "They have been drilled for hundreds of hours in flying precise formations and rehearsing set tactics for each situation they may encounter. Japanese pilots fly by the book. They have plenty of guts but lack initiative and judgment.

"They go into battle with a set tactical plan and they stick to it. Their bombers will fly a tight formation through the toughest pursuit as precisely as though they were in an air show over Tokyo. Their pursuits always pull the same tricks. God help the American pilot who tries to fight them according to their plans.

"The object of our tactics is to break their formations and make them fight according to our style. Once the Japanese pilot is forced to deviate from his plan, he is in trouble. They lack the ability to improvise and react instinctively to new situations. Their rigid air discipline can be used as a strong weapon against them."

Chennault instructed his pilots not only on Japanese tactics but also on the engineering, performance, and armament characteristics of the Japanese aircraft. He distributed mimeographed information sheets containing drawings and performance data on the newest and deadliest Japanese fighter—the Zero. None of the AVG pilots knew such a plane existed. When they learned how good it was, several found reasons to resign.

Chennault drew diagrams of every type of Japanese plane they would meet in the air, and he showed them the most vulnerable point of each. Using colored chalk, he drew circles around gas tanks, bomb bays, oil coolers, and other spots to aim at, and he repeated these lessons, over and over, drilling the information into his pilots so that in combat they would react instantly, without having to stop to think.

He told his pilots how they could win in combat, even against such a superior plane as the Zero. He described the respective advantages of the P-40 and the Japanese fighters. Enemy fighters, he told them, could climb faster, turn in a shorter radius, and operate at higher altitudes. But with the P-40, "you can count on a higher top speed, faster dive, and superior firepower."

"Japanese fighter planes were built for turning combats. If they can get you into their kind of fight, they are deadly. Use your superior speed and faster dive to make a pass at your opponent, get in a quick burst and then break away. . . . Never get into a long-continued turning combat." Chennault wanted there to be no individual dogfighting in the AVG and stressed that pilots who attempted that against Zeros would die.

He emphasized to his pilots the importance of accuracy in gunnery. At least half of them had no previous aerial gunnery experience. "You need to sharpen your shooting eye," he said. "Nobody ever gets too good at gunnery. The more Japs you get with your first bursts, the fewer are left to jump you. Accurate gunnery saves ammunition. Your plane carries a limited number of bullets. There is nothing worse than finding yourself in a fight with empty guns."

He lectured them on how to fight in pairs and how to engage in complicated maneuvers while staying together as a team, as perfectly coordinated as if both planes were being controlled by a single hand. It was the kind of flying Chennault had done with his air corps acrobatic team. Now he was taking it to war.

He drilled them on the advantages of fighting in pairs. Two P-40s attacking together focused 12 guns instead of 6 on the target. Thus, each pair of fighters had greater firepower than the single plane they would be attacking, whether a fighter or a bomber. Fighting in pairs also allowed one pilot to concentrate on the target while the other protected his tail.

Not everyone agreed with Chennault's tactics. The British were disdainful of the idea of attacking and immediately breaking away. The RAF fighter group in Rangoon issued orders that any British pilot who dove away from a fight would be court-martialed. Any pilot in the Chinese Air Force who did so faced a firing squad. Some of the AVG pilots were also skeptical. They had long been schooled in traditional dogfighting tactics in which two planes chased each other until one stayed on the tail of the other long enough to shoot it down.

Individual dogfighting was a fine technique, but it was not suitable for heavy P-40s tangling with more agile and sharper turning Japanese fighters. It did not work for Spitfires either, and in the early months of the Pacific war, a great many American and British pilots met their deaths trying to fight the Japanese in that way. At the same time, AVG pilots using Chennault's shoot-and-dive-away approach were shooting down 15 enemy aircraft for every one of theirs lost. Chennault's tactics later became the standard for the Pacific theater.

Diagrams and lectures taught the AVG pilots the theory behind

Chennault's tactics. As soon as the morning's class was over, they took to their planes to practice what they had learned. They began with an hour-and-a-half of individual dogfighting, just to get used to violent maneuvering in the P-40, which so few of them had flown before. Although Chennault was not teaching dogfighting and did not want them doing it in combat, he realized that the competition involved in a dogfight would encourage more daring flying.

Chennault watched his pilots through binoculars from the bamboo control tower and was in constant radio communication, pointing out errors and suggesting improvements. "I coached each pilot as though he were the star halfback on our football team." He dictated his observations on each pilot's performance to Tom Trumble, his secretary, and later reviewed his comments with each pilot, providing not only a detailed critique of the man's technique but also precise instructions on how to improve. In advanced fighter training in the United States, it was rare that a pilot received so much personalized instruction, and from such a superb teacher.

Flying pairs was next, with one plane protecting the tail of the other. Chennault also had them practice flying in formation as a squadron, making mock attacks on bombers, and performing strafing runs on ground targets. Day after day they drilled and practiced and corrected their mistakes, gaining confidence in their abilities and in Chennault's tactics.

When Chennault thought they were ready, he urged them to "wring out" their planes, trying every maneuver in the book until they felt at one with their machines. "He instilled the sheer love of flying in his pilots as most of them had never felt it before. After ten days or so at Toungoo they would bound out onto the field in the freshness of early morning, lift their planes into the sky, and then cavort in snap rolls, loops, chandelles, wingovers, and power dives that sent the Tomahawks screaming toward the ground."

With such intensive, daring flying occurring every day, accidents were inevitable, and they were not only the minor ones such as those on "circus day." Olga Greenlaw was shocked when she learned that among the AVG employees was a part-time embalmer. Her husband tried to warn her.

"I don't want you to become too attached to any of these kids. . . . They're out here to fight a war and you can't fight a war without somebody getting killed."

It didn't seem possible to Olga that any of them could be killed. They were all so young and so nice and having such a good time. The AVG seemed like a college fraternity party. Harvey Greenlaw thought it was a "cinch that a few of these boys will smash up before we ever get into action. A lot of them have only a couple of hundred flying hours. We've got to make tough, resourceful fighter pilots out of them—and the airplanes are hot and hard to handle. I just want you to realize some very unpleasant things are likely to happen."

The weather was clear and bright on Monday morning, September 8, as Olga Greenlaw watched the planes return from their practice flights. They were due at 11:30, and one by one they slipped into the field. But 11:30 came and went and two pilots had not returned, Jack Armstrong and Gil Bright, former navy pilots who had been stationed at Norfolk, Virginia. As Chennault was in Chungking for the day, Harvey Greenlaw was in charge.

There was nothing to do but wait for the pilots to show up, assuming they had bailed out of their planes for some reason, or to get word of a crash in the jungle. The news came during lunch. The stationmaster in a town north of Toungoo called to report a midair collision. He made no mention of survivors.

Greenlaw sent out three planes to search for the crash site, and he organized a rescue party to stand by. Before long, one of the pilots located the wreckage and radioed its location. The rescue party headed out in cars and soon came across Gil Bright, riding a bicycle he had borrowed from a Chinese civilian.

According to Bright, he and Armstrong began their morning dogfight in the usual way, making a head-on pass at each other. But this time neither pilot turned away when he should have. They remained on a collision course at a combined speed in excess of 600 miles per hour. At the last possible instant, Bright rolled over, but Armstrong's plane sheared Bright's wing off no more than one foot from the fuselage. Bright bailed out but Armstrong could not. The rescue team found his body in the wreckage of his plane, which had drilled a hole in the mud ten feet deep.

"It was all his own fault," Charlie Mott wrote in his diary about Armstrong. "He made a head-on attack and Bright tried to miss him but he pressed it home too far. . . . He just tried too hard in things like that. With me last week, I had to avoid him on two occasions."

Greenlaw telephoned Ed Pawley, in charge of CAMCO operations in Rangoon, to request a casket. It arrived by truck, with a huge array of flowers. More flowers were sent by the wives of the local British officials, and the funeral was held at 4:00 the following afternoon. Chaplain Frillman held the service in the mess hall, and Armstrong was buried in a concrete vault in the cemetery of St. Luke's, Church of England. "It was dark when we left the cemetery," remembered Olga Greenlaw, "with an oppressive black overcast deepening our gloom. The incident had definitely sobered the boys."

Two weeks later the AVG suffered its second casualty. Max Hammer, who had arrived the week before with the third group of pilots, was caught in a sudden monsoon and crashed into a mountainside 15 miles from the airfield. A search party left immediately, carrying pistols, knives, and flashlights, outfitted in rubber boots as protection against leeches and snakes. By the time they located the body, it was too dark to extricate it from the wreckage. Two pilots volunteered to stand watch over the body during the night, and the next day Hammer was buried beside Armstrong in the second tin-lined casket sent up from Rangoon.

On October 25, Pete Atkinson, a popular veteran P-40 pilot, was making a steep practice dive when the governor on the propeller gave way. The prop windmilled out of control and the plane raced toward the ground faster and faster. The men at the airfield recall hearing the telltale shriek of a propeller gone amok. To R. T. Smith it was the most "Godawful sound I ever expect to hear. An unearthly screaming roar, going up very suddenly to a high pitch." At less than 1000 feet, the tail came off and the rest of the plane plummeted to earth at a speed of 600 miles an hour.

Atkinson, a devout Catholic, had never missed Sunday services. A high mass was said for him with a bishop, 20 priests, and

100 choirboys in attendance. A cross of red roses from Chennault stood among the flowers. A Gurkha soldier played taps and Atkinson was laid to rest beside Hammer and Armstrong. Olga Greenlaw returned home, where all three fallen pilots had lain before their funerals. "The downstairs room was cluttered with withered flowers and palm leaves. The chairs were still in place. It seemed as if everything was waiting for another coffin to take the place of the one we had just moved away."

Other accidents occurred in those early months, some attributable to pilot error but others apparently the fault of the planes. Although no one else was killed, there were some close calls, shaken pilots, and wrecked P-40s that would never fly again. The accidents increased the doubts and suspicions about the aircraft held by some of the pilots before they had ever flown one. Back in the States, when the plane became operational, it acquired a reputation as a killer in the hands of all but the most experienced pilots.

When they started flying the plane at Kyedaw, some of the AVG pilots still did not like it. "It seems to climb like a brick," said Charlie Mott, "and doesn't have the performance desired in a ship to combat this type 'O' [Zero] Japanese fighter." Buster Keeton wrote of his first flight in a P-40: "The plane took off very easily, of which I was surprised and relieved. Do not like the way it handles in the air at all . . . according to all the men, they are the hardest planes in existence to land."

Robert L. Scott, who joined Chennault after the AVG was dissolved, wrote about the difficulty in just starting the P-40's engine, saying that a man needed "four hands. First your right toe had to be pressing the inertia starter pedal while your hands were fumbling with switches and working a wobble pump. There was a primer to shoot seven or eight shots into about three cylinders and you could always feel the cold of the evaporating gasoline, leaking from the plunger onto your fingers and smelling up the cockpit. After the whine of the inertia flywheel reached the right pitch you shifted pressure from toe to heel to engage the clutch and the prop made its first slow, laborious turns. The left hand was busy adjusting the critical throttle, and then poised to shove the red knob of the mixture control at precisely the right instant. Simultaneously the right one had moved to twist the crank of the booster magneto. If all that footwork and hand-changing had been correctly coordinated, the prop forgot its sluggish reluctance, caught with almost mechanical laughter and a breath of blue smoke, then smoothed to a roar of steady power."

Chennault was not all that pleased with the P-40s either. His aide, Joe Alsop, referred to them as "mongrel planes." They were mavericks, just like the men who were trying to fly them. Chennault knew how vulnerable the liquid-cooled engine would be in combat. A single bullet through the glycol coolant tank would cause the engine to overheat and shut down in minutes. The B models of the P-40 had no auxiliary fuel tanks that could be dropped when going into combat. That severely limited the range of the planes. They also had no bomb racks on the wings, which reduced their effectiveness as weapons against ground targets.

The four British .30-caliber machine guns in the wings were considered by Chennault to be worthless against the Zero, although he did recognize that the guns might be effective against Japanese bombers. The reflector gunsights on the planes were useless against any kind of target because it took too long to line them up. Because the mechanics did not have the proper tools to modify the gunsights so they could be used in combat, they were forced to improvise. Under Charlie Mott's direction, they fashioned gunsights out of iron rings, which proved to be extremely effective.

The Tomahawks also had no radios, and again the men of the AVG improvised. The best they could get was a radio transceiver, RCA-7-H, which had been built for the Piper Cub, a light sport plane. Of limited range and not engineered to withstand the shock and vibrations of a high-speed combat plane, the radios were a constant source of trouble. They were also a source of danger when pilots in the air could not be reached.

The P-40s were airplanes that no one else wanted, dangerous and difficult to fly and not as good as the main Japanese fighter they were expected to do battle with. The AVG pilots, on their voyages to the Far East, had seen another American aircraft—the Brewster Buffalo—being flown by the RAF and the Dutch Air

Force in Surabaya, Singapore, and Rangoon. The Buffalo had a much better reputation than the Tomahawk, and some of the AVG pilots were angry that they had to fight with a second-rate plane while other countries had obtained a superior plane through lend-lease.

In reality, the P-40 was far better than the Buffalo, but it took a mock dogfight to prove that to Chennault's pilots. Occasionally, RAF pilots landed at Kyedaw Field and taunted the Americans about their inferior planes. Unable to ignore the challenge any longer, AVG pilot Erik Shilling agreed to take on an RAF pilot flying a Buffalo. To everyone's amazement, the P-40 flew rings around the Buffalo. Later, when the real fighting began, the Americans saw that the British pilots in their Buffalos were being slaughtered, and they became very grateful for their P-40s.

In the last months of peace in the fall of 1941, however, many of the pilots were still unhappy with their planes, but under Chennault's tutelage they were learning to make the most of them. The American pilots were better protected than their Japanese counterparts. The P-40 had two heavy sheets of steel behind the pilot's head and back; the Zero had no armor plating. There were other advantages. The P-40's gas tanks were self-sealing and could take hits without catching on fire and with only a minor loss of fuel. The aircraft as a whole was ruggedly constructed, capable of sustaining considerable battle damage and remaining airworthy. In a dive, the P-40's heavy weight made it so fast that the Zero could not catch it.

Top speed at 10,000 feet was 300 miles per hour and at 20,000 feet, 285 miles per hour. These speeds were attainable, however, only under ideal test conditions, without the fuel and ammunition needed for combat. In daily flying over Burma, the P-40 was not that fast. Because the plane lacked a supercharger, its effective ceiling was approximately 25,000 feet.

The planes were painted in the U.S. Army Air Corps camouflage colors of dark olive green and brown on top and gray underneath. When they were assembled and flown to Kyedaw, the American insignia was replaced by the 12-pointed blue-and-white star of the Chinese Air Force. In mid-November, the now-famous shark's teeth were added to the planes. It happened because Charlie Bond, who was having dinner with some other AVG pilots at the Baptist mission in Toungoo, noticed a photograph in a British newspaper of some Tomahawks being flown by Australians in North Africa. They had the tiger shark's teeth painted on the nose of their planes.

"I'm going to paint my P-40 that way!" Bond wrote in his diary that night. "I discussed it with the others and they thought it was a good idea. Fortunately, Chennault likes the idea as well." Before long, every P-40 flew with the menacing mouth with the red eye above it and the bright red tongue between the teeth.

There was no stencil for marking the outline of the shark's mouth on the planes. As R. T. Smith recalled, "each pilot simply drew the outline with chalk and then painted the lips, teeth, and eyes according to his own taste. As a result, of course, no two were exactly alike." Nevertheless, Smith thought the shark's mouth on his plane looked "mean as hell."

Another problem limited the effectiveness of the P-40s—the lack of spare parts. Chennault called it the "most critical problem" he faced. He told his supply officer, Skip Adair, that they would not be able to last more than fifteen days in combat without more airplanes and parts. When the AVG purchased the planes from the Curtiss-Wright Company, Chennault had been informed that the company had not manufactured any spare parts. This was done under orders of the air corps, which wanted only completed planes and no additional parts. The air corps believed at the time that it was better to replace a damaged or worn-out plane with a new one than to try to rebuild or repair it. This might not be such a problem for an air force with a constant supply of replacement planes, but for the AVG, which could not obtain additional planes, it was a disaster.

Long before they got into combat, the lack of spare parts reduced the number of planes available to the AVG. The training and practice flights were hard on the planes and quickly wore out many parts, especially tail wheel tires. In addition, there were shortages of electric switches, radio tubes, oxygen bottles, carburetors, spark plugs, and batteries. Another critical item they were desperately short of were E1B solenoids. Without these tiny conductors, the machine guns would not fire. Joe Alsop even took one to Rangoon's leading jeweler to have him make duplicates of it, but they did not fit.

For a long time, the only source of spare parts was damaged aircraft, P-40s that could have been repaired—had parts been available—but that became, instead, repositories of parts for other planes. Greg Boyington described one AVG pilot who had five small American flags painted on his airplane. "He had wrecked five P-40s, which made him a Japanese ace. This became the only way of getting spare parts."

The AVG was also short of ammunition. Top army and air corps leaders still had misgivings about supporting the AVG and claimed they had no ammunition to spare. Gen. George Marshall told Lauchlin Currie on June 15, 1941, that no .30-caliber bullets would be made available for China. Currie appealed to Roosevelt advisor Harry Hopkins. "If we don't get the ammunition over there," Currie said, "there will be an international scandal and we might as well forget the rest of the lend-lease program for China." Hopkins urged Roosevelt to pressure the army into sending ammunition to the AVG, arguing that it would look bad for the United States to send planes and pilots but no ammunition to carry on their fight. The army finally agreed and by August authorized a shipment of one million rounds of .30-caliber bullets and a half million rounds of .50-caliber bullets.

On November 24, two weeks before the Japanese attack on Pearl Harbor, Alsop sent a three-page cable to his friend Bob Lovett, the assistant secretary of war for air, pleading for more equipment for the AVG. "We have neither the strength for immediate combat nor the reserves to sustain combat. Thus American air prestige in Far East as well as big human and materiel investment in daily danger. Need not point out that they have been frivolously jeopardized by penny wisdom pound foolishness."

Half measures, Alsop insisted, would not be much better than no measures at all. The planes were worthless without the parts to keep them flying. Alsop urged Lovett to inform the president of the situation. "I am only a poor newspaperman," he added, "on a private bender and nobody is asking me to fight Japanese but as an American cannot help but be deeply shocked and stirred. . . . Forgive slight peevishness if you had seen what I have seen you would be more than peevish.''

There was one benefit from the shortage of spare parts—it served to boost the morale of the mechanics. As Paul Frillman noticed, the AVG ground crew "began to treat the shortage of parts as a challenge and to enjoy improvising. They rigged up contraptions of bamboo, rope, and pulleys and used gangs of Burmese workmen instead of mechanical hoists. They taught themselves how to rip up one plane for the parts and to put several others back into the air. Filing and hammering at odd bits of metal, they began to manufacture some of the simpler parts themselves.''

But there was a limit to improvisation and home-built parts, and Chennault devoted much of his energy to scouring the Far East, from Calcutta to Manila, searching for spare parts. Brooke-Popham in Singapore was again generous with his help, offering Chennault parts for the Brewster Buffalos; unfortunately, these would not fit the Tomahawk.

At one time Chennault had more than a dozen men scattered throughout the area hunting for parts, and one of these missions led to another controversy with William Pawley. Alsop, then in Singapore, suggested to Brooke-Popham that a letter from him might persuade General MacArthur in the Philippines to give the AVG spare parts from the army air corps stockpile there. Brooke-Popham agreed, and signed the letter written by Alsop. As Alsop was about to depart for Manila, Pawley arrived and announced that Chennault had authorized him to deal with MacArthur. This was not true, but Alsop did not know it at the time. Pawley took Brooke-Popham's letter and proceeded to Manila, where he did obtain some items such as tires.

When Chennault learned of Pawley's trip, he was furious and sent a strongly worded telegram to China Defense Supplies:

PAWLEY NOT AUTHORIZED TO NEGOTIATE BY ME. . . .
THERE IS EVIDENCE HE REPRESENTED HIMSELF IN
SINGAPORE AS PREDOMINANT IN GROUP IN ORDER TO

OBTAIN MESSAGE FROM COMMANDER-IN-CHIEF FAR
EAST [BROOKE-POPHAM] TO MACARTHUR.

Chennault accused Pawley of using his AVG connections to conduct private business and suggested that Pawley's trip to Manila was undertaken only to further his own financial ambitions.

Chennault urged Soong to make it clear to all parties that he, Chennault, and not Pawley was in command of the AVG and that Pawley represented the group only when he had Chennault's express authorization.

Soong suggested that Chennault send Alsop to Manila. MacArthur helped all he could, but he had little to spare. Admiral Hart, chief of the Asiatic Fleet then based in Manila, provided navy patrol planes to fly the tires to Singapore where Brooke-Popham arranged for their shipment to Rangoon. Chennault was pleased with the tangible aid provided by these three military leaders because it demonstrated a confidence in him that was not forthcoming from military leaders in the States.

While Alsop and others were roaming the Far East looking for spare parts, the staff of China Defense Supplies was trying to help out from Washington. They succeeded in amassing a load of P-40 spares and placed them on a Pan American Airways China Clipper departing San Francisco. One of the stops en route to the Far East was the tiny atoll called Wake Island. And that was where the Clipper found itself on the morning of December 8, 1941. Chennault's supplies were offloaded and left on Wake while the Clipper returned to Hawaii with a load of Pan Am personnel. When the Japanese captured Wake Island 16 days later, they got Chennault's supplies.

It was three months before any additional materiel reached the AVG. Two tons of ammunition and parts were dispatched aboard another Clipper that flew across the Atlantic Ocean, Africa, and the Middle East to reach Calcutta. Chennault would be plagued by a shortage of parts for his airplanes until the day he left China four years later.

Despite the problems of training, organization, and supply, Chennault was whipping the AVG into a combat-ready state. In late November the group was organized into three squadrons, each composed of 18 planes with 10 in reserve. The First Squadron, led by Robert "Sandy" Sandell, included primarily former army pilots. They called themselves the Adam and Eve First Pursuit Squadron and painted figures of Adam and Eve—representing the first pursuit in history—on each plane.

Charlie Bond designed the insignia, a black snake coiled around a big red apple with a woman chasing a man across the face of the apple. When Chennault saw it, he knew it would have to be changed. "The red apple looks too much like the Japanese Rising Sun, Charlie. It won't do." Bond thought about it awhile and came to the conclusion that there were green apples as well as red ones. Chennault agreed, and the squadron planes were adorned with green apples.

The Second Pursuit Squadron was led by Jack Newkirk, who, like most of the other squadron members, had been a navy pilot before joining the AVG. The navy crew, known as the "water boys," soon acquired a reputation as the noisiest group in the AVG. Newkirk chose the incongruous name "Panda Bears" for the squadron, after the gentle animals that are native to China. To Jim Howard, the name "didn't seem to be an appropriate symbol of our mission." Others felt the same way and would not agree to having a panda painted on their planes. Cartoonist Bert Christman began to paint caricatures of each pilot on his plane, but he never got the chance to finish them.

The Third Pursuit Squadron, led by former army pilot Arvid E. "Oley" Olson, was a mix of army, navy, and marine corps pilots. They called themselves the Hell's Angels, after the popular movie about the World War I flyers, and painted shapely angels in provocative poses on their planes.

By the end of November, despite their problems, morale was high among the men of the AVG. They were ready to fight. The pilots had lost the weight they had gained on their sea voyage to Burma, and they were tanned and fit. Chennault had certified 84 of them as ready to fly combat missions.

Chaplain Frillman observed that "all day pairs of closely aligned P-40s twisted and sideslipped overhead as Chennault's maneuvers were practiced with growing skill. The men were so fascinated by them that at the bar in the mess hall they spent most of the evenings talking tactics, weaving their bodies as they swooped their aligned hands around. I used to think how odd it would look through a soundproof window, seeing these extremely tough young men behaving like a gaggle of ballet dancers."

They had learned to fly Chennault's way and to maintain a tight discipline in the air. On the ground, however, they were the same hard-drinking hell-raisers who had arrived in Rangoon months before. In Toungoo and on leave in Rangoon, these brash, noisy Americans left a permanent impression on the locals, particularly the British.

Stories—some true and some apocryphal—abounded about the men of the AVG. A Chinese reporter in Burma wrote a story, but before it was passed by British censors in Rangoon, they excised the following passage: "The most interesting thing is that the Government has recruited 200 to 300 young women who can speak English from Shanghai and Hong Kong. It is said that the duty of these young women is to relieve the monotonous life of the Americans." There was no truth to the story, but it fit the image the AVG had acquired.

Thanks to Chennault, the AVG had become a tough, lean, hard outfit. The group's problems, however, were still critical. Only 43 planes, fewer than half their supply, were ready for combat. Many high officials in Washington had written off the AVG as a folly. Reports sent to the War Department from army officers in the Far East painted a grim picture of the AVG as an undisciplined mob that stood no chance against the Japanese. Soong heard these reports and cabled Chennault, expressing his concern:

REPORTS TO U.S. WAR DEPARTMENT STATE YOUR GROUP CANNOT BE READY BEFORE FEBRUARY 1942 AND WILL NOT LAST TWO WEEKS IN COMBAT. YOUR COMMENT REQUESTED.

Chennault replied that the group would be ready by the end of November and would last as long as China needed it. He knew that war was coming and that a Japanese fighter base was only 110 miles away, about twenty minutes' flying time. RAF Group Captain Manning refused Chennault permission to install an air-raid warning net in Burma similar to the one he had installed in China. The only warning of a Japanese attack might come from a single British civilian on the Burmese border who had a pair of binoculars and a telephone. Every day, at dusk and at dawn, Chennault stood in the rickety control tower watching the skies to the east, waiting for the enemy.

SEVEN

THE BOYS ARE GOING TO TOWN

"**M**y plane is ready and so am I—and it is my dearest wish that I get my sights on one of those Jap bastards."

"We are stunned . . . we realized that we are right in the middle of one hell of a big war! . . . I wonder when we'll get a chance at them. We are very tense and prepared to do our best, but we have no replacements."

"It is unbelievable that the Japs had enough guts to attack Honolulu. . . . Everybody running around like mad wondering what will happen to us. . . . I can't help from thinking the U.S. will easily wipe up the Japs."

So wrote three pilots in their diaries on December 8, 1941—December 7 at Pearl Harbor and in the States—when the AVG suddenly found itself in the front line of America's war. The AVG was closer to the Japanese than was any other American air combat unit.

Chennault was worried on that first day of the war, more worried, he said, than at any other time in his career. He knew the Japanese could easily bypass the lone British civil servant spotter on the Burmese border. Their airplanes could appear over the nearest mountain and swoop down on the field before anyone on the ground would even hear them. The Flying Tigers could be destroyed before they got in the air! The Japanese knew where they were, and they surely knew how ill-equipped they were just then. Chennault noticed that on that day and the next, more Burmese natives than usual were wandering around the field, despite the Gurkha guards. Several Buddhist monks seemed to be particularly curious and intrusive as they examined both the planes and the men.

Pilots waited by their planes, ready to take off. Sidearms and steel helmets were issued to all personnel. The AVG cars and trucks were hurriedly camouflaged with green and yellow paint. In the HQ office, Olga Greenlaw began the first page of the AVG's war diary.

> Monday, December 8th, 1941
> Point "A"
> Weather: Sunshine, scattered cumulus clouds.
>
> It was made known this morning at 7 o'clock that the United States was at war with Japan. Great Britain also declared war an hour later.
>
> Field orders were issued from Group Headquarters for all three squadrons to stand by: the Third Pursuit Squadron to be the Assault Echelon; the Second Pursuit Squadron to be Support Echelon; & the First Pursuit Squadron the Reserve Echelon.
>
> All members of the AVG authorized to wear firearms. No leave for personnel is granted. Orders were issued for an air raid warning system. Watch for enemy parachute troops. Telephones were installed wherever necessary. . . .
>
> Complete blackout tonight & alert crew standing by. The auxiliary field four miles north of Kyedaw was equipped with red lights marking runways and white lights marking boundaries of field while Kyedaw was kept in complete darkness.
>
> This command is on the alert 24 hours daily & pre-

pared to defy hostile actions of the enemy. Alert ships
to be fully armed & kept ready to take off at any time.

The AVG was lucky on that first day of war. No enemy planes
appeared. The next day they had a half dozen air-raid alerts, but
they all turned out to be false alarms. Their air-raid alarm was an
old brass ship's bell—it was all they could get from the British.
When it sounded, Chennault grabbed his binoculars and ran to the
control tower. The staff and ground crewmen put on their tin hats
and raced for the nearest slit trench while the pilots scrambled for
their planes. Even though there were still more pilots than planes
and each aircraft had been assigned to a particular pilot, all the
men ran as fast as they could. Chaplain Paul Frillman recalled that
"the fastest runners leaped into the planes and sat there grinning,
with the rightful pilots furiously yelling and shaking their fist at
them until the alert was called off."

Chennault sent Erik Shilling in his stripped-down photo-
reconnaissance ship over Bangkok to take pictures of the Japanese buildup. Ed Rector and Bert Christman flew as escorts. All
three were under orders not to engage in combat except in self-
defense. "Get your pictures and get home," Chennault told them.
"Fly high. No fighting." Information was more important than
the possibility of shooting down a few Japanese planes.

The men flew unchallenged at 26,000 feet over Bangkok's
docks and airfields and brought back clear pictures. When Chennault saw them, he exploded with rage. At the docks, more than
two dozen Japanese ships were unloading troops, tanks, armored
cars, artillery pieces, and other equipment. At one airfield, over
50 fighter planes were lined up wingtip to wingtip. "A half-dozen
bombers could wreck the Japanese air force in southeastern
Asia," he said. "Those are the planes and men that will be moving against Singapore and Rangoon. If we only had a half-dozen
bombers we could smash that drive before it got started." The
feeling of impotence against such targets was maddening.

All Chennault could do was ensure that his own planes were not
wiped out on the ground. Patrols scrambled day and night, whenever there was an air-raid warning, and that brought a new problem—the men had little experience in night landings.

An alert sounded at 3:30 on the morning of December 10, and six planes took off into the darkness. They circled the field for an hour and a half before Chennault recalled them. He ordered the runway lined with kerosene lanterns and watched as the first plane, flown by Tex Hill, overshot the runway and crashed at the far end of the landing strip. Hill was unhurt, but the AVG had lost another plane. Chennault immediately ordered more lights for the runway, provided by the headlights of a station wagon and a Studebaker sedan, and the other pilots made it in safely.

One day passed, and another, and there was no sign of the enemy. It was a letdown, a disappointment to the men who had been so keyed up with anticipation and excitement. Charlie Bond shaved off his mustache because he was so bored. It was something to do.

"Most everyone is anxious to get a shot at the Japs and wants to get moving," wrote Buster Keeton in his diary. "Colonel Chennault gave us a wonderful talk, warning against propaganda and for us to expect anything, and expect to move anyplace on a moment's notice. . . . According to him, we are supposed to be the strongest striking air force in the Far East." But Keeton later added, "If we could get a few spare parts, ten more planes could be put into operation."

Chennault knew that the AVG was on its own for the foreseeable future. There were no spare parts or reinforcements on the way. There would be no more planes and no more men for a long time. A telegram from China Defense Supplies on December 11 informed him that the cargo of spare parts from the United States had been dumped on Wake Island. Two days later Soong cabled him with more bad news: PENDING CLARIFICATION FUTURE POLICY OF U.S.A. ARMY AND NAVY AIR FORCE ALL RECRUITMENT FOR FAVG SUSPENDED. Soong also told him that the pilots who were supposed to have departed Los Angeles on December 11 had been released for reinduction in the Army Air Corps. These were the bomber pilots who would have formed part of the Second AVG, slated to bomb Tokyo.

Soong visited all his contacts in the War Department in an effort to obtain reinforcements for Chennault, but nothing could be spared for China. One of those Soong approached in those days following the Pearl Harbor attack was the secretary of the navy, Frank Knox. Obviously forgetting Soong's ancestry in his anger at the Japanese, Knox slammed his fist on the desk and said, "By God, T. V., we are going to kill every one of those yellow bastards!"

Chennault was busy planning how best to deploy his three fighter squadrons. It was clear to him that he would have to defend both ends of the Burma Road—Rangoon and Kunming—which were 650 air miles apart. Rangoon was the port of entry, the only point from which supplies could reach China overland. Kunming was equally vital—and equally vulnerable—as the storage and distribution center from which supplies were dispersed to the various Chinese army units. Japanese bombers could destroy the effectiveness of both centers and render the Burma Road useless. Chennault had no alternative but to divide his meager forces.

On December 12 he sent Olson's Third Squadron, the Hell's Angels, to Rangoon. Olson had 15 planes, and the British forces in Rangoon had 30 Buffalos and Hurricanes, plus a dozen outdated Blenheim bombers. Chennault had fought hard with the British to make sure that he remained in command of the Third Squadron and that it not be turned over to Group Captain Manning. Had Manning been in command, he would have demanded individual dogfighting, tactics Chennault knew would be disastrous. In return for the AVG's assistance in defending the Burma Road at Rangoon, Manning agreed to provide housing, food, and communications. As it turned out, however, none of these was forthcoming. Chennault instructed Olson to make sure his planes were dispersed and hidden until the Japanese made their first air strike.

The rest of the AVG forces—minus a dozen P-40s not yet ready for combat and 25 pilots who had not completed their training— went to Kunming on December 18. A few days earlier, Chennault issued highly publicized orders that the group would move north on the 17th. He was certain the local Burmese would inform the Japanese, and they did. Throughout the day on the 17th, Japanese planes patrolled the Burma Road looking for Americans. They bombed Kunming and announced that they had destroyed 20 American planes in the bombing.

That afternoon a truck convoy carrying supplies and base personnel left Kyedaw Field for the long trip to Kunming. The next day, three transport planes of CNAC began shuttling supplies of oxygen, ammunition, and the most vital of the spare parts, plus Chennault and his staff, to their new base in China. Later in the day, the First Squadron took off and circled the field to cover the takeoff of the Second Squadron. They all headed north.

By the early morning hours of December 19, Chennault had 34 P-40s fueled, armed, and on the alert at Kunming. His headquarters was wired into the early-warning net, and the Chinese radio crewmen were monitoring Japanese radio frequencies. For the first time in two months, Chennault breathed easier. Finally, his men were in place and ready for battle.

Kunming provided a welcome change from the oppressive heat, swarming insects, and primitive living conditions of Kyedaw. Pilot George Burgard called it "really great. The quarters are splendid, soft cots, furniture, showers, good food, a nice bar, excellent reception at the hands of the Chinese, and a good field to operate out of."

The city of Kunming sat atop a plateau 6000 feet above sea level. A beautiful blue lake lay next to the city, ringed by the rugged mountain peaks that formed the foothills of the Himalayas. December was cold, and ice covered the ground in the mornings. The airfield, three miles from the city, had a 7000-foot runway that had been under construction for five years. It was still being built by an army of coolies who crushed rocks and hauled giant rollers by hand.

"I watched the coolies," Charlie Bond said, "thousands of them, trotting back and forth with their baskets of crushed stone and pots and slimy mud to complete a hard-surfaced runway down the middle of the field. How pitiful. They stared at me as much as I stared at them."

Tan-colored alert shacks made of plaster and adobe were scattered around the field, each surrounded by a dirt revetment. There were numerous machine-gun emplacements and elaborate systems of connecting trenches. The men lived in two hostels, one at the field and the other at a university dormitory in the city. Both were modern, with all the comforts of home, including tennis courts, libraries, and pistol ranges. Each pilot had a private room with a comfortable cot, chair and table, chest of drawers, a small desk, and a charcoal heater.

Even the food was good. Among the Chinese cooks was a man who had served aboard the USS *Tutuilla*, a Yangtze River gunboat, and knew what Americans liked to eat. For breakfast he served them three-egg omelets, bacon, hotcakes, butter and jam, and American coffee. Lunch and dinner consisted of soup, four vegetables, meat, and dessert. And afternoon tea, British-style, included plates of cakes and sandwiches. An ice-cream freezer, beer and whiskey, chewing gum, recent American magazines, and swing records were also available.

Although the AVG quarters and facilities were excellent, the city of Kunming was a cauldron of filth. Packs of mongrel dogs roamed freely, feasting on unclaimed corpses in the cemeteries. The people were dirty and ragged, suffering from various illnesses, especially eye diseases. The streets were narrow, crowded with pedestrians, shabby stores, rickshaws, ponies, and a few old cars and motorcycles.

Still, Kunming had something to recommend it, being one of the most secure places in the country in terms of air-raid warning. Chennault felt safer there than at Kyedaw. Thanks to the early-warning net he had established years before, the AVG could not be surprised by a Japanese air attack. The net was so widespread and effective that it provided up to one hour's warning, signaled by a large black paper ball hoisted on the airfield's flagpole. When a second ball was raised, enemy planes were known to be thirty minutes away. A third ball signified ten minutes' warning.

In the operations shack, the approach of the planes was plotted on a map mounted on a large square table. Kunming was shown at the center of the map. Around it, concentric circles drawn in red ink one inch apart represented a distance of sixty kilometers each. Symbols showed the location of radio and telephone reporting stations, each linked to the others to form a spider web so tightly constructed that no enemy plane could slip through.

Although the relocation of Chennault's force to Kunming went smoothly, there was an element of tragedy. The P-40s arrived safely, but three other aircraft did not. William Pawley had sold to the Chinese three Curtiss-Wright CW-21 Demons, the lightweight, air-cooled fighter plane that could outclimb the Zero. Chennault intended to use them in combat, but the pilots bringing them to Kunming—Erik Shilling, Lacy Mangleburg, and Ken Merritt—ran into problems when Shilling, the flight leader, lost power. He kept his landing gear retracted and made a crash landing on the side of a mountain. Mangleburg and Merritt circled the wreckage, unaware of the route to Kunming, which was less than fifty miles away on the same course heading they had been flying. Although each had about forty gallons of fuel left, they decided to try to land. Merritt made a belly landing in a dry river bed and, like Shilling, emerged with a few minor injuries. Mangleburg circled a nearby town some twenty times at different altitudes, searching for a suitable landing site. When he finally tried to put down in a stream, he did so wheels down. The propeller struck the water, and he shoved the throttle forward to gain altitude. The undercarriage hit the third level of the terraced hill beside the stream, and the ammunition in the plane's machine guns exploded on impact. The ship was engulfed in flames, and Mangleburg was killed.

Shilling and Merritt reached Kunming eight days later, after Shilling had had one of the AVG's more bizarre adventures. When he crawled out of the cockpit of his wrecked airplane, he was confronted by a group of Chinese mountain people brandishing old flintlock rifles and long knives. Their gestures were clearly menacing and Shilling obeyed their obvious desire that he remain in the cockpit. To his dismay, the mountain people began to build a fence around the plane.

The next day they brought him a little rice to eat but indicated that he should stay inside the fenced area. Bored, and increasingly uneasy, Shilling suddenly remembered that he had his windup phonograph on board. The machine had survived the crash intact, along with three jazz records.

The music caught the attention of the Chinese, and when the records stopped, they waved for him to continue. He pantomimed in return that he wanted something to eat. They brought him food and for the remainder of the day, Erik Shilling sat on the mountainside playing jazz records for his captors. By late afternoon, the needle was being ground down and the sound had become distorted, but his audience did not seem to mind.

The following morning, Chinese soldiers arrived to rescue Shilling, directed to the crash site by one of the spotters in Chennault's warning net. As a result of Shilling's experience, AVG pilots were given a silk parchment emblem to stitch on the back of their flying jackets. It showed the Chinese flag and the words, "I am a foreign aviator flying for China. Please take me to the nearest authorities."

The first day at Kunming passed quietly. Chaplain Frillman called it a day of "giddy anticlimax. . . . Sleepiness and excitement and the stimulus of being in a new country, a new climate, made everyone in the alert shacks light-headed. . . . The thinner, cooler air of a high plateau was like a shot of iced gin after the Burma jungles. Lots of horseplay, Indian wrestling, acrobatics, even tag, helped the long hours pass." No paper balls rose to the top of the mast that day. Chennault sent out three patrols as far as 200 miles to the south, but there was no sign of the enemy. Where, he wondered, were the Japanese?

At 9:45 on the morning of December 20, 1941, the telephone that connected Chennault to the Chinese code room rang. Ten Japanese bombers had been spotted crossing the border of Yunnan Province. They were flying at 8000 feet on a northwesterly course that would bring them over Kunming in one hour. More reports came in from other spotting stations, and the line extending from the farthest circles on the plotting board straight in to Kunming grew longer.

Chennault ordered one ball raised to the top of the airfield's warning mast. Those pilots scheduled for the morning alert ran to their planes, zipping up their heavy flying suits. They climbed into their cockpits, alert, tense, and excited. Off-duty pilots watched them with a mixture of envy and relief. "I was having my day-off routine," Greg Boyington said, "not having a P-40, naturally, when the real McCoy came." He raced toward the unmanned planes, but every one of them was out of commission.

Ground crews were busy. Some of the men were driving trucks off the field to places of safety where the bombs would not reach them. Others were pushing the inoperable planes behind dirt revetments designed to protect them from shrapnel. In town, the Chinese civilians headed for air-raid shelters or the open fields beyond the city's ancient walls. In the operations shack, Chennault continued to receive information, and the line of the plot drifted closer to the center of the red circles. The Japanese course remained fixed; they were 30 minutes from Kunming. Chennault ordered the second ball to be raised.

The pilots in their cockpits watched the ball ascend, swallowed hard, and made another quick check of the switches and dials on their instrument panels. Most of them were wondering what lay ahead, how they would react in combat, whether they would live through it. They did not have much longer to wait.

"Yellow flare. Signal to warm engines," recorded one pilot. "My engine coughed, then roared. The field was deserted and bare. [Chennault's] voice over the radio and the flare were my only contact with the rest of the world—the only sign of life. It was as though I were the last man left on the planet. It was a depressed and helpless feeling just sitting alone on the ground. I saw the red flare—takeoff signal. I eased forward on the throttle, taxied to the end of the runway, and zoomed off. My depression slid away like the ground below me. I retracted my landing gear and put the ship into a good climb. The air was as smooth as silk. I felt good all over and ready for anything. Just before we swung into formation I remember thinking, 'Never in my life have I felt anything like this.'"

Chennault sent 24 planes into battle that morning. The Second Squadron, the Panda Bears, was designated to intercept the enemy. Jack Newkirk, the squadron commander, had eight planes. He led half of them in search of the enemy while the others, led by Jim Howard, flew high over Kunming ready to pounce on the bombers if they got through. The 16 planes of the First Squadron, the Adams and Eves, led by Sandy Sandell, waited in reserve, west of Kunming.

As soon as Chennault had fired the red flare, sending his planes screaming down the runway, he headed for the combat operations air-raid shelter, a pyramid-shaped structure of clay and heavy timbers located in a Chinese cemetery overlooking the field. With him were Harvey Greenlaw and Colonel Hsu, his interpreter. The shelter contained a duplicate plotting board and a second set of radios and telephones to link him with the early-warning net and with his pilots, now gone from sight. It was so dark inside that Greenlaw had to keep striking matches over the plotting board so that Chennault could locate the enemy planes.

This was a critical moment for Chennault. What he had been planning for four years was about to take place. American pilots, his boys, flying American planes and using his tactics, were about to do battle with the seemingly invincible Imperial Japanese Air Force. So far, everywhere the Japanese had struck—the Philippines, Malaya, Hong Kong, Guam, Wake—their pilots had been victorious. Neither the U.S. Army Air Corps, nor the U.S. Navy, nor the RAF had been able to stop them. And now it was the turn of a handful of mavericks flying obsolete planes, using tactics the military brass had rejected.

Chennault's fate rode with his men in their cramped cockpits. If they failed, he would have failed and might never get the chance to try again. He followed their progress over the radio and watched it on a board illuminated by matches.

"I yearned heartily to be ten years younger," he wrote later, "and crouched in a cockpit instead of a dugout, tasting the stale rubber of an oxygen mask and peering ahead into limitless space through the cherry-red rings of a gunsight."

Suddenly Newkirk's voice broke over the radio.

"Shark Fin Blue calling base. Bandits sighted 60 miles east. Attacking."

A moment later Chennault heard Bert Christman and Gil Bright, who were flying with Newkirk.

"There they are."

"No, no. They can't be Japs."

"Look at those red balls."

"Let's get 'em."

After that, Chennault heard nothing. The silence was agonizing for him. Presently, he heard the sound of bombs exploding in the distance, much farther away than the city of Kunming. The Japanese must be jettisoning their bombs in the face of Newkirk's attack. A few minutes later Chennault's suspicion was confirmed. The Chinese reported that the enemy bombers had turned around and were heading back to Indochina. Chennault ordered Sandell's squadron to take up position thirty miles southeast of Kunming. If they got there in time, they could intercept the retreating Japanese.

In Kunming and around the airfield, Chinese began leaving their shelters, amazed that no bombs had fallen. But Chennault was still waiting word from Newkirk and Sandell. Minutes later, Jim Howard's covering flight landed. They had seen nothing of the enemy. Finally, three of Newkirk's four planes came in. There were no victory rolls over the field, and the men looked glum when they landed.

As they sheepishly explained to Chennault, when they first saw the enemy planes, they could not believe they were really Japanese. Chennault understood their incredulity, as any experienced hunter would. He called their reaction "buck fever," that nervous excitement felt by novice hunters the first time they actually see game. It usually causes them to delay shooting for a few seconds.

Those few seconds of delay on the part of Newkirk and his flight were just enough to allow the Japanese to get away. When they spotted the American planes, they dropped their bombs, dove to pick up speed, and headed for their base. By the time Newkirk's pilots recovered, it was too late. They were able to make only one ineffective pass and by the time they pulled out of their dives, the Japanese had opened up too great a lead. Newkirk, Christman, and Bright all thought it would be impossible to catch up with the enemy planes, but the last they saw of Ed Rector, he was streaking after the bombers at full throttle.

Now only Sandell's squadron had an opportunity to take on the enemy. If they failed too, Chennault knew it would be bad for morale. The men would lose confidence in themselves, and perhaps in him as well. Everything depended on the 16 Adams and Eves.

Thirty miles southeast of Kunming, over the town of Iliang, exactly where Chennault had ordered them to be, Sandell and his pilots were cruising at 16,000 feet, high above an almost solid overcast. Far below, they spotted ten Japanese bombers at about 3000 feet, just above the clouds. Sandell led the squadron in a dive and caught up with the enemy in about ten minutes. In their excitement, they "went a little crazy" and promptly forgot everything Chennault had so painstakingly taught them. All the long hours of lectures and chalk diagrams on the blackboard and drilling in the air above Kyedaw Field under Chennault's watchful eyes were stripped from memory at that moment. Over a distance of some 130 miles, the Adams and Eves engaged in a melee of individual dogfighting in the best World War I manner, with a total lack of teamwork as each pilot fought his own wild war. Only luck kept them from colliding or shooting each other down.

It was also fortunate that they were pitted against Japanese bombers and not Zeros. If they had tried to do battle with fighters in that fashion, few of them would have survived. As it was, in spite of themselves, they began to shoot down the enemy planes. "We opened fire, and the bombers seemed to fall into pieces," Bob Neale said. "I saw pieces of engine cowling fall off into space. Glass from the gun turrets flew in all directions. Engines smoked and caught fire. Tails just crumpled and fell off. It was the queerest thing I ever saw."

The heavy .50-caliber machine guns in the noses of the P-40s cut a swath through the enemy formation, killing the Japanese gunners before they could open fire with their shorter-range .30-caliber guns. As the Americans closed in, they opened fire with the four .30-calibers in the wings and riddled their targets from end to end.

Charlie Bond lined up a bomber in his gunsight ring and squeezed the trigger. Nothing happened. In his excitement, he had checked his gun switch so often that he had turned it off. He broke away quickly, then zoomed up and got back in position on the same plane. This time he opened up with everything and saw his tracers dig into the bomber's fuselage. He felt his control stick quiver but thought nothing of it. He bore in again and again to attack the main formation. Only seven bombers were left, and Bond saw other fighter pilots follow smoking bombers down until they crashed in fiery explosions against the mountains. When Bond returned to base, he was amazed to find bullet holes throughout the tail of his plane.

"We were hitting them from all directions—right, left, above, below. Sandy Sandell even tried a front quarter pass while attacking. On one pass I barely missed colliding with Bill Bartling. I was too keyed up to give it much thought. After another pass I pulled away and up into clouds and immediately had to go on instruments before I came out above the layer."

Louis Hoffman, the AVG's oldest pilot, got one of the bombers. After his bullets got the rear gunner, he slowed his speed and calmly stayed in place behind the plane, riddling it from tail to nose. It soon spun out of control. Sandell got a bomber in a head-on attack, chipping away at its starboard engine. It burst into flames and the entire wing fell off.

Fritz Wolf did even better—he shot down two bombers. After diving through the formation, he came up beneath one bomber and opened up at 500 yards, killing the rear gunner. At 100 yards he loosed a burst at one of the engines and the gas tanks. The engine broke off, the wing folded back, and the plane exploded. Wolf yanked hard on the stick to get out of the way of the debris. He tailed another bomber and saw the tail gunner firing at him. He ignored the gunner and pulled to within 50 yards before firing a long burst into the engine. The plane exploded almost instantly.

Ed Rector, from Newkirk's flight, showed up in the middle of the fray. The remaining enemy bombers had maintained a tight formation, and he pulled in behind one of them and started firing. He forgot Chennault's admonition to fire only short bursts and kept the trigger depressed for a full eight seconds. He seemed so mesmerized by his target that he nearly crashed into it, diving under it when he was only about twelve feet away. He came in for another pass and the bomber caught fire but hung in formation for a long moment before falling to earth.

Rector swung away and watched the other fighter pilots continue their reckless passes, thinking that was the way to get killed.

Then he did the same thing himself, three times, but his guns had overheated from the eight-second burst and wouldn't respond. He decided to return to base, but he didn't know the way. He had no navigational map and wasn't even sure of his present position. He flew parallel to the enemy bombers long enough to get their course heading, then headed in the opposite direction, hoping that would lead to Kunming. He missed it by 200 miles.

Chennault had had no radio report from Sandell's squadron and so had no idea what was happening. It was not until the planes returned and made slow victory rolls over the field that he even knew they had met the enemy! Even when the pilots landed, they were, at first, too excited to give him a coherent account of the battle. Sandy Sandell spotted Olga Greenlaw and greeted her cheerfully. "We did it," he said. "We met 'em and kicked hell out of them. That's just the beginning . . . just an appetizer." Another pilot recalled that they were all "in high spirits." Chennault was elated when he learned that three bombers had been seen to crash and that most of the others were trailing smoke when the fight broke off. But it would not be wise to let the pilots become cocky. It might make them careless in the future.

"Not a bad job," he told them, "but it should have been better. Now let's go over what happened and make sure we get them all next time."

He brought the pilots into the operations shack, calmed them down, and reviewed the details of the action, pointing out the mistakes they had made. As it turned out, the men had done better than they thought. Chinese spotters reported that only four of the Japanese planes had returned to Indochina. Three years later, when the war ended, Chennault learned from one of his pilots who had been captured in Indochina that only one enemy aircraft had survived that first battle with the AVG. The Japanese never again tried to bomb Kunming while the AVG was there.

The celebration that night was dampened by the absence of Ed Rector. He was long overdue, and there had been no word about a P-40 from the Chinese air spotters. The pilots assumed that he had crashed in some remote area and that the chances of finding him were slim. But Rector was still very much alive. When he took the course opposite to that of the Japanese bombers, he found himself over unfamiliar territory, and was running out of gas. Below him he spied a road that led to a town, but when he dove to follow it, he lost it in the clouds. Down to 1000 feet, he was forced to turn into a valley to avoid the hills that suddenly loomed before him. He realized he was flying up a canyon, and its walls were narrowing. There was no room to turn. It was too dangerous to climb because the overcast had forced him down to 400 feet and he could not see how high the mountains were.

Up ahead was a solid wall of rock. Then Rector noticed that the canyon took a ninety-degree turn. As he maneuvered his plane into the curve, he had the impression that his left wingtip scraped the face of the mountain, and then he saw he had escaped one trap only to fall into another. Two miles ahead the canyon ended, and the rocky terrain precluded any kind of crash landing. He had no choice but to climb as rapidly as possible, and at 7000 feet, to his surprise, he broke out of the overcast into a beautiful, clear blue sky. All around him the peaks of the towering mountains poked through the clouds.

A red light blinked on his instrument panel. He had only enough fuel for ten more minutes of flight. He headed for the town he had seen earlier and as soon as he got over flat ground—a field of maize—he put the flaps down. He kept the wheels up, deciding quickly that a belly landing would be safer. At an altitude of five feet, he cut the motor and braced himself. The plane skidded across the furrows of the field before it stopped, but Rector escaped injury.

Now he had a new worry. He had seen from the air that the townspeople were running toward the landing site, and he did not know whether he was in Chinese or Japanese territory. If they were Chinese approaching him, would they know he was an American? He pulled out his .45, then put it away. It would be of no help. The crowd could quickly overwhelm him.

"Megwa fegur," he shouted, hoping he was saying the right thing. Someone had told him words that sounded like that meant "American pilot." But the people did not have to be told who he was. They knew. They cheered him and gathered around, and with their help, he finally returned to Kunming.

Thus, the AVG had met the enemy, scored their first victory, and suffered no casualties. They were off to a good start.

The days that followed were an anticlimax. Though the pilots were eager to fight again and those who had missed the first battle wanted their chance, the enemy did not come. For several mornings there were alerts and the pilots on duty scrambled, ready to do battle, but each time they returned without sighting the Japanese.

At 5:00 on the afternoon of December 23, the pilots of Sandell's squadron were honored by the people of Kunming for their victory two days earlier. They stood in formation on the cold, windswept field while a Chinese band "made noises which might have been national anthems with bits of Dixie and Yankee Doodle thrown in." The governor of Yunnan Province made a speech, and fourteen Chinese officials carrying bright red silk sashes approached the fourteen squadron pilots and draped the cloths around the shoulders and waists of the Americans. During the ceremony, Harvey Greenlaw hurried over to Jack Newkirk, whose Second Squadron was on duty, and Newkirk's men broke ranks and ran to their planes. Enemy bombers were reported to be approaching Kunming. For the rest of the AVG, however, the ceremony went on as planned.

Now fourteen young Chinese girls approached Sandell's men and presented them with bouquets of flowers, hams, and fruits. More speeches followed, but the men were "getting real touchy." They did not want to be caught by the Japanese while standing on the runway listening to speeches. Then the Chinese did the worst thing possible. They set off hundreds of firecrackers, which the pilots knew could be seen for miles in the clear and dark sky. They were like beacons, luring the enemy directly to the airfield.

When the ceremony ended, the pilots raced for the operations shack to find out that it had not been a false alarm. Enemy planes had indeed been heading for Kunming, but for some reason had turned back only fifty miles from the city.

A couple of days later the Chinese threw a Christmas party for the men of the AVG. Each pilot was given a white silk scarf.

Chennault spoke "on behalf of the AVG and was highly inspiring," said George Burgard. "He closed with a pledge to fight to victory or death." The meal that followed the speeches was somewhat less inspiring. "I noticed several of the fellows sneaking away with green faces," wrote one pilot. "When I found chicken feet in one of the dishes we were served, that was the end."

On the day after Christmas Chennault joined the Greenlaws for dinner at the Kwang Sing Yang, one of the best Cantonese restaurants in Kunming, for a meal of fish, prawns, and shrimp. While they were eating, he received a radiogram from Rangoon. The Third Squadron had also met the enemy.

The men of Arvid Olson's Third Squadron, the Hell's Angels, did not enjoy the same luxuries as the AVG units at Kunming. They did not live in comfortable hostels with tennis courts and plenty of hot water, or good food in the mess. At Mingadalon Airdrome, the RAF base twelve miles from Rangoon, Olson's men sweltered in the tropical heat in old, frayed tents in an unkempt bivouac near the dusty, red gravel runway. The British had not kept their agreement to supply food and housing, and the Hell's Angels had to scrounge to meet their daily needs. They hired Burmese nationals to prepare whatever food could be found in cans because there were no provisions for storing fresh food.

Although the living conditions were awful, the men were so busy and so keyed up in anticipation of battle that they had no time to brood over it. Ground crews worked under the shelter of trees to make the P-40s ready for war and to prepare four trucks for rapid servicing of the planes. One truck was kept loaded with ammunition, one with gasoline, one with oxygen, and one with parts and tools for engine and body repairs. The trucks were stored in dirt-walled revetments beside the runway, and their crews were ready to swarm over a plane and service it quickly so that it could get back in the air in minutes.

Other ground crewmen were fashioning emergency landing strips, some as far as forty miles from Mingadalon. From the air they looked like dry rice paddies. The fields had been named "Johnnie Walker" and "Haig and Haig," after the bottles of

Scotch that had been cached near each field. The Third Squadron was prepared for everything.

The men knew they had to be fit for combat as soon as possible because Rangoon—the only remaining gateway for supplies into China—was a prime Japanese target. Supplies from Rangoon's huge, crowded port moved north by barge, train, truck, airplane, and mule. American DC-3s, operated by CNAC, could reach Chungking in hours. By truck over the Burma Road, it could take up to six weeks to cover half the distance. Without Rangoon, supplies for China would have to be brought from India. Worse, the capture of Rangoon and then the rest of Burma would permit the Japanese armies to invade India.

To the Japanese, Burma appeared to be an easy conquest. They knew the RAF had little to stop them, only a dozen Blenheim bombers and about 30 equally obsolete Brewster Buffalos. Once they eliminated that feeble opposition in the air, they could land troops and rapidly subdue the entire country. As it turned out, everything went largely according to their plan, except that the opposition they faced in the air was not so feeble after all.

The Hell's Angels saw the enemy for the first time on December 21 while on a routine patrol with the RAF, but the Japanese were not ready to do battle. When they saw Olson's fighters, they jettisoned their bombs and hurried away. Later that day, a Japanese reconnaissance plane flew over Mingadalon Field and the port at an altitude of 25,000 feet. The men knew what that meant. Chennault had told them many times that whenever an enemy observation plane spotted their location, they could expect an attack any time from 1 to 48 hours.

It was slightly less than 48 hours, at 11:00 A.M. on December 23, when the Japanese returned, 54 Mitsubishi twin-engine bombers, of the type that had tried to bomb Kunming, and 20 fighters. Eight of the fighters were Zeros and the others were Nakajima Type 97s, a nimble, open-cockpit, fixed-landing gear, 2-gun aircraft in use since 1937. Chennault said later that the small number of fighters relative to the number of bombers indicated that the Japanese expected little opposition from the Americans and British. The Japanese planes came in two formations, one to bomb Rangoon and the other to attack the airfield.

Olson had 15 operational P-40s. That morning the pilots ate a breakfast of bacon, bread, and cold tea. As the sun rose and the temperature reached 115 degrees, they took off their shirts and lounged around the alert tents in boots, helmets, and shorts. At 10:30, the telephone rang. It was the RAF reporting that the enemy had been spotted at 15,000 feet, about thirty minutes' flying time away.

All twenty of Olson's pilots ran for the fifteen planes. An off-duty pilot, dressed for a day in Rangoon in white shirt and long pants, reached one of the planes and took off. Another pilot, frustrated at seeing someone else taxi down the runway in his P-40, ran after it, brandishing his .45.

At 18,000 feet, the squadron split into two flights, one led by George McMillan and the other by Parker Dupouy. McMillan's men attacked first; Dupouy's acted as reserve. The nine planes dove in single file out of the sun and sideslipped along the long edge of the enemy's first V formation of twenty-seven bombers. Charlie Older fired at the lead bomber and scored a hit in the bomb bay. The plane exploded almost at once. The other bombers closed the gap and continued on, maintaining a perfect formation. McMillan's group made several more runs and shot down two more bombers.

On the other side of the V formation, R. T. Smith closed in on the tail of a bomber. Oblivious to the point-blank fire from the Mitsubishi's tail gunner, he crept within fifty feet before opening up with all his guns.

Years later, Smith recalled "the crackling sound of my four .30-caliber wing guns and the slower, powerful thudding of the two .50s in the nose, like twin jackhammers ripping up pavement; and the pungent smell of cordite filling the cockpit, a good smell." Smith kept firing until the bomber exploded in a huge ball of flame right in front of him. The shock wave tossed his P-40 about like a leaf in a storm. Smith tore through the debris and shouted, "By God, I got one of the bastards, no matter what happens from now on!"

Charlie Older, making head-on passes, shot down two more bombers. That was enough for the Japanese. They dropped their bombs, turned around, and dove for speed, fleeing for their base in Thailand. To keep the bombers from being pursued, the covering Japanese fighters attacked McMillan's flight, and the ensuing battle ranged over many square miles. Once again the AVG pilots, in their first contact with the enemy, forgot Chennault's tactics and resorted to individual dogfighting. The resulting confusion was so great that the pilots have never been able to agree on the details.

While McMillan's group tangled with the Japanese fighters, Dupouy's flight attacked the second wave of twenty-seven enemy bombers. Dupouy led three planes in a head-on attack, and Neil Martin led three in a pass at the side of the bomber formation. As Martin dove closer, all the Japanese turret gunners opened fire, bringing twenty-seven streams of cannon fire to bear. Most of them hit their target. For a fraction of a second the P-40 hung motionless, as though stopped in flight by the hail of fire, then it rolled over and fell to earth. Martin, a former air corps pilot from Arkansas, became the AVG's first battle casualty.

Several of the enemy bombers in the second wave were smoking and starting to lag behind, but none had yet fallen. Dupouy's group went after the stragglers and soon sent three of them spinning out of control. While the Americans were diving on the bombers, six of the Nakajima fighters dropped down and got on their tails. Four focused their fire on Henry Gilbert's P-40 and it went into a spin with fire spurting from both wings. Gilbert, from Bremerton, Washington—at twenty-one, the youngest flyer in the AVG—became the second battle casualty.

The other two Japanese fighters stayed on the tail of Paul J. Greene's plane and kept up their fire until it began to tumble. Greene, dressed only in cowboy boots and shorts, with his .45 strapped around his waist, bailed out. He had brought along another pilot's parachute, one that was too small for him. Although it opened properly, the straps pulled tightly and bruised him. That was a minor worry, however. The Japanese fighters that had shot down his plane were coming back to finish the job. The ground crew at Mingadalon could see the planes making passes at Greene and could hear the high staccato sound of the .303 machine guns. Each time a Japanese pilot took aim, Greene pulled at his parachute harness to spill air from the chute and swing out of the line of fire. Finally, he went limp. When the chute came down close to the field, a number of ground crewmen ran out. They found him lying on his back laughing. He said he just got tired of tugging at the harness and decided to play dead.

Dupouy's fighters continued to pour fire into the enemy formation, but the Japanese had the advantage of numbers and bore on to the airfield and the city. British antiaircraft fire was ineffective. Bombs rained down on the field, followed by a strafing attack by the fighters. Explosions peppered the runway and damaged the RAF operations office, a hangar, and a gas pump. The AVG office was strafed and some ten Buffalos and RAF training planes were destroyed. Forty men were killed on the ground—ten RAF personnel and thirty Burmese soldiers.

Other bombers pounded Rangoon's crowded dockside while eight Zeros strafed streets jammed with people. This was the city's first air raid, and most of the people had ignored the sirens and spurned the shelters to stay outside and watch the battle. Bombs damaged two large department stores, the railway station, and an oil refinery, as well as the docks, and hundreds of Burmese and British civilians were killed.

The Hell's Angels were low on gas and broke off the fight. The Japanese headed back to their base in Thailand. When the P-40s landed, they had to dodge the craters left by the Japanese bombs.

A returning RAF pilot came to the AVG alert tent to announce that he had seen a P-40 pilot, "a ruddy idiot," in the middle of a cluster of Japanese bombers on their way back to Thailand. He was identified as one of McMillan's flight, Robert R. "Duke" Hedman, a former army pilot from South Dakota. He had outraced the assigned pilot of a P-40 and taken off to the curses of the loser. Hedman was known as a conservative, by-the-book flyer, one who always followed regulations. The feeling among the AVG was that he would have a difficult time in combat, but he proved his detractors wrong that day by downing five planes and becoming an ace.

He had shot down a fighter and a bomber in the AVG's first diving attack, but before the bomber went down, one of its gunners fired and smashed Hedman's canopy. He was forced to fly with his head down, but that did not stop him. He tangled with several enemy fighters, shot down two, and took hits in his gas tank and gunsight. He took off after the retreating bombers, got inside their formation, and shot down the lead plane. The Japanese could not shoot at him for fear of hitting one of their own planes. As he landed at one of the outlying airfields, his P-40 had only five gallons of gas left.

When the battle was over, Olson's squadron claimed to have shot down fifteen of the enemy. They were wrong. The RAF sent out search parties around Rangoon and found wreckage from thirty-two Japanese planes. In addition, they received reports of planes going down at sea but had no wreckage to verify the losses. After careful examination of the pilots' battle reports, the RAF concluded that twenty-five planes had been shot down by the AVG, with a loss of two pilots and three aircraft. The RAF shot down seven Japanese planes, with a loss of five pilots and eleven aircraft.

The Third Squadron had ample cause for celebration, and the place for it was Rangoon's Silver Grill cabaret, a nightclub that became the center of off-duty activity for the Americans. The British, usually formally dressed for dinner, were not pleased by the sight of the Yanks in khaki shirts and spattered mosquito boots with .45s on their hips, elbowing their way into what had been a British preserve. Many of the pilots brought half-castes with them, lovely Anglo-Indian girls who would never have dared enter the Silver Grill on their own. It just wasn't done.

The men of the AVG monopolized the dance floor, teaching their girls how to jitterbug. The Americans also persuaded the orchestra to play "The Star-Spangled Banner" as well as the usual "God Save the King" at the end of each night's dancing. The British, unfamiliar with the American national anthem, remained seated the first time it was played. The AVG quickly showed them the error of their ways.

On December 23, Radio Tokyo announced that the air defenses of Rangoon had been destroyed and that they would have special gifts for the city's people on Christmas Day—poison gas and parachutists. This warning, following the carnage of the air raid, instigated a panic among the Burmese. The rich left for India. The poor, stirred up by Buddhist monks and other leaders of the Burmese nationalist movement, turned on the remaining Englishmen, attacking and looting. The Burmese workers at the airfield disappeared, leaving Olson's men with a diet of stale bread and warm beer for two days.

Most of the squadron's airplanes had sustained battle damage, and the ground crews hid them as best they could and worked around the clock to make them airworthy. The pilots analyzed the air battle they had just fought and developed new tactics. They had noticed that the Nakajima fighters could not catch up with the bombers they were supposed to protect if they were engaged in a fight. The P-40s, however, with their faster diving speed, could. Next time, the pilots decided, they would separate the fighters from the bombers and then go after the bombers. They had also observed that Japanese pilots became careless once combat had broken off. In the future, the AVG patrolled the coastline on the route back to Thailand and caught many straggling enemy planes.

The Japanese returned on Christmas Day in force. At 11:00 in the morning the RAF notified the Hell's Angels that three waves of bombers, 60 in all, escorted by 32 fighters, were heading for Rangoon. The Third Squadron could put up 12 P-40s and the British had 16 Brewster Buffalos. The odds were uneven again, as they always would be for the AVG.

The Hell's Angels broke into two flights, led, as before, by George McMillan and Parker Dupouy. Fred S. Hodges—known as "Fearless Freddy" because he was afraid of the local insects—had missed the first battle because of dysentery. He was determined not to be caught on the ground again during a bombing raid. When the alarm sounded, he ran from his hospital bed to the nearest plane, clad only in his underwear and mosquito boots.

When Duke Hedman got to his plane, his crew chief tried to stop him. The gas tank still had holes in it and the gunsight had not been replaced. Hedman yelled to the crew chief that he never used a gunsight anyway.

Shortly after the planes had taken off from Mingadalon, and only minutes before the first Japanese bombs fell, a British Blenheim bomber drifted in for a landing, its pilot oblivious to the situation. When the plane rolled to a stop, two men in dress uniforms stepped out—Gen. Archibald Wavell of the British army and Lt. Gen. George Brett of the U.S. Army Air Corps. They seemed surprised when Olson and two mechanics herded them into a slit trench at the edge of the runway. Another AVG mechanic climbed into the plane to make sure all the crew had gotten out. He was astonished to see that the bomb bay was outfitted with a rug and wicker lounge furniture for the comfort of the brass. Chennault could have made better use of that plane.

At 12:15, some of McMillan's pilots attacked the Japanese fighters in the first wave to separate them from the bombers. McMillan himself and R. T. Smith went after the bombers. McMillan shot down two bombers and got on the tail of a third. As it caught fire, the top turret gunner hit his plane with two cannon shells, one destroying the bullet-proof windshield and the other hitting the engine. Trailing smoke, McMillan glided down to a rice paddy and made a safe wheels-up landing.

Smith shot down another bomber and found himself head-on with a Japanese fighter. The two pilots opened fire at 400 yards and held it for all of two seconds, the time it took to close the distance between their ships. Neither pilot took evasive action, but the Zero passed beneath Smith's plane with a foot of clearance between the tips of their propellers. Smith turned to have another go but saw the flaming Zero dive straight for the water. When he returned to the field he counted thirty-four bullet holes in his plane, five of them around the cockpit. It struck him then that "head-on passes could be strictly non-habit-forming."

Duke Hedman shot down two Nakajima Type 97 fighters and was after a third when he was jumped by four fighters. They made two passes at him, riddling the plane with bullets and shattering the canopy. Hedman nosed over into a steep dive and kept his head down to escape the 400-mile-per-hour wind whipping through the cockpit. The Japanese pilots, evidently assuming he was dead, wheeled away. He made it to an auxiliary field and glided in for a dead-stick landing.

In Dupouy's flight, Lewis Bishop and Bob Brouk heard over their radios the order to land immediately. Assuming the message was from their flight leader, they dropped down and lowered their wheels. As they approached the end of the runway, they were jumped from behind by six Japanese fighters. The order had been a trick. Bishop and Brouk pulled up instantly, shoved their throttles forward, and zoomed almost straight up, quickly losing the Nakajimas.

Charlie Older and Tom Haywood, in McMillan's flight, flew that day by the book—Chennault's book. Following his rule to fight in pairs, they made pass after pass at one formation of bombers and shot five of them out of the sky. Haywood's plane lost an aileron and the main spars in one wing had been shattered.

Ed Overend and the rest of McMillan's flight pounced on a formation of twenty-seven Japanese bombers that had already dropped their bombs on the city. Every gun in the Japanese group opened up on them. "It was the wickedest sight I have ever seen," Overend said, "with twenty-seven cannons firing from the top turrets and flames spurting from the tail guns and dust bins under the fuselage." He fired a burst into one of the bombers' engines. The Japanese plane caught fire, and Overend followed it, firing, until its wing fell off and a huge sheet of flame flicked out from the fuselage.

Overend pulled out of his dive and climbed to make another attack. He saw two other bombers fall. As he pulled in behind another bomber, he felt a torrent of bullets strike the rear of his ship. He tried to maneuver out of the way of the Japanese fighter on his tail, but his controls jammed. His only chance was to dive. As he started down, he had the satisfaction of seeing the bomber he had been attacking spin in. Gradually he was able to pull away from the fighter on his tail, grateful for the P-40's superior speed in a dive.

He considered bailing out but decided against it, recalling how the Japanese fighter pilots had attacked Paul Greene while he hung in his parachute. Also, Overend knew how desperately Chennault needed every plane, and he thought that maybe, if he made a decent landing, his P-40 could fly again—or at least supply parts for other planes. He kept his wheels up and made a gentle belly landing in a rice field. He climbed out on a wing and saw some natives running toward him. They were carrying sickles and clubs, but as soon as they got close enough to see that he was not a Japanese, they lowered their weapons, grinned, and started him on his way back to Mingadalon.

Overhead, Dupouy's flight went after a wave of bombers flying over the airfield at 18,000 feet. The escorting fighters had stuck with the bombers and immediately attacked the P-40s. Within minutes, two Nakajimas were downed, one by Dupouy and the other by Fearless Freddy Hodges in his underwear. Dupouy and Bill Reed chased three fighters out off the coast, opened fire at 50 feet, and shot one down in flames.

On the next pass, Dupouy got too close and collided with the Japanese fighter as its pilot tried to turn away. Dupouy lost four feet of his right wing as it sheared off a wing of the enemy plane. The Japanese fighter fluttered into the sea while Dupouy managed to bring his ship under control. It took 45 minutes for him to nurse his crippled plane back to the field, where he made a perfect landing.

The battle lasted an hour and a half. One by one, the men of the Hell's Angels squadron landed, almost out of gas and ammunition and most with battle damage. Tom Haywood approached the runway with one aileron gone, but that didn't stop him from doing an unsteady but proud victory roll over the field. When the results came in, they showed that the Japanese had lost 36 planes, more than one-third of their attacking force. Furthermore, that figure included only those planes that crashed on land and could be verified. Others were reported to have fallen into the sea en route to their home base.

The RAF claimed seven of those planes, at the cost of six pilots and nine fighter aircraft, almost an even trade. The AVG was officially credited with 19 enemy planes with only two of their fighters lost. All AVG pilots returned safely. Once again the AVG had achieved a stunning victory against overwhelming odds.

The men of the Hell's Angels celebrated Christmas Day with a feast, which, following their two days on stale bread and warm beer, was much appreciated. Their benefactor was William Pawley, who happened to be at the airfield where he watched much of the action from a grove of banyan trees. He was so pleased with the results that he arranged for a panel truck full of ham, chicken, cake, pie, cold beer, and Scotch to be delivered that afternoon. Trestle tables were set up in the shade of the banyan trees, and Generals Wavell and Brett joined the men for their meal.

The AVG and the RAF had carried the day in the air, but on the ground the Japanese had won a victory. Enough of their bombers got through to Rangoon and the airfield to cause considerable destruction. At Mingadalon, the bombardiers had concentrated on the southeastern corner of the field, where most of the AVG ground personnel had taken shelter. In the city, panic was growing by the hour and hordes of people were fleeing, especially the large Indian population who feared that the Burmese would turn against them if the British were forced to leave.

"It was horrible," recalled an AVG crewman. "Sixty-five tons of bombs were dropped on Rangoon. It was worse than anything the British ever saw at London. I never want to see another like it. . . . Get on your face in a ditch, that's all you can do—and pray. You can't fight back; you want to run—anyplace, anywhere, just run. It wouldn't be so bad if you could do something; you're so helpless."

He talked about the upheaval among the population. "Rangoon is walking back to India. There are 150,000 Indians, barefooted and on bicycles, in rickshaws, some of them driving a cow, going up the road to Mandalay, then across to Assam. The coolies at the docks are gone. We can't unload the ships. I saw English regiments moving cargo."

The Hell's Angels were preparing to leave Rangoon at a moment's notice, if need be. The Japanese dropped leaflets over the city warning that their paratroopers would soon be landing. The AVG personnel were not trained as infantry, and they couldn't take the risk of being captured. They set to work, packing personal belongings and supplies into trucks that they parked by the runway for a quick departure. They even did their cooking outdoors so as not to be caught unawares.

"Continued alert duty," wrote squadron leader Olson in his diary. "Men are somewhat on edge, nervous and in a rather frayed condition. . . . No reinforcements have arrived as yet. Our planes are diminishing to a certain extent one way or another. We are still holding on with a few British planes."

To Chennault in Kunming, Olson sent a more optimistic message. His radiogram reached Chennault while he was having dinner with the Greenlaws at the Kwang Sing Yang restaurant:

ALL PILOTS RETURNED AFTER BATTLE ON DECEMBER 25 SHOT DOWN TEN FIGHTERS NINE BOMBERS. LIKE SHOOTING DUCKS. WOULD PUT ENTIRE JAP FORCE OUT OF COMMISSION WITH GROUP HERE. HAVE ELEVEN PLANES LEFT. OLSON.

Chennault looked up at the Greenlaws and grinned.
"The boys are going to town."

EIGHT

ALL HELL BROKE LOOSE

A legend was born in the skies over Rangoon and Kunming in the closing days of 1941. The men of the AVG found themselves famous throughout the world, and they had been given a new name. It was the Chinese newspapers that first heralded their victories and dubbed them *"Fei Weing,"* the Flying Tigers. In doing so, they were offering the American mavericks who fought for China the highest accolade, for the tiger had been China's national symbol since the founding of the Chinese Republic in 1911.

For the first time in China's long war with their hated enemy, the seemingly invincible Japanese had been stopped. Japanese pilots were demoralized by their staggering losses in just three battles with the AVG, after years of complete air superiority. Their leaders felt humiliated by their defeat by inferior numbers, and Radio Tokyo trumpeted their anger and frustration in an English-language broadcast: "The American pilots in Chinese planes are unprincipled bandits. Unless they cease their unorthodox tactics, they will be treated as guerrillas. Give up the fight, Americans, before you are annihilated."

It was only a matter of days before the exploits of the Flying Tigers were headlined in newspapers of the Allied nations who were hungry for a victory and for heroes to honor. After the attacks on Pearl Harbor, Guam, Wake, Clark Field, and Hong Kong, and the sinking of HMS *Repulse* and HMS *Prince of Wales,* finally a handful of American pilots· were daring to stop this litany of defeats at the hands of the Japanese.

War correspondents flocked to Rangoon and Kunming—Time-Life, United Press, Associated Press, the Chicago *Daily News, The New York Times,* and other news organizations, and with each new story, the legend grew. On December 27, the men of the AVG heard a commentator on radio station KGEI in San Francisco, broadcasting from the Fairmont Hotel, describe them as the hardest fighting outfit in the world. Three nights later the station devoted a full ten minutes to the exploits of the Flying Tigers. It made the men proud.

They were called the "wonderful knights of the air," and "lean, bronze giants with gleaming teeth." *Collier's* magazine published an article about the Japanese advances in the Far East, noting that only "one obstacle stood in the path of swift, easy victory. The Burmese heavens are full of 'sharks'." *Time* wrote that the victories of the AVG proved that "man for man, plane for plane, anything labeled USA could whip anything labeled Made-In-Japan."

Americans had reason to feel good about themselves again, which is what heroes are for. In the coming months, the Flying Tigers never let them down, not in the legends that developed about them, nor in the reality that supplied the stuff of those legends.

Even for heroes, however, not all days make for sensational press releases. Some times are filled with routine, with squabbles and bickering, with ordinary sickness. And so it was with the main group of the AVG at Kunming as the new year, 1942, began. Chennault fell ill with what he called his annual attack of chronic bronchitis. He had planned to visit his squadron at Rangoon but spent the entire month of January hospitalized in Kunming. Sometimes he had sufficient energy to work briefly in his office, but mostly he was confined to bed, a crusty old warrior with nurses fussing over him, his cigarette ashes spilling over the bedcovers, and a radio nearby so he could hear his pilots as they ranged the skies looking for the enemy.

He still maintained control of the outfit, and the first matter he had to deal with was the relief of Olson's Third Squadron at Rangoon. The pilots and ground crew were suffering from fatigue and only 11 P-40s were flyable. Chennault decided to send Jack Newkirk's Second Squadron, the Panda Bears, to Rangoon. They were still smarting over their case of buck fever the first time they met the enemy and wanted a chance to redeem themselves. On December 30, the squadron's ground personnel departed aboard a CNAC transport, and at 9:30 that morning, Newkirk's 18 planes roared down the runway and headed south. Olga Greenlaw watched them go, wondering how many would return.

Although Chennault had two combat-ready groups, he remained concerned about the pilots and planes that had been left at Kyedaw Field. They were a constant source of worry and had lost more planes in accidents than the operational squadrons had in combat. Messages from Kyedaw were guaranteed to make him lose his temper.

Buster Keeton had been ordered to remain at Kyedaw to help train the rest of the pilots, and he was not happy with that duty. He blamed CAMCO for the lack of fully qualified pilots. He believed that if CAMCO's recruiters had done their job properly, "there would not be all this training to go through. Just another headache for the Colonel, who has plenty of such."

There were also headaches for Keeton and his flight instructors. "I swear to God if it isn't disheartening to see plane after plane crashed up done through negligence on the pilot's part. The pilots are supposed to be at least fair, but I swear some of them do things that a 10-hour student wouldn't do. Adkins tried to take off downwind which is against all rules of aviation. The man in the tower was waving the red flag but he didn't pay any attention."

The airplanes were in sorry shape and getting worse every day. "Some of these planes we are putting out and flying would be grounded in the U.S. Army and Navy for a complete overhaul," Keeton wrote in his diary. "Every time I test a plane I wonder if I will get off and back to the field in one piece. We sure need spare parts, especially props. Have nine more planes we could put into commission here if we had them." The trainee pilots were damaging propellers every day. Keeton had no replacements.

While the planes at Kyedaw were becoming useless because of wear and damage from poor flying, the ones at Rangoon were becoming unfit because of combat. If they could not be repaired, Chennault would soon be left with no P-40s to fly. He had assumed that such work would be handled by CAMCO. His contract with William Pawley's company called for it to provide mechanics, tools, and equipment to repair battle-damaged planes at CAMCO's facility at Loiwing, China, just over the Burmese border.

In late December, some of the planes from Kyedaw were shipped to Loiwing, but Pawley's mechanics did little work on them. In what Chennault termed the "final blow," Pawley said that repair work on the damaged P-40s interfered with the assembly of the trainers and CW-21 Demons that he had sold to the Chinese government. On January 1, Pawley notified Chennault that CAMCO would make no more repairs on AVG planes. The Flying Tigers were on their own.

Word quickly spread that CAMCO was abandoning the AVG. Keeton noted that "if Pawley pulls out it looks to me as though members of the AVG might be left holding the bag. . . . I think it is a dirty trick for him to pull out after getting the organization set up."

Chennault lashed out in letters and radiograms to Soong and China Defense Supplies, accusing Pawley of much more than refusing to repair the P-40s. On January 11, 1942, he wrote: "I am convinced, after a long trial, that Mr. Pawley will not cooperate in any work which does not provide a generous profit or other award for Mr. Pawley. I have also come to the conclusion that he should not be given control of the revolving fund unless close supervision and frequent audits are made of his financial operations." Chennault added that despite repeated requests to Pawley for an audit of AVG expenses and accounts, it had not been provided.

He accused Pawley of selling supplies purchased by the AVG. "Mr. Pawley directed the delivery of a large portion of the groceries and sales articles, which I had purchased in New York for the use of the AVG, to Loiwing, and there authorized the sale of a considerable number of these articles. I have requested a full accounting for the articles sold, but have not been able to obtain one."

Chennault stopped just short of calling Pawley a crook, but Pawley had his own charges to make. On January 11, he wrote to Chennault. "It seems that your repeated efforts to place me in a very bad light with Chinese government officials and others is being continued. . . . We are all convinced, General, that your attacks by letter and telegram, copies of which have been widely distributed, have been for the sole purpose of discrediting both me and my organization, thereby depriving us of even a small portion of the credit which might have been due us as a result of the AVG's success."

Then Pawley began making accusations to anyone who would listen. A radiogram from the CDS office in Rangoon alerted Chennault:

YOUR REPUTATION VERY HIGH HERE AND I WISH TO PROTECT IT. W. PAWLEY MAKING SEVERE CRITICISMS OF YOUR HANDLING OF AVG AND MINIMIZING YOUR PART IN AVG PERFORMANCE.

Pawley charged in a letter to Chennault that the AVG's shortage of spare parts and its lack of an adequate staff were due to Chennault's negligence and his refusal to accept Pawley's advice. He criticized Chennault for remaining in the safety of Kunming during January while all the fighting was occurring in Rangoon. He added that Chennault offered no leadership to the squadron at Rangoon and that the pilots there had accomplished magnificent work without Chennault's "assistance or support. . . . Many have wondered why neither you nor any of your executive staff made an appearance at Rangoon, and why the full responsibility was left to young squadron leaders."

There was no victor in this little war, nor did it make headlines or end in a truce. More charges and countercharges were made during the winter of 1942 and into the spring, but other events soon overtook them. When Burma fell, Pawley went to India to attend to his other business interests. And Chennault was too busy with the real war and with the army's attempted induction of the AVG. When World War II ended, however, Claire Chennault and William Pawley battled each other again, this time over who should receive credit for starting the AVG.

There was also bickering within the Flying Tigers that winter, unrest in Sandy Sandell's First Squadron, the Adams and Eves. The pilots and ground crew were unhappy with their squadron leader. "An undercurrent of dissatisfaction seems to be growing in our squadron," Charlie Bond wrote. "Neither the pilots nor the airmen seem to like Sandell." The problem apparently was due to Sandell's somewhat cold and aloof manner in dealing with his men. A group of the pilots had spoken to him about the morale problem and of their desire to introduce more discipline and military organization into the outfit, but nothing had changed and discontent remained high.

Pilot George Burgard believed the men were close to mutiny and needed a more stable commander. "He is a terribly inefficient squadron head," Burgard said. Everyone realized that the squadron had a problem, but no one knew what to do about it.

After many discussions, Bond and Boyington decided to approach the Old Man and ask his advice. At the time, unfortunately, Chennault had just been hospitalized for bronchitis and was too ill to see them, so they took the problem to Harvey Greenlaw and Skip Adair. They would not help. It was up to the Adams and Eves to deal with Sandell themselves.

The pilots drew up a petition asking Sandy to step down as squadron leader. Every man in the outfit signed it. Sandell read it without saying a word, took out his pen, and added his signature to the list. Then he went to tell Harvey Greenlaw.

"Well, what are you going to do?" Greenlaw asked. "Lose your squadron?"

"Yes, if they want it that way. Maybe they will be better off with someone else as squadron leader."

When the men learned that Sandell had signed the petition himself, they tore it up and never broached the subject again. Sandell never commented on it either, and he continued to lead his squadron exactly as before. Nothing had changed except that by adding his signature to theirs, he had shown them a human side.

Perhaps the unrest and dissatisfaction within the squadron was not so much the fault of Sandell as of boredom. After the initial success in the battle of December 20, the Adams and Eves had seen no action. They knew that the Hell's Angels were fighting hard in Rangoon, and when the Panda Bears were sent to join in the action in Burma, Sandell's squadron was left to patrol the empty skies over Kunming. On January 12, eight of the Adams and Eves pilots were sent to Rangoon as reinforcements, but the rest waited, and fumed, in Kunming.

"Our Adams and Eves might just as well have been back in the United States blowing bubbles in the bathtub," Boyington said, "for nothing came over Kunming or even near it. Damn it to hell! Stuck here. Our First Pursuit Squadron seemed to be worse than second-best, maybe third-best." Almost every day throughout the month of January, reports came from Rangoon of AVG victories, but there were no victories for the First Squadron.

"This sitting on my fanny is getting me down," Charlie Bond said. "I wish we had some action." The men spent their time prowling the filthy streets of Kunming, searching for something to do. "A few of the group ran across a Chinese prostitute in town last night and they are daring any of us to go look at her. Pus and scabs in her navel and all over her belly. Left breast wrapped in a swath of bandages. Cripes, what's happening to us?"

Nothing was wrong with the men of the First Squadron that combat would not cure, but they would have to wait awhile for that. Some refused to wait and used the lack of action as an excuse to quit. In the middle of January, 11 pilots decided to go home. Chennault gave them all dishonorable discharges for leaving while their country was at war.

But a few days later came a reason to celebrate—the AVG's first wedding. Emma J. "Red" Foster, a tall, pretty nurse, married Johnny Petach, a pilot with the Second Squadron who flew back to Kunming from Rangoon for the ceremony.

"Newkirk said I better get married while I was still in one piece," Petach said.

Emma and Johnny had met and fallen in love on the ship *Jae-*

gersfontein on their way to the Far East, and became formally engaged at the end of December, just before the squadron went to Rangoon. Chaplain Frillman conducted the wedding ceremony, and the men of the AVG, wearing their full-dress uniforms for the first time, provided the military escort.

"I've got to pile up a lot of bonus money now," Petach said. "Have to shoot a lot of Zeros to keep Emma in style."

Days of boredom, days of routine. Each passed slowly in review for the men in Kunming—until the morning of January 22. Instead of waiting for the Japanese to appear overhead, the First Squadron was going to take the war to the enemy. Pilots and crews of the Chinese Air Force would fly 18 Russian-built SB-3s—twin-engine, single-wing bombers—to Indochina, to bomb Japanese installations there. The Adams and Eves would be their fighter escort.

The bombers left early in the morning from their base at Chang Yi, 60 miles north of Kunming. The Flying Tigers took off at 8:30, refueled at a base near the Indochina border, and rendezvoused with the bombers as they headed toward Hanoi. The operation was a fiasco. As Sandy Sandell described it, the Chinese pilots "flew all over the landscape—it was twice as crazy because they flew in two formations of nine each. Right after we joined them their second flight dropped back and remained a mile behind the first. We couldn't decide which ones to escort."

The weather also worked against them. Broken clouds obscured the ground. The fighter pilots were not sure what the Chinese bombardiers were aiming at, if anything, when they dropped their bombs 20 miles east of Haiphong and headed for home. The pilot of the lead bomber immediately increased speed, leaving the others behind. "Scattered from hell to breakfast," Sandell said.

The First Squadron barely reached Kunming safely. Because the bombers were so slow, the P-40s had to maintain a cruising speed back and forth over the formation to protect it. The action consumed most of their fuel. If Japanese fighters had found them and attacked the P-40s, they would not have had enough gas to get back to base.

The next day, the men felt exhausted from the trip and frustrated because they had not met the enemy. "That trip yesterday took more out of us than we thought," wrote George Burgard in his diary. "Five hours at 20,000 feet, like we spent yesterday under constant strain, really hits you the next day."

Two days later the mission was attempted again, with the same disappointing results. Arvid Olson's Third Squadron, back from Rangoon, provided the fighter escort. As before, the Chinese pilots did not maintain formation, and the P-40s had to keep circling above the slow bombers to provide protection. Hanoi was under a heavy cloud cover. The Chinese dropped their bombs through the clouds southeast of the city and headed home. Chinese officials later told Harvey Greenlaw that the raids gave the Japanese something to think about. "You can't beat 'em," Greenlaw answered, "simply by giving them something to think about."

Apparently, the raids also gave Chennault something to think about in his sickbed. Two days after the second raid, he revived his plan to bomb Japan. He dispatched a secret radiogram to Madame Chiang, requesting that copies be sent to the Generalissimo, T. V. Soong, and Lauchlin Currie:

CAN BEGIN ATTACKS ON JAPAN'S INDUSTRIES AT ONCE IF YOU CAN SEND REGULAR OR VOLUNTEER BOMBARDMENT GROUP EQUIPPED WITH LOCKHEED HUDSONS AS SPECIFIED BY ME IN JUNE 1941 AND AMERICAN KEY PERSONNEL TO OPERATE UNDER MY COMMAND AND CONTROL OF THE GENERALISSIMO ONLY.

It was wishful thinking on Chennault's part. There was no chance that additional planes and crews could be shipped to China. He could not even get propellers and spark plugs to keep his own planes in the air. The bombing of Japan was a dream that would not be fulfilled for a long time.

On the day of the second Chinese bombing raid, January 24, Sandell's First Squadron finally got the news they had been longing for. They would leave Kunming in the morning to join the fighting in Rangoon. "What a moment!" said Boyington when he heard. "I couldn't seem to swallow, now that the time was here. A hard lump stuck in my throat, lasting until the following morning, until after I started my P-40 rolling down the dirt runway."

Many of the pilots said they had lumps in their throats. They were excited, and a little fearful, too. Would they acquit themselves well? Would they come back?

Sandell visited Olga Greenlaw to tell her he was leaving. He was wearing his army air corps dress uniform tunic with his silver wings pinned to the front, and he took the jacket off and handed it to her, reminding her that she had talked about getting a coat like it for herself. It fit her perfectly, but she said she would keep it only long enough to have a tailor copy it.

"Well, all right," Sandy said, "but maybe I won't come back."

He asked her for the leather flying jacket she had had made for herself. "I'll wear it," he told her, and added that he was disposing of his most prized possessions, three Oriental rugs she had helped him choose.

"I am going to have my three carpets rolled up. As soon as I take off tomorrow, you go to my quarters and get them. If I don't come back, you keep them. . . . I have a couple of books that I like. . . . Tomorrow I'll bring them to Operations. You will be there to see me off?"

"You are acting damn silly," Olga said. "What's come over you anyway?"

Sandell put his arms around her and said quietly, "Good-bye, Olga. Take care of yourself. Think of me now and then."

The next morning Olga went to the operations shack and found Sandell and his pilots studying a map of their route to Rangoon. He came over to her and handed her the books, *The Anatomy of Revolution* and a biography of Mozart. A curious combination, she thought.

Sandell was not the only pilot planning for the possibility that he might not come back. Albert E. "Red" Probst went to Olga and gave her a large gold ring set with a two-carat ruby. "If I don't come back," he said, "take it home with you and send it to my mother." He gave her his mother's address along with a slip of paper containing the names of all the AVG men who owed him money from bridge games, poker, blackjack, and craps. He asked Olga to collect his debts and to deposit the large sum of money involved in his account in the finance section, where it would be sent to his next-of-kin. Looking pale, Probst shook Olga's hand and headed for his plane.

The other pilots left the operations shack. Sandell shook hands with the six clerks in the room and said good-bye. When he came to Olga, she reached up and kissed him.

She walked to the control tower to watch the First Squadron take off. They formed up overhead, then one plane pulled out, "made a circle and dove over the operations shack, pulled up and made another circle, flew low over the shack again and tipped its wings. Sandy was saying good-bye."

Throughout the month of January, the men at Rangoon found little boredom or routine. Jack Newkirk and the Second Squadron, the Panda Bears, found that out as soon as they arrived to replace Olson's Third Squadron. Both the city and Mingadalon Field were dangerous places to be. Newkirk's men had only to look around them to see how extensive the bombing and strafing had been. The alert shack, a former RAF barracks, had just enough of its roof intact to provide a bit of shade from the searing heat of the sun. Other buildings around the field had been reduced to rubble. Craters filled with debris pockmarked the surface of the runway. Slit trenches, the only places of refuge in a bombing raid, scarred the surrounding fields.

The primary reason for the danger was the lack of an adequate warning system. Usually, the alarm could not be raised until the enemy planes were heard or sighted as they neared the field. Despite Chennault's protests, the British had never instituted a reliable warning net. Worse, even when the British did detect the approach of enemy aircraft, they often told only their own pilots and failed to notify the AVG.

When Greg Boyington first arrived at Mingadalon, he asked about the air-raid alert procedures. "Long before the RAF gets around to announcing the alert," he was told, "you will see two

Brewsters take off in a westerly direction, regardless of the wind sock. That's the signal."

Something better had to be done, and, as usual, the men of the Flying Tigers had to improvise and do it themselves. Alex "Mickey" Mihalko, the Second Squadron's communications chief, developed a simple but effective system. He started to hang around the British radio and telephone office to get to know the RAF personnel who worked there. Whenever the telephone rang, he tried to be the one who answered it, helping out his new friends who were busy with their other work. If the caller reported the approach of enemy planes, he obligingly handed the phone to an RAF clerk. Then he would turn on the microphone and, in a voice that could be heard all over the field, would yell, "Go get 'em, cowboys!" When the AVG pilots on duty in the alert shack heard Mickey's shout, they ran for their planes and usually got airborne before the British.

The Panda Bears quickly settled into life at Mingadalon and were ready for action, but no enemy planes came. After three days, Newkirk decided that if the Japanese were not coming to him, he would go to them. On January 3 he led Tex Hill, Jim Howard, and Bert Christman on a mission east toward Thailand. Their objective was the Japanese air base at Tak, 170 miles away.

Christman's plane developed engine trouble, and he was forced to turn back. "Planes were getting worn down," Hill recalled. "It got to where a plane was just as likely to go down from engine failure as from the Japs." The three remaining Flying Tigers arrived over the enemy airfield at 10,000 feet and were delighted to see rows of twin-engine bombers lined up neatly on the runway. It looked as though they had caught the Japanese by surprise.

The P-40s roared down out of the sun and began their strafing run. Suddenly, Hill noticed they were not alone. Three other planes were in the traffic pattern with them—Nakajima Type 97s. One got on Howard's tail and started firing. Hill whipped into position and shot the plane to pieces with a stream of machine-gun fire. As he flew through the debris, he came face-to-face with another enemy fighter. "This was before they learned that it could be painful to do that," Hill said. "The Japs soon learned that the

P-40 had too much Allison engine and armor plating up front for their 7.9-mm rounds to get to the P-40 pilot and that his .50-caliber machine guns put them in reach long before they were in firing range. But for this Jap in my sights it was too late." Hill shot the plane out of the sky, but he took some hits and his plane started vibrating.

Newkirk shot down the third fighter in a head-on pass, and Howard continued his strafing run, seemingly oblivious to the battle behind and above him. Concentrating intently on the task at hand, he destroyed five planes on the ground.

After they returned to Mingadalon Hill walked over to the tall, serious Howard.

"Good thing I shot that Nip off your tail, Jim," he said.

"Whose tail?" Howard asked, surprised. "There was nobody on my tail."

"Take a look at your ship, Jim. It's full of holes."

They examined Howard's plane and counted eleven bullet holes, but then they checked Hill's and found thirty-three. They also learned why Hill's ship had vibrated so much. Bullets had stuck in the propeller blades, forcing it out of balance.

Following this successful raid on Tak, the Flying Tigers held a bigger than usual party at the Silver Grill in Rangoon. Newkirk and two other pilots commandeered the floor show and offered two hours of barbershop harmony.

The Panda Bears did not have to wait long to meet the enemy again. Humiliated at losing their planes on the ground at Tak, the Japanese sent twenty-seven fighters on a mission of revenge the next day. The AVG had some advance warning, and fourteen P-40s took off, assembling in two groups at 21,000 feet, to look for the enemy. They circled through large, scattered clouds but didn't find the Japanese.

The ground crew at Mingadalon, however, saw the Japanese clearly through their binoculars, approaching from the southeast at 18,000 feet. They tried to warn the pilots but their radios had gone dead. While eight planes remained at 21,000 feet as cover, six others began to descend in large circles. The Japanese pilots saw them but remained screened by the clouds.

They waited until the six P-40s were below them at 11,000 feet and then dove. The surprise was complete, the battle swift and deadly. Within fifteen minutes the landscape was dotted with the wrecks of three Japanese planes—and three P-40s. It was the only battle in the AVG's history in which they just broke even.

George Paxton was the first to be hit. "All hell broke loose in my cockpit—awful thuds of bullets hitting everything—glass, armor seats, everything. It was deafening. My plane seemed to hang still in the air. . . . The crashing of the bullets never seemed to quit. I knew I had been hit—shoulder, leg, and arm. They all burned."

He managed to push the stick forward to dive but felt himself going into a spin. Smoke filled the cockpit and Paxton wondered if he was going to burn to death. The Japanese plane hung on his tail, pumping more bullets into his ship. His windshield and instrument panel were covered with oil. For a moment he thought it was his own blood.

The spinning stopped and so did the pounding of bullets. To Paxton's amazement, the P-40's controls responded to his touch and he decided to stay with the plane, although he did not know his altitude or how much longer the plane might hold together. As he leveled off, the windshield broke apart, giving him a clear view. He was over a lake not far from the airfield, flying at 1000 feet.

Paxton steered for the field, put his wheels down, and touched the runway. The plane veered sharply to the right. He kicked the left rudder pedal hard, too hard, and overcorrected. The P-40 skidded down the runway and the landing gear collapsed. He tried to open the canopy but it was jammed, and he sat there helplessly, not knowing what would get him first, the fire or the strafing Japanese fighters. Then one of the ground crew—he never learned who it was—pulled him out and rushed him to the hospital. He had five bullet wounds and his plane had sixty-one holes, but it had brought him back and he would live to fly again.

Bert Christman's plane was also shot down. He bailed out and landed in a rice paddy. His jaw was creased in two places from Japanese bullets. Another had hit the left side of his earphones and had torn it away without leaving another mark on him.

Gil Bright, who had survived the midair collision over Kyedaw in which Jack Armstrong had died, took a hit and was forced to make a wheels-up landing in a rice paddy. He jumped from the plane and ran away as fast as he could. Unfortunately, he chose to run a straight line from the nose of the P-40. When it burst into flame and exploded, the machine guns started to fire. Bright became the only Flying Tiger to be shot at by his own plane. Luckily, he suffered only burns on his face.

The covering force of eight P-40s continued to circle at 21,000 feet throughout the battle. They had no radio contact, and the clouds prevented them from seeing the action 10,000 feet below them.

The Japanese returned early the next morning, approaching from three different directions. It was the beginning of a five-day onslaught to wipe out the AVG and the RAF. The enemy tried massed assaults; decoys of bombers with large numbers of fighters hovering above, ready to pounce; waves of fighters to engage the Allies while the bombers tried to slip through; false orders broadcast in English over the AVG radio frequency; and low-flying formations of fighters slipping in to strafe the field once the AVG and RAF had been drawn away.

Both pilots and ground crew came under fire. The operations center was moved off the field and hidden beneath a stone bridge a quarter of a mile away. A new ground-to-air radio system was installed with the ground transmitter placed in a jeep. Mickey Mihalko, the communications chief, took the jeep out during every air battle, racing around the field as he followed the combat through binoculars and warning the pilots aloft of new waves of planes bearing in on them.

As the P-40s landed, mechanics and armorers worked rapidly to get them ready to return to the battle as soon as possible. Under huge banyan and mango trees on the perimeter of the field, other ground personnel worked to restore badly damaged planes to flying condition. Still others bent to the task of constructing fake P-40s out of wood and canvas that they lined up along the runway to serve as targets for enemy strafing runs. The dummy ships were stuffed with dry straw so they would flare up quickly when hit by tracers, convincing the Japanese that they had destroyed real planes.

The Japanese sent over a few bombers at night to harass the AVG and keep them awake. Exhausted pilots and ground crew had to abandon their beds, pile into cars and trucks, and drive away from the field, where they tried to catch some sleep.

On the sixth day Mingadalon was quiet. The Japanese, overwhelmed by their losses, had decided to regroup. For two weeks the enemy lacked a bomber force large enough to mount a daylight attack. Once again the AVG had beaten back a determined assault by a much larger force, and they had done it at a cost of six P-40s. The Japanese lost at least thirty fighters and bombers, whose wreckage was found on the ground, and thirty more had been reported going down at sea or in the jungles. Clearly the Flying Tigers had scored another resounding victory.

During the lull in the daylight bombing, the Japanese raided Mingadalon and Rangoon at night. Although the airfield sustained little damage, the city was devastated. Anti-British Burmese nationals lit fires to pinpoint targets for the Japanese bombers. The Japanese made methodical and accurate runs, knowing that no fighters would challenge them. By the end of the first week, it was no longer necessary to light fires. The city was burning continuously.

The AVG pilots were angry, not only because their sleep was being disturbed, but also because they could not do anything about the raids. The bombers roared overhead as unmolested as if they were on a training exercise. Three of the Panda Bears pilots—Jim Howard, Pete Wright, and Gil Bright—decided to attempt some night flying tactics. They had observed that the Japanese flew in ragged formations of five to seven planes and just before they reached the target, they closed up in a tight V formation, turning on their running lights so that they could see one another clearly.

On the night of January 8, the three Panda Bears pilots took off and circled Rangoon, waiting for word from the ground that the enemy's running lights had been spotted. No lights were seen, however, and the Japanese bombed the city and sped away undetected. Finally, at 4:00 A.M., the trio radioed the field that they were ready to land, a dangerous undertaking in the darkness. Cars and trucks had been lined up along the left side of the runway so that their lights could be turned on just as the fighters came in to land. Ken Merritt was resting in one of the cars. Three weeks before, he had survived the crash of his CW-21 Demon fighter while ferrying it to Kunming and had been in almost constant action for several days. While he waited to help light the runway for the returning fighters, he fell asleep. The other cars in line turned on their headlights, but a gap of darkness remained around Merritt's car.

Pete Wright lowered his wheels and flaps, preparing to land. He set his prop in low pitch and his mixture in automatic rich as he made the final turn and lined up on the runway. At 300 feet with an airspeed of 120 mph he approached the landing strip and a rubber gasket in a valve handle in the cockpit blew out. Thick, greasy hydraulic fluid sprayed over his face, smearing his goggles. "I tried to wipe off my goggles with my sleeve, but found that impossible. I pushed them up from my eyes and stuck my head as far out of the left-hand side of the cockpit as possible. I still couldn't seem to get away from the blinding, stinging fluid."

He sensed that he was over the edge of the runway about 50 feet high. He pulled back on the stick and his ship hit the ground in a left skid, careering directly toward the row of headlights. Wright spotted a gap and steered for it, thinking that if he headed anywhere else, he would plow into one of the parked vehicles.

"Suddenly, there was a terrific crash," he recalled, "and I violently cracked my head against the windshield. The plane spun around and stopped with a jar. For a moment I sat stunned and blind in the cockpit. I heard a shout, and hands dragged me from the plane. I quickly came to, and when I had wiped the blood and oil from my eyes, I was amazed to see, by the lights of an approaching truck, the wreckage of a Chevrolet sedan, that had been completely sheared in two."

No one yet knew that Merritt was in the car. Some time later, when an AVG pilot asked the RAF clean-up crew if the wreckage had been removed, the man in charge said, "Sir, we are attending to that. But what shall we do with the body in the car?"

January 8 was a day of double tragedy for the Flying Tigers in

Rangoon. A flight of four—Charlie Mott, Percy Bartelt, Bob Moss, and Gil Bright—went on a mission to strafe an enemy air base in Thailand. Mott led the formation out of the sun, sending bullets spurting into the rows of Japanese planes on the runway. The Panda Bears zoomed up and swung around for another pass. This time only three P-40s pulled up. Mott's plane had been hit, but he was able to bail out. He landed in a tree, thirty-five feet off the ground, slipped out of his parachute harness, and fell, fracturing his ankle. He was captured by the Japanese, and another name was erased from the AVG duty roster.

Strafing missions continued over Thailand almost every day as the Second Squadron shot up planes, hangars, and vehicles. When the Japanese began to maintain fighter cover for the air bases, the AVG had to change tactics. Instead of all the planes participating in the strafing, half would remain overhead as cover.

A raid against the Japanese base at Tak caught the enemy in the middle of a formal ceremony in honor of local Thai officials. The three AVG pilots—Newkirk, Howard, and Hill—spotted a grandstand full of people, who did not stay seated for long when they saw the shark-nosed planes bearing down on them. The pilots lined up their sights on a row of seven Brewster Buffalos that had belonged to the Thai air force, but which now sported Japanese insignia.

As they bore in on them, Newkirk spotted a Japanese fighter plane coming in for a landing. He pulled back on the stick, fired a burst into the fighter, and continued his strafing run while it crashed in flames behind him. Two other enemy fighters were disposed of just as quickly, and they crashed on the field in view of the crowd. The Thai officials being honored that day had been told they would witness a demonstration of air power. They did.

Things were going well in the air and, by the middle of the month, conditions on the ground had improved. The men no longer had to live in tents. During the two-week lull in the daylight bombing, the citizens of Rangoon had been asked to open their homes to the Flying Tigers. Having seen how well the AVG was defending their city, the British and the rest of the local population felt more kindly toward the Americans, so the pilots were assigned to private homes where they could sleep safely through the nighttime raids.

Charlie Bond and George Burgard stayed with a Danish oil company executive whose wife and children had been evacuated. The men had a comfortable bedroom and servants who addressed them as "master" and catered to their needs. They ate and drank well with their genial host. "We were up at 6:00 A.M. and had a quick breakfast. Mr. Jensen's number-one boy fixed me a little Thermos bottle of coffee to take to the field. Off we went in our jeep in the dawning light of a new day in this war. I thought to myself how I liked this life."

Greg Boyington and five others stayed in the palatial homes of two Scotsmen—Jim Adam and Bill Tweedy—who lived a half mile apart. They had driven out to the airfield to invite the pilots to live with them. "Jim and I have spent most of our lives in comparative comfort," Tweedy explained, "but we know what the other side is like. And we decided it was awfully selfish of us, not sharing our homes with you fellows, who are the only reason we are able to live in them."

After a hard day of flying, Boyington and the other pilots would drive to their new homes to enjoy a double Scotch-and-soda (a "burra peg") on the patio while rehashing the day's events. A hot tub would be drawn for each man, to the proper temperature, with cigarettes and matches and another burra peg within easy reach. Fresh, clean clothes would be laid out in their spacious, private bedrooms, and they would then join their hosts for a lavish meal.

Boyington particularly appreciated mornings in his new surroundings with "no clanging alarm clocks, no bugler, merely the delightful aroma of freshly brewed tea. This came from a teapot and a poured cup upon a table beside my pillow. And for once in my life I was able to get out of bed by degrees and enjoy myself. The cup of tea was very nearly consumed by the time I had finished a cigarette and had gotten my other slipper on a foot. Then into the bathroom for a shave and a toothbrush I went. Upon returning to my bedroom I found fruit, ham and eggs, marmalade and toast, and more tea, placed upon the little table beside my bed. What a way to live! How could I ever forget this part?"

By the last week of January, the lull in the daylight bombing came to an abrupt end. The Japanese had rebuilt their air force considerably. According to British intelligence, the Japanese had 300 planes, including 120 fighters, which they were ready to hurl against Rangoon and Mingadalon in an effort to eliminate the air defenses. The campaign began on January 23 and continued for six days, during which time Sandell arrived with the First Squadron from Kunming.

On the morning of the 23rd, a formation of twenty-three Nakajima fighters approached the airfield. The AVG was nearly caught by surprise. Only two P-40s got into the air for the first ten minutes of the attack. Tex Hill and Frank Lawlor took on the entire enemy formation until five RAF planes and three more P-40s could join them. Lawlor shot down four planes in succession, Hill got two more, and Bill Bartling brought down another. That was enough for the Japanese and they turned back, minus almost one-third of their force.

The pilots landed and grabbed a quick lunch, buckboard style, while the ground crew swarmed over their planes, readying them for the next battle. The air-raid alarm sounded just as the pilots finished wolfing down their food. A force of thirty-one bombers was on the way. The Japanese hoped to catch the AVG on the ground with their fuel and ammunition not yet replenished. Thirty Japanese fighters flew in support.

Against this force of sixty-one planes Jack Newkirk led ten P-40s. They charged the enemy bombers and fighters and began knocking them out of the sky. Bartelt shot down three fighters before a failing engine forced him to return to the field. Bob Neale dove through both formations and shot down one plane in each as he sped by.

Newkirk damaged one bomber and destroyed two others. A flock of Nakajimas jumped him—he was never sure how many there were—but he caught one in his sights and shot off its wing. He had taken so many hits, however, that he had to try to land. It wouldn't be easy. His flaps had been shot away so he could not slow down to a safe landing speed. He overshot the runway and crashed, nosing over. Unhurt, he found a patched-up plane that would have been declared unsafe in the States, took off, and brought down two more enemy planes.

All the pilots were doing well. Gil Bright damaged a bomber, newlywed Johnny Petach earned the bonus for one plane, and although Bill Bartling and Bob Neale were forced down, neither was injured.

Ed Rector and Bert Christman operated as a team, with Christman serving as wingman. About forty miles from the field, they saw twenty-seven dive bombers and a large number of fighters in two V formations, with the fighters to the rear. Rector waggled his wings and gestured to Christman, whose radio was dead, indicating that he should stay close as they dove toward the rear of the formation. They made one quick pass across the top of both Vs, pulled up, and began a pass at the dive bombers. Rector got one and watched Christman make his pass.

The Nakajima fighters were catching up with them. Rector flew at them, blazing away, with Christman right behind him. Suddenly they were surrounded by enemy fighters. Christman's plane was hit in its big Allison engine and in the fuselage. It was finished, too torn up to try to ride down. Christman raised himself in the cockpit and prepared to dive over the side. A Japanese fighter plane zoomed in and fired, hitting him in the chest. Rector saw him tumble out of the plane and fall 12,000 feet to the rice paddies below. His parachute did not open.

Christman had been one of the most popular of the pilots. Even though the Flying Tigers had shot down twenty-one enemy planes that day, the loss of Bert Christman seemed too high a price to pay.

The next morning, George Paxton led a search party to find the body. Others set out to avenge Christman's death. Bob Neale and Tex Hill were cruising at 15,000 feet when they spotted seven Japanese bombers on a heading for Mingadalon. As they dove at their prey, they saw two RAF Brewster Buffalos attack the formation. The British shot down one of the bombers and Hill and Neale hit the others. "We just knocked them off like moving targets in a shooting gallery," Neale said. They each knocked down a plane and the RAF got another. The lead plane exploded even though no one had fired a shot at it. Five down and two to go.

No one knew who downed the last two because both the Flying Tigers and the RAF were firing at them when they went down. Far below, in the jungle, Paxton and his search party watched the burning bombers plummet from the sky. "They all fell in a straight line," he said, "as though somebody was dropping smoke pots. In a couple of minutes there was a row of seven columns of black smoke rising from the wrecks in the jungle." It was a sight, Paxton added, that Christman might have enjoyed seeing.

Christman was buried in a military cemetery near the airfield that afternoon. Chaplain Frillman flew in from Kunming in the AVG's utility plane, a beat-up Beechcraft, to perform the service. Many British residents of Rangoon attended to pay tribute to their American defenders. A squad of British soldiers fired volleys over the grave and the old Beechcraft flew over in a final salute.

The following day, the AVG lost another popular pilot, Louis Hoffman, the oldest flyer in the group and surely one of the best. He was called "Cokey" because he was always hunting for Coca-Cola. He had arrived at Mingadalon in mid-January as part of an eight-man contingent of the First Squadron. On January 26, he met the enemy for the first time, flying as Bob Prescott's wingman. They were hit by five Japanese fighters while they were climbing away from the field after takeoff, sitting ducks at their climbing speed of 110 miles per hour.

Prescott shoved his stick forward and nosed over into a dive. The P-40 picked up speed fast and in seconds was doing 450. He knew the wings might not hold at a greater speed, but he kept going anyway until he pushed 515. The Japanese fighters had been left far behind, but there was no sign of Hoffman's plane. No one knows exactly what happened to him. His body was found in the wreckage of his plane two days later.

Charlie Bond was one of the pallbearers at Hoffman's burial and he never forgot the experience. The body "had not been embalmed, and the stench was sickening. His coffin was covered with an American flag. We had to delay the rites in order to lengthen the burial hole; the coffin was too long." Greg Boyington also remembered the funeral. "I became nervous and perspiring, looking into the open grave with Cokey's coffin beside it. We stood there listening to an English minister drone on in the hot sun, and he seemed to be stretching the ceremony out for too long." The service was too vivid a reminder of what could lie ahead for any of them, or for all of them if they remained fighting a war by themselves, with no help from the United States.

During the funeral, the pilots on alert duty had to scramble. A flight of fifty-five enemy fighters had been detected. The AVG found them and shot down ten. Sandell accounted for two and left a third spouting smoke when his own cockpit filled with smoke. His coolant temperature zoomed to 150 degrees. He cut off the engine and glided down, but as he landed, an enemy fighter circled and started to dive on his plane. Sandell jumped from the cockpit and ran to a slit trench. The Japanese pilot did not pull up. He dove right into the tail of Sandell's plane.

Each day brought more air-raid alarms, but even a false alarm meant stress, both to the tired men and the worn-out P-40s. Every takeoff was a heart-pounding prelude to a possible battle.

The next day brought more of the same. Charlie Bond rose early in his lavish quarters at the Danish oilman's home to get to the auxiliary field named Johnnie Walker. Some planes were always left there at night in case the Japanese tried a night raid on Mingadalon. At dawn, Bond and his group took off on the five-minute flight to Mingadalon, to spend the day on standby alert.

There were two alarms that morning. The eight pilots on duty took to the air but found no enemy planes. The third scramble was more successful. The men took on 35 Nakajima Type 97s and destroyed 16 of them, all confirmed. One P-40 was damaged and forced back to the field. The pilot, Matt Kuykendall, had a lucky break. A bullet just grazed his forehead, knocking off his goggles. Bond got his first two planes, content that he "had done something in this war."

Newkirk's Second Squadron, the Panda Bears, had been in

almost continuous combat for a month. At the end of January—perhaps fearing a recall to Kunming—he sent a message to Chennault:

THE MORE HARDSHIPS, WORK, AND FIGHTING THE MEN HAVE TO DO THE HIGHER OUR MORALE GOES. SQUADRON SPIRIT REALLY STRONG NOW.

The men had reason to feel good. They had beaten back the enemy in every encounter and had destroyed more than 150 Japanese planes, at a loss of four pilots—three killed and one a prisoner. Even Winston Churchill praised them. "The magnificent victories these Americans have won over the paddy fields of Burma are comparable in character if not in scope with those won by the Royal Air Force over the orchards and hop fields of Kent in the Battle of Britain."

Their morale may have been excellent, but physically, the men of the Second Squadron were worn to exhaustion. They looked gaunt and haggard, with unkempt beards. Most had not had the time or the extra energy to shave. Their planes were wrecks and only six, damaged and patched, were reasonably fit to fly. Control cables had been spliced with whatever wire could be found. Fabric-covered control surfaces on wings and tails were held together with adhesive tape. Patches cut from tin cans or from any other metal that could be scrounged covered holes in the metal fuselages. Bullet holes in propeller blades were filed smooth—there were no replacement props. Furthermore, all the engines were long overdue for complete overhauls. It was amazing that the planes held together in combat. That miracle was due to the skill of the ground crews, who worked around the clock to make sure that the AVG faced each day with at least some planes on the line.

Neither men nor machines could continue much longer. The Panda Bears had to be taken out of combat for a while. Yet there were enemy raids to counter every day and strafing missions to perform. On January 30, they were assigned to strafe the enemy air base at Tak and the Japanese troops who were closing in on Moulmein, on the Gulf of Mataban. The mission was not expected to cause much damage but to remind the Japanese that the Flying Tigers were capable of attacking anywhere at any time.

George Burgard called the mission "stupid." He said, "our ships are so few, and our pilots so valuable, it is complete nonsense to use them for such senseless missions." Many pilots agreed that strafing runs were a poor use of their limited resources. The First Squadron, which had originally been assigned the Moulmein mission, had refused to go.

It was up to two pilots of the Panda Bears. Then Tommy Cole, who had a habit of volunteering for dangerous missions, offered to accompany them. The three P-40s roared low over the enemy field at Tak, made a quick strafing run, and made one pass at the Japanese troops outside of Moulmein on their way home. That was all they were supposed to do, but eager Tommy Cole turned back for another pass. The two other pilots saw him disappear below the treetops, then the nose of his ship leaped up at the end of his run, and the plane shuddered and seemed to hesitate. It fell to the ground, leaving a column of smoke as a fleeting monument.

Four days later, the Panda Bears were ordered back to Kunming.

(Left) Three Men on the Flying Trapeze. From left: Billy McDonald, Chennault, Luke Williamson. *(Courtesy Mrs. William C. McDonald)*

Below) Curtiss Hawk II biplane flown by the Chinese Air Force in their war with apan when Chennault arrived in China, 1937. *(Smithsonian Institution Photo)*

(Above) Vought Corsair biplane used as bombers by the Chinese Air Force. *(Smithsonian Institution Photo No. 3B-9855)*

T.V. Soong. *(National Archives)*

FLYING TIGERS

AMERICAN VOLUNTEER GROUP • CHINESE AIR FORCE

ROSTER

1st SQUADRON

C. L. CHENNAULT
Group Commander

2nd SQUADRON

3rd SQUADRON

Insignia of the AVG and the three pursuit squadrons: Adams and Eves, Panda Bears, and Hell's Angels.

(*Above*) AVG personnel en route to Burma aboard the *Boschfontein*, September 1941. From left: Charlie Bond, Lewis Bishop (partially hidden), Bob Prescott, Dick Rossi, Ralph Gunvordahl (partially hidden). (*Courtesy Charles R. Bond*)

(*Below*) Chennault at AVG headquarters, Kunming, China, May 1942. (*Smithsonian Institution Photo No. 83-4558*)

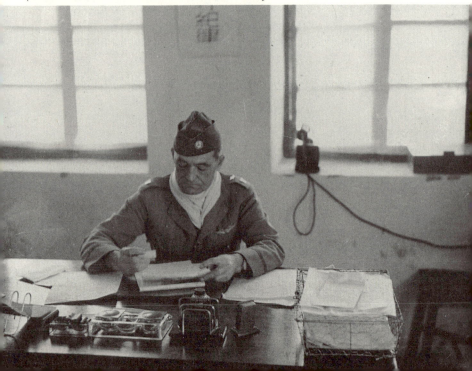

(Left) Generalissimo and Madame Chiang Kai-shek with Chennault, 1942. *(Courtesy Robert M. Smith)*

(Right) Pilots' barracks at Toungoo. *(Courtesy Robert T. Smith)*

Below) Fuselage assembly room for AVG P-40s and, later, for the U.S. Air ⁻orce. *Smithsonian Institution Photo No. 74250AC)*

(Above) First Squadron pilots at Kunming. From left: Bob Neale, George Burgard, Bob Little, Charlie Bond, John Blackburn, Mac McGarry. *(Courtesy Charles R. Bond)*

(Below) Second Squadron pilots at Rangoon. From left: Jack Newkirk, Hank Geselbracht, Bill Bartling, Jim Howard, Bob Layher. *(Courtesy Robert T. Smith)*

(Above) The Third Squadron at Kunming. *(Smithsonian Institution Photo No. 83-4560)*

(Below) P-40s lined up at Hengyang airfield, July 1942. *(Smithsonian Institution Photo No. 83-4566)*

(Left) Bert Christman. *(Wide World Photos)*

(Above) Arvid "Oley" Olson and his personalized "angel" P-40. *(Smithsonian Institution Photo No. 83-4570)*

(Above) A P-40 approaches the field at Kunming. *(Smithsonian Institution Photo No. 74274AC)*

(Right) Mitsubishi Zero fighter plane. *(Courtesy Robert T. Smith)*

(Left) Pilots' alert tent at Mingadalon. *(Courtesy Robert M. Smith)*

(Above) The bar on the second floor of Hostel Number 1 at Kunming. *(Courtesy Robert M. Smith)*

(Below) A famous photo of the Flying Tigers taken by Clare Boothe Luce at Kunmir Sitting on the P-40 (left to right): Erik Shilling, Bill Bartling, Joe Rosbert, George Paxton, Frank Adkins. Standing below: Charlie Bond, Bob Little. *(Courtesy Charle R. Bond)*

(Above) Chaplain Frillman conducts an AVG funeral service at Toungoo. *(Smithsonian Institution Photo No. 83-4575)*

Greg Boyington.

Tex Hill. *(Smithsonian Institution Photo No. A81098AC)*

Chow time at Loiwing. *(Courtesy Robert T. Smith)*

(Above) The Hweitung suspension bridge over the Salween River. *(Courtesy Robert M. Smith)*

(Right) First Squadron pilots with Japanese aircrew prisoner, Kweilin, China, June 1942. On wing: Joe Rosbert, Dick Rossi. Below left: Robert H. Smith; right, Bill Bartling. *(Courtesy Robert T. Smith)*

(Above) Chennault at bat. He regularly played baseball with his men while based in China. *(Smithsonian Institution Photo No. 754720)*

(Left) Hap Arnold and Chennault inspect P-40s at an air base in China, February 1943. *(Smithsonian Institution Photo No. 74291AC)*

(*Above*) Arnold, Chennault, Stilwell, the British representative Sir John Dill, and Bissell at an air base in China, February 1943. (*Smithsonian Institution Photo No. A23480AC*)

(*Below*) Chiang Kai-shek and Chennault at Fourteenth Air Force headquarters. (*Smithsonian Institution Photo No. 56822AC*)

(Above) Chennault, commanding the Fourteenth Air Force, is promoted to major general, March 1943. Pinning the second star on Chennault's shoulder is his chief of staff, Edgar E. Glenn. *(Smithsonian Institution Photo No. 69164AC)*

(Right) Chennault receives the Distinguished Flying Cross from George Stratemeyer, commanding officer of the Tenth Air Force. *(Wide World Photos)*

N I N E

WE HAVE BAD NEWS

Rangoon was doomed. Its fall was as inevitable as the sunrise and had been ordained years before, more by the British than the Japanese. They had neglected to prepare defenses for Burma, just as they had in Malaya and Singapore. British planners had never considered the possibility that Burma could be invaded overland through neighboring Thailand. As a result of their lack of foresight, the British would soon undergo the longest retreat in their history, all the way to India.

By the end of January, Japanese troops had driven the poorly equipped force of British, Burmese, and Indian troops out of Moulmein—made famous by Kipling—and around the Gulf of Mataban toward the peninsula on which Rangoon was situated. The only barriers facing the Japanese were natural ones: three rivers, the Salween, the Bilin, and the Sittang. Ordinarily, these were wide, fast-moving streams that would slow down an army, but February was the dry season and the waters were shallow and slow. The Japanese troops did not even need boats to ford two of the rivers.

Rangoon was dying long before the Japanese captured it. Thousands of its residents had fled. For weeks, every road, trail, and river leading north was jammed with refugees. Trains left the central railroad station covered with humanity as people climbed onto the roofs of the cars and clung to their sides. No danger seemed greater than staying in the city. Fires burned and smoldered constantly, and the obsolete fire department had little equipment to deal with them. Each new bombing raid brought fresh showers of incendiaries, and orange and red flames brightened the tropical sky every night.

Law and order broke down completely. Mobs of Burmese roamed the city at night looting and torching British houses and Hindu shops. Before long, they turned to killing the few Hindus who had not already left, then the British, too, when anyone was caught alone. The men of the AVG stopped coming into the city singly, only in groups and well armed with .45s and submachine guns. They moved fast in convoys of jeeps and more than once had to shoot their way through a mob. Rangoon as a social organism ceased to exist.

The AVG pilots had little time to visit Rangoon, anyway. The air war claimed all their attention. Sandell's First Squadron, the Adams and Eves, were on their own. The remainder of Newkirk's squadron pulled out for Kunming on the third of February. The Japanese continued their night raids, coming over Mingadalon and the auxiliary fields as many as four times a night. No P-40s were destroyed, but several were peppered by shrapnel.

The pilots, kept awake at night, also had to scramble during the day, usually for false alarms, and their tiredness was sometimes overwhelming. The night of February 4 saw a particularly heavy raid that destroyed eight more blocks of the city. Bombs fell within a mile of the house in which Bond and Burgard were staying, but both men were so tired they slept right through it. They were amazed when told of the raid the next morning.

Two nights later, the Japanese came over four times. About a dozen bombs hit the runway, but by sunrise, the natives had already filled in the craters. The runway was ready for use when the alarm sounded. This one was for real. A force of thirty-five Nakajima Type 97s was approaching. Scrambling to face them were six P-40s and two Hurricanes of the RAF—almost five to one. The usual odds.

Bob Neale and Charlie Bond fought one enemy plane for about ten minutes. "He must have known he was done for," Bond said, "but he was a game little guy." The Japanese pilot was excellent. Once he flipped around in an amazingly tight turn and headed straight for Bond. The Type 97 pulled up, Bond dove, and in seconds the Japanese was on Bond's tail. Bond jammed the throttle forward and hoped the engine would hold together. When he looked back, he was relieved to see Neale on the enemy's tail. That was the end of that Japanese pilot. The tally for the day was seven Japanese planes destroyed and five damaged. No Allied planes were downed.

The following day, February 7, Sandy Sandell took off at 8:00 in the morning for a test flight. The damage to the tail of his airplane, done when the enemy fighter had crashed into it on the runway, had been repaired, but he was dissatisfied with the controls and wanted to check them out.

Harry Fox, the squadron line chief, cautioned Sandell before he took off.

"Take it easy, Sandy," he said. "You know what we have to use for spares."

Sandell grinned at him. "Sure," he said, and he climbed into the cockpit.

He roared down the runway in the morning haze and was quickly lost to view, but then he returned in a power dive, pulled out, and flashed over the hangar, barely missing the wind sock. He pulled up to 2500 feet and began a series of slow rolls. Several people watched from the ground as the P-40 rolled once and started over a second time. The ship rolled onto its back, apparently stalled, and went straight in. Sandell died instantly. The only parts that could be salvaged from the plane were the tail wheel and the right wheel.

In Kunming, Olga Greenlaw was working in her office. A little after 8:00 she thought she heard familiar footsteps and turned to say hello. No one was there. Some time later, Bill Wyke, the assistant group adjutant, told her there was a telephone call for her from the airfield. She instantly felt queasy and ran down the hall to the phone. It was Harvey.

"We have bad news," he said, "from Mingadalon."

"Don't tell me," she said. "I know it. It's Sandy. He's dead! Did it happen this morning—about eight o'clock?"

"Yes," Harvey said.

That afternoon Olga went to Sandell's room to itemize and pack his belongings. With her were C. E. Smith, the adjutant, and Mel Ceder, the provost marshal. They found a bottle of whiskey, poured themselves a drink, and toasted the memory of Sandell in silence, each lost in thought. As was customary, some of Sandell's belongings were sent to his next-of-kin, while items such as phonograph records and guns were auctioned off.

The auction was held that night following dinner. Olga Greenlaw never attended it. "It seemed to me as if we were vultures, picking up stuff when men got killed. I didn't like it at all. I was reading some papers when I heard the shuffling of many feet coming down the stairs—some went on down the hall to the bar or recreation room. Talking, laughing—there was always fun at these auctions, so they told me. The dead man was forgotten—life went on."

It was not that the men of the AVG were cold, callous, or uncaring, but when life could be snuffed out in a second, any day, and when it could strike any man in the group, they could not afford the luxury of a public grieving and mourning. It was too great a reminder of the fragility and vulnerability of their own lives. And so they laughed and drank and got on with the business of living. Tomorrow night it could be their possessions being auctioned.

In private, death was a different matter, and each man handled it in his own way. Some got more drunk than usual in the quiet of their quarters. Some found a woman for the night. Others spent the time alone. Charlie Bond sat out on the lawn of the Danish oilman's home, looking at the stars and "wondering about everything in general: life, death, love, Mom and Dad, Doris, and my being in Rangoon, halfway around the world, and involved in war where people are shooting at each other and trying to kill each other. And what for?"

Chennault sent a radiogram to Bob Neale when he heard of Sandell's death:

TERRIBLY SORRY LEARN SANDY'S DEATH. ENTIRE
GROUP SENDS DEEPEST SYMPATHY TO FIRST SQUAD-
RON. YOU ARE APPOINTED SQUADRON LEADER EFFEC-
TIVE THIS DATE. CARRY OUT INSTRUCTIONS ALREADY
ISSUED FOR SANDELL. RECOMMEND DEPUTY LEADER
FOR APPOINTMENT. CHENNAULT

Bob Neale, a twenty-eight-year-old ex-Navy pilot from Seattle, was a good choice to replace Sandell. He was jovial and well liked by the pilots and ground crew and was an excellent flyer. He recommended Greg Boyington to be his vice squadron commander and Chennault approved. Neale took charge of the squadron aggressively, but there was little to do, just what had become the usual round of false alarms and missions to escort RAF Blenheim bombers to Moulmein in which they went unchallenged by the Japanese. Enemy troops continued to approach Rangoon, so Neale asked Bond to draw up an emergency evacuation plan for the squadron so that they would not be trapped. They should be ready to leave on a moment's notice.

The men did lots of flying over the next several days, answering false alarms and running escort missions, but had no contact with the enemy. The pilots were growing restless and bored, and, as a result, their parties were becoming more boisterous. On Friday the 12th, Bond, Burgard, Neale, and a few others tried to drink the RAF under the table and apparently succeeded. The resulting hangovers were described as memorable, and Bond wrote in his diary that he would never do it again. But the next night a bunch of them did do it again, and the following morning five pilots scheduled for alert duty failed to show up. One was Boyington. Neale was furious with his deputy squadron leader, and they had "one hell of an argument."

The next day brought a blow to everyone's morale when they got the news that Singapore had fallen. "The report arrived shortly before noon," reported George Burgard, "and it spread gloom throughout the field. Everyone is disgusted as hell the way things are going and at the inadequateness of the British in all respects. Rangoon is certainly much more of a soft touch than Singapore and here we sit, twenty-two FAVG pilots trying to defend it against a nation. What prize chumps we are, holding down the hot spots for the British. . . . Sometimes I'm pretty disgusted at the way this life goes—but all in all it hasn't been a bad war— for us.''

But it was an increasingly bad war for the civilians. With Singapore gone, more of them decided it was time to leave Rangoon, including those who had been housing American pilots. Jim Adam and Bill Tweedy, who had been host to Boyington and others, were preparing to get out. Boyington could continue to use the house—the servants were willing to stay on—but he had to promise to shoot Angus, Jim Adam's Great Dane, before the Americans pulled out.

Boyington recalled their departure. "The most pitiful sight I ever saw was when these two old Scots were leaving Rangoon. They had said farewell, and were to travel by foot with light bundles over their shoulders. As they walked down the road, they looked much like two of our own Knights of the Road back home. Before they started, I asked: 'Anything I can do for either of you after you go?'

"And Jim had said: 'Set a match to it. It's too good for the Japs.' ''

Jensen, the Danish oilman who had been host to Bond and Burgard, was also leaving. He turned his house and servants over to the Americans and told them to treat the place as their own. The two pilots, after scouting the air base for canned goods from the British to make sure they'd have enough to eat, settled in, wondering how long it would be before they, too, evacuated Rangoon.

The city was collapsing, all sense of order and discipline nothing but a memory. The only organized activity, which quickly generated into chaos, was taking place on the docks. They were piled high with thousands of tons of lend-lease supplies and military equipment. Some of the native laborers refused to work on the docks because of their fear of the Japanese bombs, so there were few people to unload the ships and move the massive amounts of materiel.

There was too much equipment even to inventory. Estimates include close to 1000 half-assembled GM trucks, 5000 tires, jeeps, staff cars, ammunition, blankets, antiaircraft guns, machine guns, rifles, hand grenades, canned foods, cases of liquor (Scotch, sherry, and gin), medical supplies, uniforms, spare parts for the RAF Hurricanes, and new Brewster Buffalo fighters still in their crates. A fortune in materiel was waiting on the docks to be destroyed in air raids or captured by the Japanese.

China desperately needed those supplies and so did the AVG. Chennault arranged for his men to take anything they could use, including trucks, and send it north to Kunming. For weeks, every man who could be spared sweated his days and nights away on the docks. Even Chaplain Frillman said he worked like a Chinese coolie. "I spent every day there, with whatever ground crewmen could be spared from the airfield, smashing open crates and barrels, loading our trucks with spare parts for planes and vehicles, tires, tools, radio equipment, guns and ammunition. We tried to round up a three-month supply of canned goods and liquor for the whole AVG. When time ran short we just snatched whatever crates were handy and portable, with no idea of contents.

"Trips to and from the docks were weird. We traveled in convoys because Japanese agents or Burmese nationalists were reported sniping at stray Westerners. Nearly everyone had fled or was in hiding, and we roared through empty sun-baked streets under a burning blue sky. Over the roofs we could see the pale gold spire of the Shew Dagon [pagoda] and the great black and red pillar of smoke and flame from the docks. Smaller plumes of smoke rose from every part of town; twenty-five blocks were said to be burning. The air-raid cleanup squads had eventually fled, for masonry lay tumbled out onto the pavements and the sweetish smell of decay hung over many fields of ruins. For blocks we could see nothing alive except the scavenger dogs, crows, and buzzards."

AVG personnel were flown down from Kunming to drive convoys of trucks north to the Burma Road and then over that winding, traffic-filled stretch to Kunming. Chennault arranged with Chinese customs officials at the border with Burma to pass all AVG trucks and convoys without inspection, having assured them that the only supplies being brought into China were for the AVG's use and not for sale on the black market.

It was inevitable, however, that some of the men involved in the transfer of goods from the Rangoon docks to the air base at Kunming would seize the opportunity for personal gain. And so, trucks headed north laden with personal booty. Because China had been almost completely cut off from foreign goods for years, virtually anything could be sold. There was considerable money to be made with little effort.

"Some of the men have begun to go down to the docks," wrote Charlie Bond in his diary on February 18, "drive their trucks up to a pile of whatever they are interested in, speak in a commanding voice, and direct the Burmese laborers to load the stuff onto their truck. Then they merely drive off with it. . . . The men have caches of canned fruit, rifles, shotgun shells, soap, radios, and whatnot. John Dean picked up three more jeeps for the men yesterday the same way. Hell's bells! No wonder war costs so much!"

A few days later he noted that "Looting is completely out of hand. Many of the men are getting their share also. We have at least a hundred cases of various kinds of liquors, box after box of cigarettes, toothbrushes, talcum powder, cheese, canned goods, anything that might be of use in China. I saw one jeep loaded with cases of sherry."

One of the ground crewmen brought a British radio to George Burgard and told him how much more there was to be had on the docks. It would all be lost to the Japanese if they did not do something about it. They got a ten-ton truck and "piled up so much stuff it would not be believed if I listed it. Included were 15 radios and two bolts of wonderful flannel. We are sending it north on a convoy and figure to make over $1500 on it in Kunming. It's mad—but true. Can you believe it? . . . The men have picked up tons of stuff—all we can take in the convoy in addition to our own supplies. It is pitiful—the altogether miserable organization of the British here. The city is gone because of it. Perhaps it will be hours, maybe days, but it's gone."

At Mingadalon the air war continued, and the tension grew over the possibility of being caught by surprise by the enemy. The ground crew began to kid among themselves about finding Japanese in the cockpits of the P-40s when they warmed up the engines in the morning. They placed bets on who would be the last to leave. They tried to joke about it, but they all realized how precarious their situation was.

On February 20, the Japanese crossed the Bilin River, the second of the three water barriers between them and Rangoon. Notices were posted throughout the city urging all civilians to leave within forty-eight hours. The RAF was preparing to evacuate, and Neale's First Squadron was getting ready to move to the airbase at Magwe, 250 miles north of Rangoon.

The 21st was, for the Adams and Eves, "a wild and hectic day." Six P-40s were ordered to escort four British Blenheims on a raid against Japanese troops north of the town of Bilin. The formation assembled and flew over enemy lines at 16,000 feet, dropping down to 12,000 as they approached the target. Suddenly they ran into a flight of forty Japanese fighter planes escorting twelve bombers. The AVG had no chance to think about going after the bombers because the fighters pounced on them from above.

There was no pattern or order to the fight. Bond recalled veering, diving, and climbing, trying to outmaneuver the agile Type 97s, and not seeing another P-40 the entire time. Burgard got only two in a full hour of fighting. "It was a wild scramble. They have no rhyme or reason to their method of flying."

The Flying Tigers claimed six enemy planes downed with no losses themselves, although Burgard's ship was hit by a bullet through one wing and another through the right tire. John Farrell took a bullet through his canopy that left him with a cut near his right eye. They landed at Mingadalon and Bond was still writing the combat report when Neale ordered him up again. The mission was to lead a flight of five planes to cover Neale's six that were escorting more Blenheims over the same target.

When the bombers dropped their loads, the P-40s roared over the enemy troop concentrations strafing long columns of trucks. The AVG pilots noticed that British troops were already retreating over the Sittang River, the last natural barrier before Rangoon, only seventy-five miles from the city. As soon as they landed, Neale ordered Bond to lead three planes back to continue the strafing. Two turned back with engine trouble, but Bond and the other P-40 went on. They zoomed over the same road and started firing at the column of trucks. At one point they flew so low that Bond's propeller grazed the topmost branches of a tree.

His plane started to vibrate, and he nursed it back to the airfield. He examined the propeller and found a one-inch hole through the middle of one of the blades. It was from the nose guns—he had almost shot himself down. Later that night, Bond put his thoughts on paper.

"I had really been in combat—a lot of it, and all day. I had seen war at its worst. That Jap column had been wrecked by .50-caliber slugs tearing the trucks to bits. I saw one Japanese on his horse ducking for cover and I had grinned as I passed over to get a bead on a truck down the line. I'm sure I would have gunned him down just like a truck had I been in the right position. What a business. Like beasts. No thought for life whatsoever. Instead, a feeling of hatred for the Japanese that becomes deeper day by day."

On the 22nd, the men of the AVG were put on one-hour's evacuation notice. They loaded their jeeps with their personal possessions and sat on the field, waiting to pull out. By noon, the threat had lessened and they were put back on twelve-hours' notice. The following day they sent a large convoy of supplies north to their new base at Magwe. Most of the mechanics went along, and six P-40s were transferred to Magwe from which they could patrol the highway and protect the convoy.

General Wavell issued orders to the British on February 24 that Rangoon was to be defended to the last, and AVG squadron leader Neale told his remaining men that they would stay to the end. Six of his remaining 11 P-40s strafed the Japanese airbase at Moulmein, destroying 3 planes. For the rest of that day and the next, the Flying Tigers were in the air almost constantly, escorting bombers and strafing enemy troops. Late in the day on the 25th, they intercepted a large enemy force of 40 fighters and 12 bombers.

All 11 P-40s and 8 Hurricanes—the entire Allied fighter force—took them on. The RAF recorded 6 kills and the Flying Tigers, in their best day of the war, shot down 19 confirmed and 8 probables. One P-40 was missing. The pilot, Ed Leibolt, had been seen bailing out. Other pilots had returned hours, even days after being shot down, so there was reason to hope that he was alive.

Chennault sent his men at Rangoon some good news on the 26th: orders to pull out on March 1. There was, however, some question about whether they could stay that long. Japanese troops were getting closer by the hour. Neale radioed Chennault that they might have to evacuate before the first. Chennault replied: EX-PEND EQUIPMENT. CONSERVE PERSONNEL UTMOST. RETIRE WITH LAST BOTTLE OXYGEN.

All that day and the next, the Japanese came over in force, with raids of more than 100 planes each. The AVG had been reduced to six flyable aircraft, and these were in terrible condition. Nevertheless, they flew combat missions on both days and accounted for twenty-three confirmed enemy planes and eight probables. Jim Cross caught a burst of bullets through his windshield, oxygen bottle, and the left side of the cockpit. The shrapnel and flying metal cut into his left shoulder and cheek, but he brought his ship back to the field safely.

The AVG could not keep up the pace much longer. Planes and pilots were wearing out. They were out of spare tires. If one more threadbare tire blew, that plane would be lost. The last of the oxygen bottles was already in place in a plane. They had no more.

Pilot Fritz Wolf described the situation: "Planes at Rangoon are almost unflyable. Tires are chewed up and baked hard. They blow out continually. We are short on them, and battery plates are thin. When we recharge them, they wear out within a day. There is no Prestone oil coolant in Rangoon. British destroyed the battery-charging and oxygen-storage depots without any advance warning to us so we could stock up. We are completely out of auxiliary gear shifts and they are wearing out in the planes every day.

"Fresh food of any kind is completely lacking. We are living out of cans. Water is hard to get. Most of the city water supply has been cut off.

"Dust on the field fouls up the P-40 engines considerably. It clogs carburetion so much that it is dangerous to increase manifold pressure when the engine quits cold. Entire carburetion systems are cleaned on the ground, but they are as bad as ever after a single day's operations. This tendency of engines to quit makes it hard to dogfight or strafe."

Nothing worked in Rangoon, either. Even the telephones went dead when the British evacuated all the operators. The British also released from institutions the lepers, the insane, and the criminals.

On Rangoon's docks, the British set about destroying the remaining lend-lease equipment, using bulldozers to shove much of it into the harbor. Other items were burned, including the new General Motors trucks and 5000 tires, which the Chinese Army could have made good use of. The trucks could have been driven north and saved, but there was no organizational apparatus left to arrange the operation.

Then the supplies and the docks themselves were blown up, and ships at anchor were sunk. The city's water system was wrecked, and the oil refineries on the outskirts set afire. For three days, a column of smoke and flame reached as high as three miles, a giant pylon inviting the Japanese to add to the destruction.

Chaplain Frillman and others risked their lives amid the bedlam of Rangoon to hunt for supplies for the AVG. They recorded some strange and horrifying sights. "One day we came upon a leper at a downtown gas station. It was an American station, exactly like all those selling this brand in the United States. The leper with his filthy rags, his great lion head and thickened features, looked as if he had escaped from a medieval dungeon. He was laughing insanely as he pumped the gas into the street, shaking the hose above his head to make the fluid scatter and sparkle in the sunlight."

On one of their forays, the chaplain and his group took a detour through the city to escape a fire. They found themselves passing an automobile dealership with three beautiful new Buick sedans in the showroom window. The place was deserted, but the keys had obligingly been left in the cars. They drove them off the showroom floor, but one of the men was so excited at driving a powerful American car that he wrecked it after only a few blocks. They drove the other two back to the airfield.

No one who saw Rangoon during its final days would ever forget the horror. Historian Russell Whelan wrote: "From a hundred fires a great pall of black smoke stretched across the sky. Wharves, factories, rice and teak mills, oil storage plants, vessels in the river and homes and buildings in town were in flames. In the streets lay hundreds of bodies of Indians who had fallen in the pogrom declared by the Burmese against these resented foreigners when doom closed down upon Rangoon. Over these bodies stumbled ragged, bedlamite bands of looters and rioters, loosed from the jails and asylums. . . . Here were imbeciles, maniacs, criminals, cripples, victims of every disease of mind and body known to the East. They roamed the city, shrieking in crazy choruses, throwing burning brands into the windows of buildings, destroying and desecrating. The smells of Rangoon were now the smells of embers and of death."

On the night of the 27th, with Rangoon and all of southern Burma about to fall under the heel of the Japanese, the RAF gave a party to dedicate their new officers club at Mingadalon. The AVG was invited. Chaplain Frillman remarked that it seemed crazy to be dedicating a club that the Japanese would be using in a day or two.

An RAF officer regarded Frillman with an expression of disdainful amusement.

"You Americans," he said, "always getting the wind up."

The party was grand, and everyone had a terrific time. The AVG staggered off to bed about 2:00 A.M., only to be awakened two hours later by the sounds of aircraft and trucks on the move. The RAF was leaving—and taking their radar air-warning equipment with them. Now the Flying Tigers had no way to detect incoming planes. To stay any longer would be suicidal.

Bob Neale made last-minute preparations to evacuate. Four planes took off in the morning for Magwe. Greg Boyington flew one of them. Before he left, he remembered his promise to his host—to burn the house and shoot the dog so they wouldn't be left for the Japanese—but he didn't have the heart to do either. He asked pilot Robert H. Smith, who had also lived in the house, to do it for him.

When the flyers caught up with each other later, Boyington asked Smith if he'd taken care of Angus. Smith replied, rather weakly, "I shot at him. But I missed him. He got away."

The remaining ground crew quickly loaded the trucks and jeeps. Neale sent for Frillman and gave him some unwelcome news.

"You're it," he announced. "You are taking the first convoy up the road."

"You're out of your mind," Frillman said. "I'm the chaplain. I'm not taking any convoy anywhere."

"The Old Man says so," Neale told him, and he showed him the radio message from Chennault: CONVOYS START THIS MORNING. FRILLMAN TAKES THE FIRST.

The Japanese were fewer than twenty miles away. The road north could be cut at any time. Frillman found the convoy waiting for him at the end of the field. It consisted of "twelve jeeps and eighteen trucks, loaded to the hilt with goodness knew what. Beside most drivers sat pretty Anglo-Indian girls dressed as for a picnic, with frilly blouses and harlequin sunglasses. I had a twinge of morality, then thought what might happen to them if they didn't come with us. I got my Buick, which I luckily had already loaded to the roof, and led the parade through the deserted smoke-hazed streets."

Other, smaller convoys left later in the day, but Neale and his wingman, Robert H. Smith, stayed on, hoping to hear something from Ed Leibolt, the missing pilot. Neale took the radio out of his ship and ripped out some panels to make room for a stretcher in case Leibolt was injured. Chances of finding him lessened with each hour as the Japanese advanced beyond the area where he had been seen bailing out. Neale and Smith waited throughout the day but gave up the next morning. They could not afford to risk losing their P-40s by staying around too long. They stuffed two cases of whiskey into Neale's radio compartment and took off, circling the burning city before heading north to Magwe. Leibolt was never found.

While the First Squadron was being chased out of Rangoon, the rest of the Flying Tigers were being wined, dined, and decorated by Generalissimo and Madame Chiang Kai-shek in Kunming. The men had seen no action during the month of February, so the Chinese festivities were the only activity that broke the monotony. The Japanese were concentrating on Rangoon and had left Kunming alone. The pilots took their daily turns in the alert shacks and passed the time playing gin rummy and acey-deucy. They went hunting for duck and other game, slept, undertook marathon poker games, and drank. Because they had so little to do, some of them managed to get into trouble.

There were outbreaks of petty jealousy and minor disagreements between pilots and ground crew. Some of the men—three or four troublemakers—caused problems in the city of Kunming by getting drunk, insulting women, beating up Chinese civilians. Once they tried to break into the YWCA. When Harvey Greenlaw was called to the quarters of the AVG clerks to quell a disturbance, he told the men that if they wanted out, they should resign at once. He would arrange to get them home as soon as possible. No one wanted to resign, although Greenlaw persisted and said that he would be glad to be rid of certain of them. The prospect seemed to sober them up, at least for a while.

Another problem for the AVG during February was the increasing presence of American army officers. No one in Kunming knew who they were, or why they were in China, but almost every day one or more would arrive in crisp dress uniforms on their way to Chungking. The men of the AVG, who had been fighting on their own for two months, looked upon the army officers as noncontributing intruders in their war, and they resented their presence. They also worried that the arrival of so many American officers meant that the AVG was about to be inducted wholesale into the U.S. Army Air Corps. None of them wanted that, especially not the large contingent of former navy and Marine Corps pilots. With little else to occupy their minds, the men at Kunming began to brood about the possibility of finding themselves in the military again. It turned out to be a legitimate concern.

The AVG received one bit of good news midway through the month. Five Pan American Clippers arrived in Calcutta with the first spare parts the Flying Tigers had received since landing in Burma eight months before. Included in the precious cargo were tires, batteries, propellers, solenoids, oxygen, and ammunition. When Chennault got the news, he arranged for CNAC transports to pick up the supplies and bring them to Kunming. One of the ferry pilots was his old friend and aerobatics partner, Billy Mc-Donald.

The only other big event of February was the celebration that took place on the 28th, when the men of the AVG were the guests of honor of the Generalissimo and Madame. The pilots were excited and impressed by the high honor being paid to them. Throughout the day, houseboys and coolies decorated the front of the Number 1 hostel with potted plants and Chinese and American flags. The downstairs hallways were covered with embroidered silk banners, and the auditorium on the second floor was draped with hundreds of yards of colored crepe paper.

Chennault arrived at the Greenlaws' quarters as they were getting ready for the evening.

"Better look me over," he said to Olga. "Do I look all right?"

"He stood in front of my large mirror," she wrote. "I straightened his tie, pulled his coat, smoothed it out until there wasn't a wrinkle left, and told him he looked as if he had just stepped out of *Esquire* and that regardless of age, he had the best figure for a uniform of any man in the outfit. He smiled, winked happily at Harvey and left the room abruptly."

Everyone wore dress uniforms and was on his best behavior. The bar had been closed all evening to ensure that everything would go smoothly, but when the festivities began, there were still two empty chairs in the auditorium. It was too much to hope that "a party of this importance could go off without a hitch." The missing pilots showed up later, while two Chinese women were singing, and disrupted the song with drunken applause. They had missed the speeches, particularly Madame's pointed comments about the need for discipline.

"Without discipline," she had said, "we can accomplish nothing, and I, as your Honorary Commanding Officer, am going to din more discipline into you. I mean discipline of our inner selves. However, I am not going to make out of you little plaster saints, and I am human enough to like interesting people, but I do want you boys to remember one thing, the whole of the Chinese Nation has taken you to its heart, and I want you to conduct yourselves in a manner worthy of the great traditions that you have built up. I want you to leave an impression on my people, a true impression of what Americans really are. . . . Perhaps I should be very polite and say, 'Boys, you are just grand. You are little angels, with or without wings.' "

As she finished, the men of the AVG rose to their feet, cheering. She had charmed them, as she charmed everyone. "Her speech was very impressive," recalled Buster Keeton, "and all the AVG liked her tremendously." Pilot John Donovan wrote to his parents, "She absolutely captured our hearts. Colonel Chennault had always adored her and now she has the adoration of every member of the AVG. . . . She gathered the entire group into her arms and called us 'her boys.' This, despite the fact that she doesn't look a day over twenty-eight. . . . She was at once a mother, an attractive bewitching girl, a counselor, a wit, a sternly disciplined person who encouraged us to discipline ourselves. We cheered her to the rafters time and again. She earned the respect and admiration of all."

The presence of Madame Chiang and the Generalissimo at Kunming was a great success, but their departure a few days later was a disaster for the Flying Tigers. It started with what Keeton called "a hare-brained idea" of Harvey Greenlaw's concocted just ten minutes before the Chiangs were to leave on a CNAC plane. Greenlaw decided that the pilots would put on an air show.

Six pilots had already volunteered to provide fighter escort for the transport plane. They included Greg Boyington, who had arrived in Kunming on March 1, and five other pilots from the First Squadron. Boyington looked upon the flight as an honor, like escorting President and Mrs. Roosevelt. "The catch was that no one told us where we were going. Each thought the other might know, or at least that the leader might know, so we did not bother to find out. I look back on the whole thing as some experienced old man might at some damned-fool things of his childhood."

While the pilots were waiting to take off, a jeep pulled up with Greenlaw's message to put on a show and make it look good. The pilots took off and watched as the official party arrived at the DC-2 waiting on the runway. While the people on the ground were bowing and shaking hands, the P-40s started to dive. They approached the far side of the field in line and started to roll over, so that each ship would be upsidedown as it roared over the dignitaries.

The first two planes, flown by Frank Lawlor and Robert Layher, came in too low. Everyone in the official party fell flat on the ground. The baggage compartment door on the lead plane had come open just as the pilot started his roll, and the second pilot had great difficulty pulling up. Both came close to plowing in and killing the leaders of China and the AVG.

The excitement was far from over. The flight leader had to land because of the open baggage door, and he motioned for Boyington to take over. The transport took off, gained altitude, and was joined by the five escorting fighters. But Boyington was worried. Not only was he unaware of their destination, but he also discovered that his compass was not working and he could not hear anything over his radio.

He was already in trouble with Chennault because of an incident four nights earlier when he and his ground crew had thrown a party in Hostel Number 2, with a large supply of whiskey and some willing girls who had come from Rangoon in one of the truck convoys. They were all engaged in target practice against the hostel's adobe walls when a bullet ricocheted too close to a civilian representative of the Allison Engine Company. He complained to Chennault, and Chennault chewed out Boyington. "My punishment was—a limit of two drinks per evening. [Chennault] hadn't said how large, however. So I assumed this to mean two full water glasses." It was too soon for Boyington to get into trouble again.

The group flew without incident for two hours until they encountered a strong headwind and thick clouds. They didn't carry enough gas to fight such headwinds for long, so Boyington decided they should return to Kunming. The cloud cover would protect the Chiangs' plane from Japanese fighters. The AVG pilots, however, were lost. They had no compass and no working radio and were flying over unfamiliar terrain with their gas gauges dropping ever lower.

For a moment luck was with them. They broke out of the clouds and spotted a flat hilltop just as they were about to run out of gas. The field, which turned out to be a Chinese cemetery, was too short for a proper wheels-down landing—if they tried one, they would wind up in the valley 300 feet below. The five planes made wheels-up belly landings, but the damage to the aircraft was greater than what the enemy had been able to cause in a single day. One radio worked then, so they were able to notify the base.

"The Colonel was awfully broken up about the whole affair," said Buster Keeton, "and will give us a lecture tomorrow morning." He did—on how to navigate in China and how to recognize features of the local terrain.

It took Boyington and the others a week to reach Kunming from their crash site some 200 miles away. While they were making their way through the mountains, the Flying Tigers suffered another loss. Chennault dispatched five planes of the Third Squadron to Magwe in Burma. They left at 11:00 A.M. on March 9. At 8:00 that night, Chennault received a report that they had gotten lost and been forced to crash-land. Three P-40s were wrecks. The other two could be salvaged. "Lord, what a mess," George Burgard wrote. "Ten airplanes in less than one week. The Colonel will die." Buster Keeton added, "That is really destroying us. A lot of equipment for no reason except stupidity on the part of the flight leader. The poor Colonel will probably go crazy."

Boyington volunteered to try to salvage some of the planes he had lost on the hilltop. A team of mechanics straightened out propellers and wings, emptied the planes of all surplus weight, jacked them up so the wheels could be let down, and put thirty gallons of gas in each tank, just enough to get Boyington to an auxiliary field sixty miles away—if he survived the takeoff. The ground crew raised the tail of the first plane to a horizontal position. Boyington stood on the brakes and shoved the throttle forward. The plane leaped ahead when he released the brakes and raced toward the sheer drop at the edge of the field. When he reached it, the plane dropped about fifty feet with its nose high, almost in a stall, until he brought it under control. He managed to pull up in time to clear the mountains. When he was in sight of the auxiliary field he ran out of gas but was able to glide in and make a dead-stick landing. He repeated the adventure twice and was thus able to reclaim three of the five planes he was responsible for losing.

Morale continued to plummet at Kunming during the month of March. The bickering, fighting, and drinking increased. Keeton wrote in his diary: "Morale of the outfit is getting low due to inactivity and numerous rumors. The men have been raising hell in town; shooting up places, getting drunk, and raising hell in general."

On March 10, two pilots got drunk and began shooting off their .45s. A bullet bounced off a wall and struck the same Allison representative who had almost been shot by Boyington and his group the week before. He asked the pilots to be more careful. They jumped him and beat him up.

A truck convoy from Rangoon arrived and with it came the rumor that the pilot in charge, who had stopped flying and been given a staff job, had made several thousand dollars on goods brought into China and sold on the black market, an easier way to make money than shooting down enemy planes. The other pilots were resentful.

More pilots and ground crew began talking about quitting, and on March 12, five of them did. Chennault gave them all dishonorable discharges. The remaining Flying Tigers began to feel they had been abandoned by the United States, left on their own to be killed off one by one. They realized they were fighting a losing battle and, no matter what they did, it was inevitable they would soon be chased out of Burma and perhaps out of China, too—if they lived that long.

Olga Greenlaw observed the changes. "Almost every member of the group was beginning to show signs of war weariness. Pilots and ground crews had taken a terrific pounding and their nerves were starting to fray along the edges. Wear and tear on the planes was enormous and our general situation was growing steadily worse. We didn't have enough of anything—plane replacements, spare parts, anti-aircraft weapons. The odds that the boys fought against were consistently so overwhelming as to be almost ridiculous. No matter how many Jap planes they shot down an equal number—or more—appeared on the next raid. And look as we might—and we did—we could see no relief in sight."

Charlie Bond recorded his thoughts on the morale problem. "Seems like most of the guys have started thinking about making money rather than fighting the war and that everyone is disgusted about one thing or another. . . . What in hell is happening to the outfit?"

Chennault was wondering the same thing. He called the men together for a talk on March 12 and told them how upset he was about the low morale and the five resignations. He tried to allay their concern about being inducted into the army by telling them he had persuaded the U.S. military authorities that the AVG would operate more effectively if it remained independent. That was wishful thinking on Chennault's part. He had not convinced the army of that, and he may have said so as much to boost his own morale as that of his men.

The poor morale even affected the First Squadron when they returned to Kunming after their month of combat in Burma. A week after Chennault's speech, Bond returned to his room to find Boyington, Red Probst, Bill Bartling, and Matt Kuykendall drunk on his supply of sherry, gin, and Scotch. Bond tried to get them to leave because they were all scheduled for an early alert in the morning, but Boyington was looking for a fight.

Bond had to pull Boyington away from Bartling and ended up telling him off. Boyington was angry at Bond because Neale wanted to give Bond Boyington's job as vice squadron leader. In the morning, some of the pilots did not show up for alert, and Neale raised hell, particularly with Boyington for setting a bad example.

Chennault himself was in low spirits about the situation. The air force he had fought so hard to get and to train—and which was proving the success of the tactics he had advocated for so many years—was in danger of being knocked out of action, if not by the Japanese then by its own internal dissension. Without replacement planes or pilots, the AVG had a limited future.

Even if they did survive as a group, Chennault had another cause for alarm. He was more bothered by the growing number of army air corps officers in China than were his men because he knew their presence meant the end of his own war. As the formal American military establishment in China expanded, the likelihood that his unorthodox style of fighting could survive diminished. No army commander was going to allow a group of civilian mercenaries to operate in his area.

The army was bound to take over, either by inducting the AVG or by sending them packing and replacing them with regular air corps units. And where would that leave Claire Chennault, a beat-up ex-army captain, now a civilian, whom few in the air corps liked or trusted? Sidelined, cast off, sent home to Waterproof, Louisiana, to sit out the war he had spent his entire career training for? He could envision a new commander, a West Pointer no doubt, with a tailored dress uniform, shiny brass buttons, and tact and polish, but who had never before seen a Japanese plane.

Chennault had to fight back, and the only weapon he had was his connections with the China Lobby in Washington. He had recognized the potential problem as early as January 20, and had cabled Madame Chiang of his concern:

> COMBAT EFFECTIVENESS OF AVG WILL BE GREATLY LESSENED FOR MONTHS IF INDUCTED INTO US ARMY. IF DESIRED I WILL ACCEPT US REGULAR APPOINTMENT AS GENERAL OFFICER AND APPOINTMENT BY THE GENERALISSIMO AS AIR OFFICER COMMANDING IN CHINA.

Chennault noted that he would then be in a position to command not only the AVG but also any additional U.S. air corps units sent to China. Thus, his future would be more secure. With appointment as a general officer and the commanding air officer in China, he would be the highest-ranking and most experienced airman on the scene when the American military presence became more visible.

Five days later, Chennault wrote to his friend Leland Stowe, a journalist, to complain about the possibility that the AVG would be forced to become part of the army. He said that all the reports and regulations and paperwork would leave him no time to operate against the enemy. He believed that jealousy was the motivation behind the idea of inducting the AVG into the army. The War Department resented the publicity the AVG had received and was annoyed that no air corps unit could match the AVG's record. There was also, Chennault added, a personal element.

"Certain high-ranking Air Corps officers are intensely jealous of my success in training and operating this group. I attempted to teach sound methods of pursuit employment and tactics for years, but my efforts met with such disfavor that I finally retired in disgust. These same officers would willingly sacrifice this group in order to end my opportunity for proving my doctrines were and are sound."

By March, the threat from the army was clearer, and on the 17th Chennault composed a long radiogram to T. V. Soong stating his complaints, making an outright bid to be placed in charge of all air activities in the China–Burma–India theater. He threatened to quit and to take his story of War Department blunders and ineptitude to the public. It was a bold gamble on the part of an old poker player whose nerve was much stronger than his hand, but he felt he had nothing to lose.

He told Soong he was discouraged by the War Department's failure to take advantage of opportunities to conduct offensive air warfare against Japan. If the bombers he had been promised had arrived, he could have inflicted serious damage on the enemy. Had he been able to carry out his original plan to bomb Tokyo, the course of the war in China would have surely been altered.

As for the future of the war, Chennault told Soong—knowing that Soong would pass the message to his friends in the U.S. government—it was imperative that one man be immediately placed in charge of all aviation in the Far East. That man should have a thorough knowledge of Japanese air tactics and of the situation in China, Burma, and India. Only one person in or out of uniform fit that description: Claire Lee Chennault. It was only a matter of time before an overall air commander would be appointed, and Chennault saw clearly that he was the only man for the job.

As for the present situation, he told Soong, it was grim. Exaggerating some, but not much, Chennault said that the AVG had only enough airplanes for one effective squadron, which diluted the value of their overall effort. There were no plans for replacements or reinforcements. Most of the air corps officers who came through Kunming with their bulging briefcases offered hastily conceived plans for future operations, but none of these men had the authority to implement the plans and no one asked Chennault for his advice or recommendations. Chennault concluded his March 17 cable to Soong with the following remarks:

> MY RECOMMENDATIONS UNSOUGHT OR DISAPPROVED BY ALL. CONVINCED MY USEFULNESS AND AVG FINISHED APRIL 15 UNLESS IMMEDIATE ACTION TAKEN. REQUEST PERMISSION TO DEMOBILIZE AND DISCHARGE GROUP THIS DATE OR APPOINT NEW COMMANDER. MY PATRIOTIC DUTY TO RETURN STATES AND REVEAL TO AMERICAN PUBLIC WAR DEPARTMENT PROGRAM OF INDECISION, OBSTRUCTION, NONSUPPORT, AND PASSIVE INACTIVITY FAR EAST. AWAIT YOUR ORDERS.

There is no record of a reply from Soong. Perhaps he knew Chennault well enough to know that he was bluffing, that he would never voluntarily step down as commander of the AVG or demobilize the group as long as there was even one plane and one pilot left. But Soong also knew that Chennault was not bluffing about taking his case to the public. If he were stripped of his job, that was exactly what he would do. It is believed that Soong made this threat of Chennault's known to his highly placed friends in Washington. The press was treating Chennault as a hero and would give widespread coverage to his views on the conduct of the war in China. No one in government wanted the embarrassment that would cause.

The following week Chennault dispatched another message, this one to General C. J. Chow, commander of the Chinese Air Force. The content was less volatile and threatening and was directed to other influential contacts, both in Chungking and Washington. Chennault told Chow that the message was for Madame Chiang, and he asked that a copy be sent to Lauchlin Currie, whose views were respected by President Roosevelt:

AVG RAPIDLY BECOMING INEFFECTIVE DUE TO EX-HAUSTION EQUIPMENT AND PERSONNEL LOSSES. GROUP HAS BORNE BRUNT IN DEFENSE RANGOON, BURMA AND YUNNAN. INITIALLY EXPECTED GROUP ENDURE ONE MONTH BUT HAVE HELD ON OVER THREE MONTHS MERELY BECAUSE SUCCESSFUL EFFORTS YOU AND MINISTER SOONG SEND SPARE PARTS BY AIR. PER-SONNEL REPLACEMENT NOW EQUALLY SERIOUS AS EQUIPMENT. . . . SUGGEST TRANSFER MEN AND EQUIPMENT NEEDED FROM US AIR CORPS GROUP NOW ARRIVING KARACHI.

Chennault was trying to get the new air corps units being sent to the area before they got him. He would much rather induct the air corps into the AVG than the other way around. The days of his maverick war were clearly numbered, and he knew it, but he was fighting to hold on, however tenuously, for as long as possible.

Magwe was "a hell of a hole," according to George Burgard. The airfield to which the First Squadron had fled after evacuating Rangoon was far more primitive than Mingadalon. The RAF had hastily hacked it out of the jungle, hoping it would not be discovered by the Japanese. It had no dispersal or revetment facilities, no protection for aircraft on the ground. There was only one operating radar set, and it covered only the southeast approaches. Thus, it could warn only of attacks coming from Mingadalon, now in enemy hands. There were no spotters on the ground, and the only other early-warning system was provided by a Blenheim bomber that circled during daylight hours at 10,000 feet about eighty miles from Magwe. That was the only way to detect air strikes coming from Thailand, where most of the Japanese planes were based.

The operation of the field was chaotic. For a time, no one in authority seemed to know where the supply of gasoline was stored. The pilots of the Adams and Eves took to sleeping by their planes when scheduled for morning alert, so as not to be caught by surprise. They figured that with the lack of a decent warning system, they would be lucky to get ten minutes' warning time. To complicate matters, the RAF used the field as a center for evacuating British and Indian personnel to India. Transport planes, and bombers pressed into service as transports, were frequently taking off and landing, making a quick scramble by the Flying Tigers a dangerous proposition.

The runway of packed dirt seemed constantly to be covered by a cloud of dust raised by the transports. The alert shack was nothing more than a tent, and the ground crew lived in tents pitched on a nearby polo field. When the men first arrived from Mingadalon in trucks, they were exhausted and dirty and their morale had hit bottom. Their first reaction to Magwe was to threaten to quit on the spot. Charlie Bond gave them a pep talk to try to cheer them up. The nearest trappings of civilization, meaning an American-style club with a bar and a swimming pool, was 30 miles distant in Yenangyaung, a town in the middle of an oil field. Several Americans lived there, and the pilots made arrangements to stay with them while off duty.

Bob Neale and Robert H. Smith, the last pilots to leave Mingadalon, took a long time to reach Magwe. Neale had told Bond that it was easy to find Magwe because it was right on the Irrawaddy River, but Smith landed a hundred miles to the north and Neale came down forty miles north, both landing in open fields. Neale had run out of gas, but otherwise his plane was undamaged. Smith's plane needed a new wheel and a new cylinder for the landing gear retraction system. Gas and parts were sent to the pilots and they finally reached Magwe, although Neale almost overshot the runway while landing. Bond razzed him about getting lost. "Famous last words," he said. "It's on a river. You can't get lost."

Not far north of Magwe the convoy of eighteen heavily laden trucks and twelve equally full jeeps, led by Chaplain Frillman in his new Buick, was on its way to Kunming. It would take them seventeen days. "My memory of that trip has blurred," Frillman wrote twenty-six years later, "each day being equally strenuous, uncomfortable, and exciting." They drove by day, ever on the alert for Japanese planes, and camped by the roadside at night. They had to stay near their vehicles at all times to guard them from Burmese nationalists attempting to sabotage all vehicles belonging to Westerners.

The first night on the road, when they began rummaging through the cargo to find food for supper, they learned just what was in some of the crates they had grabbed off the docks at random. The men found a five-year supply of shoelaces, a year's worth of facial tissues, and a small mountain of kitchen cleanser. For dinner they unearthed a huge quantity of canned asparagus and Harvey's Bristol Cream sherry.

On the second day of the journey they caught up with Rangoon's refugees, bringing the convoy to a crawl amid the high-wheeled bullock carts, the cars that looked like they belonged in junkyards, and every other kind of vehicle imaginable—taxis, buses, ice trucks, fire engines, and hearses. The Americans caught a brief glimpse of exotic Mandalay, still untouched by war, and north of that city took the one paved road leading northeast to the Chinese border. They stopped overnight at Maymyo, a British hill station in which everyone was properly dressed and the gardens were carefully tended, and Frillman saw "two proper blondes in long-skirted evening dresses, one blue, one pink, walking sedately with two young British officers. Off to a dance, I supposed. They looked strange as Martians to me," as though there were no war raging to the south.

A few nights later the men camped near Chinese troops who were heading south to try to stop the Japanese advance at Toungoo, the AVG's first base. Their commander told Frillman that an American general was coming from Washington to command the Chinese Army. His name was Shih Ti-wei, but none of the Americans knew who that might be.

The closer they got to the Chinese border, the more Americans they saw. They recognized some of them as former AVG personnel who had quit early on and gone into the black market. These men formed their own convoy of cars and light trucks, trailing Frillman's group by a mile or two. Frillman knew they would tag along when they all reached the border so they could enter China as part of the AVG and thus escape inspection by customs officials.

When they crossed the border they found the road still jammed with refugees. The inns were so crowded and dirty that the Americans did not attempt to buy anything, not even water. "We found Bristol Cream sherry could be used as eau de cologne and tooth water," Frillman said. "Even today I sometimes imagine a toothpaste flavor in sherry." The first sizable city they came to was Paoshan. The men were ready for a good time—they wanted restaurants and bars and brothels. The convoy parked outside the city walls and most of the men went into town. No sooner had they left when 18 Japanese bombers came over, plastering the city and the adjoining refugee camps. Hundreds were killed, hundreds more wounded.

No one in the AVG was hurt, but everyone was shaken by the close call and the carnage he witnessed. Some felt guilty, thinking it was probably their convoy that had led the Japanese to Paoshan. They decided to move on, but as they pulled away, with flames spreading through the city, scores of children ran alongside shouting *"Ting hao! Ting hao! Mei-kuo-ren ting hao!"* Very good! Very good! Americans very good!

As they neared Kunming, the ex-AVG black marketeers became more brazen, following more closely during the day and coming into camp at night to make deals with Frillman's drivers. He noticed that the cargos were shrinking. Tarpaulins that had been stretched out over full loads now sagged. Radios, tires, and cartons of cigarettes were missing. There was nothing he could do.

Another incident on that journey stood out in Frillman's recollections. One night before they crossed the border into China, they came upon two U.S. army sergeants who told them the new American general commanding the Chinese army, Shih Ti-wei, was Joseph Stilwell, and that he had just arrived at Lashio. Frillman had met Stilwell years ago when he was a missionary at Hankow and Stilwell was the somber, austere military attaché.

Frillman decided to take his convoy to Stilwell's compound in the hope of getting baths, clean beds, and American food.

The convoy pulled up to the camp in a great honking of horns, clashing of gears, squealing of brakes, and high-spirited shouting, stopping, by chance, directly in front of Stilwell's quarters. He immediately stormed outside, looking as though he had dressed for a meeting with the president. His decorations were lined up neatly on one side of his chest and his dress uniform was immaculate, accented with knife-sharp creases.

"We could not have looked worse or less military," Frillman said. The men were dirty and unshaven, dressed in outlandish combinations of civilian clothes and army uniforms, cursing loudly as they climbed out of their jeeps and trucks and stared at Stilwell. The Anglo-Indian girls, also looking worse for wear, primped for the general, fussing with their hair and clothing. The group looked worse than a band of gypsies to Stilwell, and it was clear to him who they were. The initials *AVG* were painted in large, white, glaring letters on each vehicle.

Frillman approached Stilwell and quickly learned how appropriate the nickname "Vinegar Joe" was for the man. Stilwell did not recognize the chaplain and before Frillman could explain, he launched into a diatribe, calling them, among other things, a disgrace to the United States Army, which, of course, they were not part of.

The drivers began to mutter about desk-bound generals and Frillman kept trying to apologize for their appearance, when a station wagon skidded to a halt beside him. The driver, an ex-AVG black marketeer, got out, along with his fat Anglo-Indian girlfriend, her mother, and a batch of children of several hues. The back of the car was filled with bottles of gin, and it was obvious that the occupants had been drinking all day. They crowded around Frillman and Stilwell, waving empty bottles in the air.

"See what I mean?" Stilwell said, with all the sarcasm he could muster. He turned on his heels, marched back into his house, and slammed the screen door. His first encounter with the AVG did not bode well for them.

T E N

PLAY BALL OR ELSE

"That whorehouse of mine," Chennault said to Theodore White. "That's worrying me." It was early 1943 and White, an old friend from Chennault's Chungking days, was writing an article for *Time* magazine. He had asked Chennault how his feud—his open warfare—with General Stilwell had begun.

By then Chennault was back in the U.S. Army Air Corps, and his outfit was under Stilwell's command. The Flying Tigers had been disbanded. Their replacements were contracting venereal disease in Kunming's Slit Alley in record numbers. The girls were keeping more of his men out of combat than the Japanese were. Chennault had to do something. He couldn't pen the men up in stockades, but he had to keep them healthy enough to fly.

And so he established the whorehouse. "The boys have got to get it," he told White, "and they might as well get it clean as get it dirty." He had sent an army transport plane over the Himalaya Mountains (the Hump) to India with a medical crew to bring back twelve healthy Indian prostitutes to serve the morale and protect the well-being of his men.

Stilwell knew nothing about it, and Chennault, aware of his commander's puritanical nature, thought it best not to ask for authorization. The official provision of brothels, where the girls were regularly inspected, was common in some armies but not in the American army, and when Stilwell did find out about it, he was irate. "Not the U.S. Army, goddamn it." White described Stilwell's reaction. "The U.S. Army would not fly whores across the Hump in Air Corps planes; it established no brothels for its men. . . . Stilwell had the morality of Oliver Cromwell—he was pure, absolutely pure, of graft, adultery, lying, thievery, or any transgression of the Ten Commandments."

There could hardly have been two generals in the same army more different than Joseph Warren Stilwell and Claire Lee Chennault. The fortunes of war placed them in each other's way, seething at the other's actions, and trying every way they knew to get rid of each other until their superiors finally solved the problem by getting rid of them both.

It had started well, that most rancorous of relationships. Chennault said that Stilwell was "uniquely qualified" to lead the growing American military presence in China, to undertake what he called the most difficult diplomatic job given any American officer during the war. Indeed, in all the U.S. Army, there was no one other than Stilwell who had the formal requisites for the post. He had sufficient rank, the three stars of a lieutenant general, to deal with his counterparts in the Chinese and British armies; years of experience in the training of troops for combat; and nearly a decade of service in China. He had been an army language student there, then a construction engineer, a battalion commander in a regiment commanded by George Marshall, and military attaché in Peking in 1937–1938. Even Chennault agreed—and said so even after they became enemies—that Stilwell was a great and courageous field soldier.

It was no wonder that General Marshall, the army chief of staff, recommended Stilwell for the job of chief of staff to Chiang Kai-shek and commander of all U.S. forces in China. In addition to Stilwell's positive qualities, however, he possessed certain negative attitudes and characteristics that would eventually undermine his work and lead to his downfall. Despite his years in China, Stilwell lacked the tact and diplomacy needed to deal with Chiang. He quickly came to dislike Chiang and openly ridiculed him to others, referring to him as "the Peanut," a nickname that eventually reached Chiang's ears. Stilwell did not think highly of the Chinese people in general, regarding them as incapable of conducting their affairs without American direction.

Because he had no respect for Chiang, Stilwell had even less for those Americans whom he saw as being allied with the Chinese leader. It did not take him long to learn of Chennault's wholehearted devotion and loyalty to the Generalissimo. And that knowledge made it difficult, even impossible, for Stilwell to trust Chennault. In addition, Stilwell had little understanding of the uses of air power. He was a foot soldier, one of the best the army had ever produced, but he seemed to be prejudiced against any weapon more complicated than a sidearm, a rifle, or a bayonet.

But all this enmity and distrust between Stilwell and Chennault was in the future. There were no signs of it when they met in Kunming on March 4, 1942, shortly after Stilwell's arrival from the States. The two men had met once before, also in Kunming, on December 31, 1938, when then Colonel Stilwell was military attaché and Chennault was a civilian consultant to the Chinese Air Force. They had a long dinner at the Hotel du Lac, where, according to Chennault's recollection, they spent the evening discussing the status of the Chinese Air Force.

Their respective situations had changed radically by the time of their second meeting in 1942. Chennault, although still a civilian, was leading a highly effective fighting force. His outfit was one of the few anywhere in the Pacific that had been able to defeat the enemy. The Flying Tigers and their leader had become heroes back home. Stilwell, with his three stars, was new to the war in China, but he was there to command the American part of it, and that would include Chennault.

"Had a long talk with [Chennault] and got him calmed down," Stilwell wrote in his diary after their March 4, 1942, meeting. What he apparently calmed Chennault down about was the future of the AVG as a civilian operation. Chennault's pilots could not continue to function with that status. The outfit would have to become part of the army. Chennault may not have liked the idea, but he recognized its inevitability. The choice was his. He could protest and threaten and argue in an attempt to continue fighting his own private war. He knew, however, that if he did so, he would soon run out of planes, parts, and men. There would be no replacements for him once the army was in charge of the war in China. A formal air corps unit would be established, and he would be given no part in it. His war would be over.

The alternative that would keep him in the fighting was to agree to the induction of the Flying Tigers and hope that he would be appointed its commanding officer. He would have to take orders again, to deal with the chain of command and all the other bureaucratic restrictions he had chafed under before, but at least he would still be in the war. And so he agreed when Stilwell spoke to him about incorporating the AVG in the American army. "He agreed to induction," Stilwell wrote, "and said he'd be glad to serve under me. That's a big relief. . . . He'll be okay."

There was only one thing wrong with Stilwell's rosy assessment. Chennault may have agreed to induction, but the majority of his men were dead set against it.

A few of the AVG pilots also met General Stilwell that day in March 1942. Charlie Bond was in Kunming with another pilot to swap two of their wornout P-40s for better ones. Bond and some others introduced themselves to the general as he stood near a DC-3, discussing the war situation with his staff. Stilwell was interested in the fighting the men had been in around Rangoon, but, overall, his mood was pessimistic. He told the pilots that the situation was bad and that MacArthur's stand in the Philippines and the victories of the Flying Tigers provided the only good news in the entire war.

He didn't talk to them about their future. Nothing was said about becoming part of the U.S. Army. "Met a group of the pilots," Stilwell wrote. "They look damn good." Likewise, Bond and the others seemed impressed with Stilwell, particularly with his promise that the Japanese would surely pay for their aggression.

Just before he was due to fly back to Magwe, Bond was called to Chennault's office and told that his squadron, the First, would soon be replaced by Olson's Third Squadron. Bob Neale's Adams and Eves needed a rest, and it would do the Hell's Angels a world of good to escape the boredom and dissension at Kunming.

In those early days of March 1942, the nature of the air war over northern Burma was changing. The Japanese were becoming much more cautious in the air, not wanting to tangle with the AVG even though they outnumbered them by almost twelve to one. Fewer than 30 P-40s were based at Magwe, and not all of them were able to fly every day. To oppose them the Japanese had 14 air regiments comprising 450 planes at bases in Thailand and at the former AVG and RAF fields in southern Burma. Even with those odds, Japanese leaders ordered their pilots to avoid air battles with the Americans.

The new Japanese strategy was to hit the AVG only when their planes were on the ground. They sent high-speed, high-altitude reconnaissance planes over the field at Magwe, hoping to find all or at least most of the AVG aircraft on the ground at the same time. If they could not beat the Flying Tigers in the air, they would try to do so on the runway, or to capture their bases so that they could no longer menace Japanese operations in Burma. In early March, after the fall of Rangoon, Japanese army leaders planned their advance north. It would take them no more than eight weeks to capture the rest of Burma and to begin their move into southern China.

The Japanese were not the only ones to change their tactics in the air. Chennault knew the size of the enemy air force facing his men in Burma, and he realized how vulnerable Magwe was. One well-timed surprise raid could wipe out the AVG there. So he shifted from defensive to offensive tactics. He ordered quick hit-and-run attacks on Japanese airfields in the hope of destroying as many planes as possible on the ground before they showed up in the skies over Magwe.

The first raid took place on March 5, the day after his meeting with Stilwell. Bob Neale led the First Squadron to Namsang, an RAF field just north of the Thai border. There they were to refuel and join a force of eight Blenheim bombers, three Brewster Buffalos, and six Hurricanes, a major striking force for the Allies.

The British force, coming from another field, appeared overhead, but instead of circling to give the Flying Tigers time to take off and join them as planned, they kept on going. Neale led his pilots aloft and turned south into Thailand, but he saw no sign of the bombing force. When the fighters returned to Namsang, they learned that the bombers had gotten lost and never made it to the target.

After that fiasco, no more large-scale raids were planned for two weeks. Gradually, men and planes of the Third Squadron filtered into Magwe as replacements, and on the 13th, the last of the First Squadron left in a DC-2 bound for Kunming. Olson's Hell's Angels were now the AVG's fighting force in Burma and the action, on a small scale, began to pick up again. On most days the men patrolled over enemy lines, observing Japanese troop movements and reporting their positions to the British. After noting the location of the enemy troops, they often went in and strafed them. On the 15th, four AVG pilots strafed trucks and barges in southern Burma, and on their way back shot down a Japanese fighter.

The next day another mission was scheduled, this time with Hurricanes and Blenheims, all taking off from Magwe. They strafed and bombed Japanese positions and returned safely, having encountered no opposition in the air. Although they suffered no battle damage, the precious supply of aircraft continued to dwindle. One P-40 ran into a jeep while landing. The landing gear on another ship collapsed as it touched down. Tires blew and batteries wore down and the ground crew kept patching up the planes as best they could.

Off-duty hours were not very exciting, not like the good old days—and nights—in Rangoon. "We go swimming in the Irrawaddy River to get clean and some of us wash our clothes there," Olson wrote. "The food is good and we sleep well, getting up early in the morning. It's so hot in the afternoon that one can hardly work. There was a dance at the American club at Yenangyaung, Burma, about thirty miles from the field, last night; a number of our members attended but not much dancing due to lack of girls for partners."

A few members of the squadron used the old AVG base at Kyedaw as a refueling stop to increase the range of their missions from Magwe. At dawn on March 19, Bill Reed and Ken Jernstedt took off from Kyedaw and headed south toward a Japanese field located ten miles from Moulmein. That was 250 miles from Magwe, and the Japanese, convinced they were far beyond the range of P-40s, had made no attempt to camouflage or even disperse the 20 fighters on the field.

The two P-40s screamed over the field six times and destroyed 15 of the fighters. Not a single shot was fired at them in return. The Japanese were too stunned to react. The Americans then swung over the Moulmein airbase and made one pass, destroying three bombers and one transport. This time the enemy returned fire but so ineffectively that each ship sustained only one bullet hole. Reed and Jernstedt recorded the largest number of kills on any one mission in the AVG's history.

On the following day, the RAF scored a major surprise victory against the Japanese at their old base at Mingadalon. A force of Blenheims and Hurricanes hit the field in bombing and strafing runs and destroyed 12 fighters and 16 bombers. Several Japanese fighters scrambled and inflicted some damage on the Blenheims, but all the British planes returned safely to Magwe.

These two raids infuriated the Japanese, and they struck back with a terrible vengeance. Their target was Magwe and they set out to obliterate it. Over the course of more than twenty-five hours a total of 266 Japanese aircraft bombed and strafed the field.

The first wave, a force of 27 twin-engine bombers and 20 Zeros, struck at 1:30 in the afternoon. They were followed closely by a wave of 17 bombers. Explosions, flames, shrapnel, and bullets filled the air. Hangars and barracks were flattened. Blenheims loaded with fuel and bombs were set afire with incendiaries. They burned slowly at first, until the fire reached the gas and the bombs, then the planes detonated in sheets of flame and showers of shattered parts. Hurricanes and P-40s went up in quick, bright bursts. The Japanese bombardiers were accurate that day. Few of their explosives were wasted.

When the bombers finished their runs, the Zeros roared down to strafe the field. In the midst of the chaos, a British pilot crash-landed on the runway. Two AVG ground crewmen—mechanic

Henry L. Olson and crew chief John E. Fauth—left the safety of their slit trench and raced to the Hurricane. The plane was on fire, but the pilot was still in the cockpit. They grabbed hold of him and dragged him to the trench, though he screamed and fought their efforts to save him. Olson and Fauth ran back to the plane to try to douse the fire. The mechanics hated to see a ship lost, even a British one, if there was a chance of saving it. While they trained a fire extinguisher on the flames, a Zero spotted them and opened fire. Olson wasn't scratched, but Fauth was hit in the shoulder by a large-caliber bullet that almost tore his arm off. Olson rushed him back to the slit trench.

No sooner had he gotten Fauth safely back when he leaped out and started running across the bullet-splattered runway. He had seen pilot Frank Swartz get hit as the third wave of bombers flashed over the field. Olson got into a jeep and headed toward Swartz. A bomb exploded nearby and tossed the jeep into the air, throwing him clear. He slid thirty feet down the runway on the seat of his pants, unhurt. He found a sedan and drove back to the trench to get his crew chief, Fauth, then crossed the runway to where Swartz lay wounded.

Bombs peppered the field around the speeding car. Shrapnel broke some of the windows. Fauth yelled from the rear seat that Olson was "a damn fool to try to drive to the hospital during the raid." He kept saying that they "ought to get in a ditch." Olson knew, however, that Fauth might not survive if he did not get to a hospital, and when they reached Swartz, he knew he had no choice. Swartz's jaw had been almost completely blown off.

At the hospital Dr. Lewis Richards, one of the AVG flight surgeons, operated on both men. John Fauth had been wounded too seriously to save. He knew he was dying and asked Olson to write to his mother and to pay off a debt. He died at 4:30 in the morning, the first AVG ground crewman to be killed. Swartz was evacuated to Calcutta but later died of his injuries. The Americans sustained one additional casualty. Crew chief Wilfred R. Seiple was almost hit by a bomb that fell beside his foxhole. The concussion bruised his chest, causing internal bleeding, but he survived.

As the third wave of bombers pulled away, the men were

rounded up to see who else was missing. All were accounted for, but they were badly shaken by the experience and developed a fear of bombing that lasted a long time.

Not all the action took place on the ground that day. When the bombing began at 1:30, Parker Dupouy was leading a flight of six P-40s back to Magwe from a reconnaissance patrol they had been flying to the south. They heard the news of the attack over the radio and intercepted the first wave of twenty-seven bombers and twenty Zeros as they were heading back to their base. The P-40s dove right through the formation and in a brief fight shot down four fighters and damaged at least one bomber before their low fuel and ammunition forced them to break it off.

Two of the pilots, Dupouy and Ken Jernstedt, landed at Magwe during one of the Japanese bombing runs. As Dupouy lined up on the runway and throttled back, two Zeros got on his tail and sent a stream of bullets into the cockpit. The canopy shattered, showering him with glass splinters, and a bullet raked his arm from elbow to wrist. He landed with the Zeros still on his tail and ran to the shelter of a slit trench as more fighters swooped down and destroyed his plane.

Jernstedt made a forced landing among the exploding bombs and the burning wreckage of the planes. As he came in, bullets from a Zero smashed his windshield. The fragments bloodied his vision, but he touched down, steered the ship around the craters, and got out safely.

Several of the ground crew were firing at the strafing planes with tommy guns and .45s. Their chances of shooting anything down were slim, but it made them feel better to fight back. Crew chief Wakefield Manning did hit a Japanese fighter that may have gone down, but it was never confirmed.

When Chennault received word of the raid, he radioed Olson's Third Squadron to expect a repeat the next day. He knew the Japanese liked to take advantage of a victory and would try to wipe out whatever was left. Even with Chennault's warning, however, the men at Magwe were operating at a disadvantage. During the night, the British dismantled their radio warning equipment to prepare it for shipment to India. The system had not been all that satisfactory, but without it, there was no warning at all.

The Japanese arrived at 9:00 on the morning of the 22nd. The ground crew was working on the damaged planes, which had been dispersed to various points around the field. The pilots had gathered in front of the wreckage of the alert shack when they heard the sound of the approaching engines. There were 17 bombers and an uncounted number of fighters. The pilots raced for their planes, but the bombs were already falling. The men piled into jeeps and cars and roared away from the field.

At 2:30 that afternoon the enemy came again with twenty-seven bombers in the first wave and twenty-six in the second. As with the morning raid, there was not enough time for any of the Flying Tigers or RAF pilots to take to the air, and the destruction was enormous. Magwe ceased to exist as a viable air base. All the facilities had been damaged. The AVG was reduced to four flyable airplanes. The British were left with six Hurricanes.

That night Chennault ordered the squadron to evacuate north to Loiwing, China, more than 300 miles away. Some of the men immediately loaded up trucks and drove fifty miles away to spend the night alongside a mountain road so they would be far removed from the field in case the Japanese returned in the morning. The others headed out the next day in a long convoy for the two-day trip to Loiwing. The four pilots who still had planes flew out that morning. Each carried one bottle of oxygen and only a few rounds of ammunition, all that was left. They were grateful that they did not run into any Japanese fighters. They would not have stood a chance. In little more than a day, the AVG was finished in Burma.

Now Chennault wanted revenge. He was angry and humiliated at being chased out of Burma and he intended to strike back at the Japanese pilots who had destroyed Magwe. He suspected, on the basis of reconnaissance flights, that they had come from two air-fields in the far north of Thailand—Chiengmai and Lampang. He chose men from both the First and Second Squadrons to under-take an extremely hazardous long-range mission. Jack Newkirk would head a flight of four from the Panda Bears and Bob Neale would lead six from the Adams and Eves. Only ten planes were considered to be capable of holding up for that distance.

Not all the pilots were optimistic about the mission. Buster Keeton considered it to be "the most dangerous undertaking the AVG had done, going 120 miles into enemy territory where if you have to force land and the Japs didn't get you the jungle will." Jack Newkirk had a premonition that the mission would be his last. He went to see Chaplain Frillman and changed his will to provide for his bride, whom he had married just one week before leaving for the Far East. On the night before the pilots were to leave from Kunming, Newkirk told George Paxton that it was only a matter of time on strafing missions before someone would get killed. He gave Paxton his whipcord cloth to make himself a new uniform. "I don't think I'm going to need it," he said. Greg Boyington noticed that Newkirk seemed to clam up later that night. Normally so open and amiable, Newkirk refused to talk at all, about anything.

Everybody at the field at Kunming got up early on the morning of the 23rd to watch the takeoff. The planes flew to Loiwing to refuel and went from there to the RAF base at Namsang, near the Thai border. They reached Namsang just before dusk, took on additional fuel, and grabbed a few hours of sleep.

The plan called for them to arrive at the enemy fields at dawn. Newkirk's assignment was to hit Lampang and Neale's flight would attack Chiengmai. Takeoff from Namsang was set for 4:00 A.M.

In the primitive bamboo hut that served as the RAF washroom, the men cleaned up before going to bed. Greg Boyington was standing with Newkirk when a British sergeant stuck his head in the door and cautioned them about the water. It was all right to wash with, he said, but too polluted to drink or to use to brush their teeth. No sooner had the door closed when Newkirk dipped his toothbrush into the water and brushed his teeth.

"Jack, didn't you hear what that guy said?" Boyington asked.

"Well, after tomorrow," Newkirk said, "I don't think it'll make any difference."

There was no moon at 4:00 in the morning. A couple of old trucks were driven to the edge of the runway and the pilots took off by the dim glare of the headlights. They reached their targets at the first faint light of dawn. Neale's flight found more than 40 enemy planes neatly lined up on the Chiengmai runway. The sight reminded Boyington of the way planes used to be arranged at Pensacola, Florida, during his training days. Ground crews swarmed over the aircraft and crew chiefs were warming up the engines preparing them for another raid against the Allies. The Japanese pilots lounged nearby.

The Flying Tigers dove for the field. Charlie Bond was amazed at the target spread out before him. It looked like the entire Japanese Air Force had crowded onto the field. The AVG pilots roared down the lines of enemy planes, so low it appeared that their props might hit the Japanese pilots as they clambered into their cockpits.

Down the men came, pass after pass, setting at least 20 planes on fire and riddling a dozen others. The field was quickly engulfed in flames from one end to the other. Although no enemy planes were able to take off, the antiaircraft fire was getting heavy. It was time to head for home. The six fighters climbed and joined up in formation. No one was missing, but suddenly one of the P-40s started to waggle its wings. It was William "Black Mac" McGarry's ship, and it was rapidly losing altitude and speed.

Charlie Bond and Ed Rector tried to stay with him, steering him to the north. The Salween River that separated Thailand and Burma was not far ahead. If they could get McGarry that far, at least he would not go down in enemy territory. McGarry's plane started to trail smoke. Black Mac pushed back the canopy, rolled the plane over, and bailed out, no more than 100 feet above the trees. He landed in a small open area, got to his feet, and waved to his buddies. Bond dropped a map and another AVG pilot dropped him a chocolate bar. McGarry picked them up and ran into the trees.

He did not return to the AVG. McGarry wandered alone for four weeks in the teak forests of northern Thailand before being captured by the Thai police. They did not turn him over to the Japanese but kept him interned in a Bangkok jail where an American OSS team found him in early 1945.

Newkirk's flight of four P-40s found the Lampang field empty, so he decided to head for Chiengmai. On the way, they strafed some buildings and truck convoys on a highway. They set some storehouses on fire and inflicted other damage. Then Newkirk went after a Japanese armored car. The return fire hit the swooping P-40, and Buster Keeton saw a large fire spread quickly along the road for a distance of some 200 yards. It was Newkirk's plane. He had hit the ground at nearly 300 miles per hour. He never had a chance.

Despite the loss of two pilots, Chennault considered the mission a success, having destroyed most of an entire enemy air regiment. The remainder of the Japanese unit returned to Japan for replacement pilots and planes. Thus, the enemy striking forces that had been pounding Magwe and other British bases in Burma were placed on the defensive, and this allowed the RAF to complete their evacuation to India.

Chennault received thanks from RAF Air Vice Marshal D. F. Stevenson "for the breathing spell furnished us by your magnificent attack," and newspapers in the United States heralded the raid as a major victory. Some of the Flying Tigers were less enthusiastic. Charlie Bond agreed that the raid was a success but wondered if it was worth the price of two such excellent pilots as Newkirk and McGarry, as well as two airplanes. When Oley Olson of the Third Squadron heard about the losses, he called the mission "foolish," and Keeton, who had seen Newkirk go down, agreed. "From a military point of view it was a success," he said, "but not from my point of view for the AVG."

That night the survivors celebrated in a bar. "Everyone was laughing and enjoying the moment," Bond recalled. "Yet Jack was gone and we weren't sure of Black Mac. It makes one wonder about the nature of human beings." Greg Boyington thought about Newkirk, about how quiet he had been two nights before, and how indifferent he had been to brushing his teeth in the polluted water. Boyington came to the conclusion that Newkirk "had gotten the word."

Loiwing, the new base for Olson's Third Squadron, was an American paradise in the midst of the primitive Chinese wilderness. It had all the comforts of home and then some; few Americans in the United States could afford such luxury. What a difference from the shattered base at Magwe they had been forced to leave. Most of the elegance, however, was reserved for William Pawley's CAMCO employees. Loiwing was the site of the factory and repair facility.

Surrounding the factory was a model American town consisting of rows of neat white cottages laid out in an orderly pattern. The machinery in the factory and the furnishings and plumbing in the living quarters were of the latest American design. Paul Frillman commented that "it was eerie to drive from the primitive countryside into this patch of modern efficiency and comfort." The cottages were for CAMCO's married personnel. Bachelors lived in dormitories within an enormous clubhouse that was equipped with a jukebox complete with bubbles and a comfortable lounge with draperies, sofas, and chairs all covered in matching flowered chintz. At one end of the lounge stood a massive fireplace and at the other end, a plate glass window overlooked the mountains. There was even a housemother. Ma Davidson stood ready to take care of every need and to provide plenty of good American food and hot water.

Olson's tired Third Squadron was permitted to use the clubhouse facilities, but they were housed less luxuriously down by the airfield. Compared with Magwe, however, it was like being at a plush resort.

At the airfield they made do with a flimsy bamboo operations shack on which they painted a sign to announce their presence: OLSON & CO.—JAP EXTERMINATORS—24-HR. SERVICE.

Not only were they more comfortable at Loiwing, but they were also safe from surprise attack. Chennault established 18 mobile warning net units in the areas south and east of the field. The Hell's Angels would get ample warning of a raid, at least until enemy troops got close enough to overrun the spotters.

They had been at Loiwing only a few days when they saw a long-awaited sight—replacement aircraft—new P-40s of the latest model, the P-40E Kittyhawk, with a longer range, greater speed, six .50-caliber machine guns, better radios, and auxiliary bomb racks. There were only six of the new planes, two at Loiwing and the others at Kunming, but even one was like a miracle.

It had taken a lot of prodding from Chennault's contacts in

Washington to get the RAF to agree to give up the six P-40s from a shipment bound for Libya. But it was Chennault's responsibility to get them to China from Accra on the West African coast, some 2500 miles away. He selected for the job six pilots: George McMillan, Tom Haywood, R. T. Smith, Charlie Older, Chauncey Laughlin, and Paul Greene. They flew to Calcutta aboard a CNAC plane and from there to Africa on a series of Pan American and BOAC passenger planes and American Ferry Command transports. It was a long, tiring trip, but the hardest part lay ahead, more than 50 hours flying in the cramped P-40 cockpits over deserts, mountains, and open water. The British thoughtfully provided a pilot in a Lockheed Hudson bomber to guide them.

The AVG pilots rose at dawn every day on the return flight, setting down at remote RAF bases long enough to refuel, eat a sandwich, and check the weather for the next leg of the trip. At dusk they settled in for the night to maintain their engines and to grab some sleep. The flight took them across the Sudan, up the Nile River valley, and over the uncharted Arabian desert and the Persian Gulf to Karachi. From there it was over the Hump and into Kunming. The round trip lasted three weeks, and the men delivered the new planes without mishap.

The pilots at Kunming were eager to try them. "On alert today and checked out in the P-40E," George Burgard wrote. "It [is] a great airplane with lots of speed, much better visibility and lands much more stably." "What I loved most," wrote Charlie Bond, "is the sound of those six fifties firing out front. What a swath they cut in the target on the lake. Look out, Japs!"

Toward the end of March, more pressure was brought to bear on Chennault to induct the Flying Tigers into the army. He had already told Stilwell that he agreed to the idea, but he had to find out how his men felt about it. Rumors had been circulating for weeks about the possibility of induction, but Chennault had never formally talked about it. On the night of March 26 he called a meeting of the men stationed at Kunming.

He told them that at the moment they were safe from induction and that they would remain a volunteer group "until the U.S. government freezes us out by not sending reinforcements in personnel and equipment." Keeton recalled that Chennault said "he would fight to the end to keep us a volunteer group." Chennault asked how many were in favor of the idea of being inducted. The majority loudly opposed it. Most of the men told Chennault they would prefer to resign and return home at once, or at best stay only until their contracts expired. Some indicated a willingness to be inducted if they were given leave to go home first.

The men were in poor shape by then, physically and emotionally, worn out by more than five months of combat and by the strain of believing they had been abandoned by their country. Many had come to dread their flying missions and to fear the possibility of getting killed in the final weeks before their contracts expired.

After the meeting, Chennault sent a radiogram to Madame Chiang:

CAREFUL CHECK MAJORITY MEMBERS OF AVG RE-
VEALS THAT NINETY (90) PERCENT WILL TERMINATE
CONTRACTS RATHER THAN ACCEPT INDUCTION INTO
US ARMY AIR FORCES IN CHINA. THIS ATTITUDE FIRM
DESPITE MY EARNEST PLEAS MAINTAIN GROUP RE-
GARDLESS. MEN NOT UNPATRIOTIC BUT ALL HOPE GO
HOME BRIEF VISIT BEFORE FINAL ENTRY US ARMY OR
NAVY.

Now Chennault had even more reason for concern about his future. If the majority of the Flying Tigers did not stay on to become the nucleus of a new air corps unit, then the chances of his being chosen to command such a unit were slim. The air corps would have less need of him if the unit were not composed mostly of ex-Flying Tigers whose personal loyalty he commanded. Two days later he expressed his bitterness about the proposed induction in an interview with Harrison Forman of *The New York Times*. He complained to Forman that converting his group to a military unit would mean the loss of its effectiveness for a minimum of four months while the change was taking place.

The Chinese people did not want to see the AVG broken up, he said, nor did the Americans. Only the Japanese would be pleased, and they would celebrate throughout Japan if it occurred. Chennault made several angry remarks to Forman, but the American public never had the opportunity to read them. The article was censored by an air corps colonel who had recently arrived in China to serve as Stilwell's air officer. He was Chennault's old adversary from the Air Corps Tactical School at Maxwell Field—Clayton Bissell—and he was now the ranking air corps officer in China.

Chennault had fought Bissell's appointment when he first learned about the possibility almost two months before, during the first week of January. Ever since America's entry into the war, Chiang Kai-shek had insisted that Chennault—his loyal and trusted air advisor—be the senior air commander in China, a demand apparently agreed to initially by General Marshall. But Hap Arnold insisted that the post go to Bissell, a regular—and regulation—officer. Soong agreed, without consulting with Chiang.

Chennault did not give up easily. He called on his friends and supporters in Washington, particularly presidential advisor Lauchlin Currie. On February 5, he had sent a cable to Currie, pleading his case:

> PERSONALLY AM WILLING MAKE ANY SACRIFICE FOR SAKE OF CHINA AND ALLIED CAUSE BUT CANNOT UNDERSTAND HOW EITHER WILL BE BENEFITTED BY SUPERSEDING ME AS SENIOR AIR OFFICER CHINA. PARTICULARLY WHEN OFFICER SELECTED, BISSELL, WAS JUNIOR TO ME UNTIL MY RETIREMENT. IN ADDITION HE HAS NO KNOWLEDGE OF CONDITIONS IN CHINA SUCH AS I HAVE GAINED IN ALMOST FIVE YEARS AND HE AND I HAVE ALWAYS DISAGREED UPON PURSUIT TACTICS AND EMPLOYMENT. IF METHODS USED IN TRAINING AND EMPLOYING AVG REQUIRE IMPROVING, SUGGEST SELECTION OF OFFICER WITH WHOM I CAN WORK HARMONIOUSLY. . . . AM MOST DISCOURAGED BY ATTITUDE WAR DEPARTMENT AND QUITE WILLING RESUME PRIVATE LIFE AS HEALTH CONTINUES POOR.

Four days later, Currie met with Arnold to intercede on Chennault's behalf and to urge that, if Chennault were not appointed senior air commander, someone of Chennault's choosing be selected instead of Bissell. Stilwell was present at the meeting in Arnold's office and witnessed Arnold's reaction to what they considered civilian interference in a military matter. "Arnold hit the ceiling," Stilwell reported. "I spoke for Bissell, and insisted that he rank Chennault. Currie pulled in his horns. I told him my opinion of Chennault had dropped a lot since hearing that. It was arranged for Currie to send Chennault another wire telling him to get in the game and play ball or else. They are acting like a couple of kids, and they'll both have to behave." It was settled. If Chennault wanted to stay in the war, he would have to work with Bissell, a man who, to Chennault, represented everything negative about the military.

Chennault—and other officers as well—considered Bissell to be more concerned with proper paperwork, detailed reports, and adherence to army regulations than with fighting the war. General Lewis Brereton, who commanded the Tenth Air Force, in India, complained to Arnold that Bissell was "saturated with peacetime routine and is unable to adapt himself to war conditions. . . . He calls for all sorts of detailed reports and asks far too many detailed questions that simply clutter up the communications lines to no purpose."

Bissell was, to a combat man, the quintessential, and detested, officious staff officer. Chennault described him as carrying his "military fetish for parade-ground discipline and the spit and polish of garrison life into a situation where combat results were the only real measure of success. I always felt that Bissell prized a snappy salute from a perfectly uniformed staff officer more than a Japanese plane shot down in flames."

Later in the war, pilots in Chennault's Fourteenth Air Force came to hate Bissell so much that they hired a non-English-speaking Chinese coolie to shout, "Piss on you, Bissell," to everyone getting off incoming transport planes. The Chinese man had no idea what he was saying, believing it to be a standard American greeting since so many people laughed when he uttered the words. According to Chennault, Bissell was not amused when one day he received the greeting himself.

On March 29, Chennault and Bissell met for the first time in many years at a crucial conference in Chungking to decide the AVG's fate. Also present were Stilwell and Generalissimo and Madame Chiang. Bissell and Stilwell made it clear that unless the AVG became part of the U.S. Army, it would be cut off from all supplies—gasoline, ammunition, parts, and aircraft. It would soon be unable to maintain itself or to fight.

Chiang reluctantly agreed to give up the Flying Tigers in return for Stilwell's promise to replace it with a complete American fighter group to be commanded by Chennault, who would be made a brigadier general. Chennault observed that throughout the meeting, both Stilwell and Bissell were more concerned with the process of getting rid of the AVG than with the problems of obtaining replacements or maintaining the air war against the Japanese. He knew there was just no place in the military organizational structure for his civilian, maverick outfit. For procedure's sake alone, it had to go—and as soon as possible.

Stilwell and Bissell wanted the AVG dissolved by April 30, only a month away. Chennault wanted to keep it going as long as he could, and with the support of Madame Chiang, got them to agree to the Fourth of July, the day when the AVG contracts would begin to expire. That was the day the AVG would lose its independence.

On April Fool's Day, the AVG had its second wedding, this one at Loiwing. Fearless Freddy Hodges married Helen Anderson, the daughter of a British warrant officer. They had met months before in Rangoon, where Helen worked in a department store, and had courted in the AVG hangout, the Silver Grill. She left Rangoon just before it fell and rode to Kunming in one of the AVG convoys. When Hodges was transferred to Loiwing, she joined him there.

"I was here three days," she recalled, "when Freddy and I talked it over. He said that it wouldn't do for me to be here as people would start to talk. But having no place to go, and not knowing where my mother and father are, I didn't know what to do. Freddy suggested we get married."

There was no minister in Loiwing so Freddy told Helen it was an old American custom to elect someone as mayor who would then have the authority to perform marriage ceremonies. The pilots elected M. D. Walsh, the manager of the CAMCO factory, inevitably known, because of his initials, as "Doc." That afternoon, while the wedding preparations were being made, the air-raid alarm sounded. Greg Boyington, on alert duty, climbed into his P-40 and sped down the runway. The engine sputtered and quit a second or two after he got airborne but before the wheels had been retracted, and he slammed into the ground so hard that his seat belt snapped, forcing his knees into the instrument panel.

The surgeon, Dr. Richards, taped Greg's knees with yards of adhesive tape and he was able to get to the wedding ceremony. His bandaged knees were so huge that he was unable to pull his trousers on, so he arrived dressed in a bathrobe. Still, he had no trouble getting himself "full of whiskey for the celebration."

No sooner had the ceremony ended when the alert sounded again, and everyone left the CAMCO lounge, running for cars and trucks to get away from the base. Everyone but Boyington. He decided to hobble out behind the building where he remembered seeing some slit trenches. He fell, of course, and had to be repaired all over again. Dr. Richards asked Boyington to do him a favor.

"I want you to stop drinking," he said, "because if you don't, I'm afraid you'll end up dead."

"Don't worry, Doc," Boyington said. "I promise. I've had enough."

A few days later, Boyington was sent to the base hospital at Kunming to recover, and a proper British clergyman was found to marry Freddy Hodges and Helen Anderson.

Things were slow at Loiwing until the afternoon of April 8. There had been an air raid alarm at 9:00 that morning, but, as had been the case for a week, no enemy planes appeared. Twenty of them came over at 12:45—Zeros on a strafing mission. Thanks to

Chennault's early-warning network, the AVG had a flight of twelve P-40s patrolling at 17,000 feet. Unfortunately, they were too high to see the Japanese fighters, who swooped low over the field and wrecked a Blenheim and a P-40 and wounded two Chinese soldiers.

Under fire, AVG radioman Harvey Cross called the P-40 patrol down. They pounced on the enemy and shot down ten fighters, half of the attacking force, and damaged two others, with no losses themselves. Not a bad day's work.

It was a bad day for Chennault in Kunming, however. Two crew chiefs had beaten up some of the pilots, and Chennault called a meeting of all AVG personnel that night. No one had ever seen him so angry. He told the men he would not tolerate any more such behavior and that he was kicking the crew chiefs out of the AVG immediately.

Then he turned to the topic of induction and made two inflammatory statements that may have been fueled by his momentary anger. Neither was true, and he must have known that one of the statements would antagonize his men. First, he told them they would not be inducted into the army. Second, he said that a new law passed in Washington prevented them from resigning from the AVG. The pilots and crewmen were stunned. Discussing the matter later, they agreed that Chennault's remarks sounded more like a threat than a fact. They were correct. No such law had been passed or even considered. Chennault's efforts, whatever their motivation, did nothing to improve the poor morale of the Flying Tigers at Kunming.

There had not been any combat for the Kunming flyers since the raid on Chiengmai on March 23. "Getting sort of restless sitting around," noted Buster Keeton. "This drag is getting thoroughly monotonous," echoed George Burgard. "We turned on the radio to listen to Bing Crosby and got homesick as hell. What a day. . . . Nothing doing all day except the usual cribbage and acey-deucey games. After work we played a little basketball, then a late shower and supper."

Occasionally something broke the cycle of boredom and it became the focus of conversation for days. One morning a pilot was found asleep in the alert shack with an exquisite Eurasian girl he had brought from Rangoon. The officer of the day added her name to the duty roster in big red letters, just beneath her lover's name. Everybody got a big kick out of that.

One night the governor of Yunnan Province gave a banquet for the AVG at his mansion in the hills overlooking Kunming. The men enjoyed the champagne and the absinthe, but not the Chinese rice wine. Those seated near the windows passed their wine outside to the Chinese guards. The governor toasted the AVG and President Roosevelt. Skip Adair, representing Chennault, who was in Chungking, made the governor an honorary member of the Flying Tigers.

Beautifully robed Chinese civilians staged plays throughout the dinner, and three of the pilots, dressed in Chinese costumes, put on their own skit. The Americans howled with laughter at their antics, but the Chinese guests seemed confused. As Burgard described it, they "got pretty well lit up" and enjoyed themselves. "Home late and almost out of control."

On April 9, ten pilots of the Second Squadron were ordered to Loiwing to bolster the forces there. Chiang Kai-shek had arrived at Kunming that morning for a hurried conference with Chennault. The situation in Burma was worsening. The Japanese were pushing the British and Chinese armies north from Rangoon, and they were already near Toungoo. Chiang wanted the AVG to fly daily missions over the front lines. If they saw enemy planes, they were free to shoot them down, but their primary mission would be to fly low over the Chinese troops in the hope that the sight of the planes would improve the soldiers' morale. It was the kind of mission the AVG pilots quickly grew to hate. Before long, it would lead them to mutiny.

Shortly before dawn on the morning of April 10, ten Zeros caught the Flying Tigers at Loiwing on the ground. It sometimes happened that atmospheric conditions in the early morning hours interfered with radio transmissions, so no reports had been received from the early-warning net. Most of the P-40s were widely dispersed, but two planes were being warmed up on the runway for the dawn patrol, with mechanics Dan Keller and Robert A. Smith at the controls.

Smith felt the controls of his plane go limp. The control cables had been severed by a burst of machine-gun fire. In the fraction of a second it took him to figure out what was happening, he heaved himself out of the cockpit and ran for a slit trench, with Keller not far behind.

Not a single P-40 got off the runway, and the Japanese pilots came over again and again, raking the field. "They took their merry time and shot a lot," Keeton said. The men on the ground fired back with tommy guns but didn't hit anything. The Zeros hit nine P-40s. Eight sustained minor damage and were able to fly again by noon. The other P-40 needed a new engine block.

At 11:00 the air-raid alarm sounded. The spotters reported that twenty-seven twin-engine bombers were on the way. The base was heavily overcast, and the Japanese flew aimlessly above the clouds, looking for a hole. A flight of P-40s, expecting low-level strafers, remained below the clouds. Finally the enemy bombers returned to their base.

At 3:00 that afternoon, twenty Zeros returned, intent on another strafing mission. Six P-40s and three Hurricanes were waiting for them. When the battle was over, seven Zeros were down—six accounted for by the AVG—and neither the Americans nor the British had lost a plane.

This was the kind of combat the men had signed up for, but it was getting increasingly rare to meet enemy planes in the air as the month of April wore on. Almost every day the men were called upon to fly what they called the "morale missions" over Chinese troops in the front line, sometimes two or three missions in a single day. The low-flying P-40s were an easy target for Japanese antiaircraft gunners, and sometimes the Chinese opened up on them by mistake. Every mission was dangerous, of course, but these flights did not even offer the consolation of an opportunity to shoot down enemy planes and thus earn a bonus. The men felt the same way about another kind of mission they were now flying regularly—escorting the slow, lumbering Blenheim bombers. Even if the bombers showed up for the rendezvous at the proper time and place, more often than not they could not find the target. It was all very discouraging.

Chaplain Paul Frillman paid a visit to Loiwing in the middle of

April and noted that the atmosphere was "most depressing. The Second and Third Squadrons were there and pilots and ground crewmen alike had dropped into a pit of disgust and exhaustion. It wasn't just the different work the AVG was now expected to do. They had been through months of tension and combat without any break. Few new planes or supplies, and no personnel replacements, had ever arrived, so they felt they were stranded and forgotten, expected to go on until they dropped."

On April 18, American airplanes bombed Tokyo. Chennault's long-held wish had come true, although it was not his mission. He was happy that the raid had taken place, but his pleasure was marred because he was deliberately not told about the mission in advance. Years later, at a reunion of AVG personnel, radioman Robert M. Smith asked Jimmy Doolittle, who had led the famous Tokyo raid, why Chennault had not been informed. Smith later wrote that Doolittle had told him "the American military leaders did not want to tell General Chennault about the raid, since he was so close to the Chinese and they feared that too many people would learn of the proposed date." Washington believed that Chennault could not be trusted with the information.

In addition to the blow to his pride, Chennault was bothered by the mission for a practical reason. He believed that if he had been informed, lives could have been saved, and he was probably right. The plan called for Doolittle's B-25s to land in China after the raid on Tokyo, and the planes were to be turned over to Chennault. The schedule for the mission called for takeoff from the carrier USS *Hornet* at a time that would put them over China during daylight hours so that the pilots could find the designated landing fields.

When the *Hornet* was spotted by a Japanese patrol boat, Doolittle's raiders were forced to take off earlier than planned. As a result, they arrived over China at night and in bad weather. Chennault remained convinced that had he known of the mission, his East China warning net plugged into one AVG radio station could have guided the planes to safety. As it was, all the aircraft were lost and the crews had to bail out or crash-land. One B-25 actually flew close to several safe airfields before coming down in enemy territory, where three of the crew were executed. "My bitterness over that bit of bungling [has] not eased with the passing years," Chennault wrote.

He always blamed Clayton Bissell for keeping him in the dark about the Doolittle raid, but the decision had been made in Washington. And another decision in Washington returned Chennault to active duty on April 15, 1942, as a temporary colonel, five years after having been retired as a captain. Nine days later he was promoted to temporary brigadier general, and so was Bissell, although Bissell's promotion was dated one day earlier than Chennault's. Thus, although Chennault had been senior to Bissell in their days together in the regular army, Bissell was now senior to Chennault. It was an old and effective army maneuver and it angered Chennault.

Now that he was back in uniform, however, certain behaviors were expected of him, one of which was a letter of congratulations to a commanding officer who has received a promotion. How it must have rankled Chennault to write such a letter to Bissell. He put off the chore for three weeks before writing on May 12.

> Dear Clayton:
>
> May I offer my sincere though belated congratulations upon your promotion? I never see official orders and only hear of them by chance. I know no one more richly deserving of promotion to the grade of general officer nor do I know any one else who has so thoroughly prepared himself for the duties of that grade.
>
> With my very best wishes for your continued success and advancement, I am
>
> > Yours most sincerely,
> > C. L. Chennault

Chennault did not have the silver stars of his new rank to pin on his uniform, and there was no PX in Kunming at which to buy them. On May 5, Jimmy Doolittle stopped there on his way to the United States, via Calcutta. He, too, had been promoted to brigadier general. Learning that Chennault had no stars, Doolittle gave him his own. Doolittle later noted where he had obtained the stars he gave Chennault—they had been given to him by Clayton Bissell. (He did not tell Chennault.)

Chennault's new rank and military status increased his desire to see the Flying Tigers inducted into the U.S. Army Air Corps, and it deeply affected his relationship with his men. Paul Frillman wrote that Chennault "made no secret that he thought all his men should follow him in, and this raised a barrier between them." Buster Keeton reflected on the change: "All the pilots in the group have had the most respect for the Colonel of any one man in the world, but it's beginning to change. We are beginning to feel as though he has changed and is using us as a means to the end. He has changed a great deal and we have found out why. He was made a Brigadier General in the U.S. Army Air Corps and has to take orders the same as anybody else."

The relations between Chennault and his men would never quite be the same. "Something had gone wrong," Olga Greenlaw said. "The place was not the same. The Army was moving in."

E L E V E N

LIKE A MAN EATING BITTERNESS

The pilots at Loiwing mutinied just three days after Chennault was recalled to active duty. He called it the "pilots' revolt," and it was a major crisis in the life of the AVG and in the changing relationship between Chennault and his men. The disgust and exhaustion that Chaplain Frillman had observed at Loiwing, combined with the growing frustration and anger at the continuing morale and escort missions, finally exploded in outright rebellion, a refusal to obey orders, and a threatened mass resignation.

The morale missions were becoming increasingly dangerous. By mid-April, the dry weather had sparked giant forest fires all over northern Burma, covering the landscape with a smoky haze. It grew so bad that pilots often had to fly on instruments when they descended below 10,000 feet. They could not maintain formation in the haze and found that it was too easy to become lost. Even when the sky was clear, the situation was hazardous. There was no communication between the AVG and the Chinese troops and poor intelligence information about their precise location. More than once the American pilots found themselves flying into heavy flak over an area they had been told was still in Chinese hands.

The Japanese took advantage of these morale missions and several times pounced on the low-flying P-40s. No one was shot down, but some close calls were reported. The Japanese now occupied the old Flying Tiger base at Toungoo, fifteen minutes' flying time from the front line, which meant that Japanese troops could call up their fighters quickly, as soon as they spotted the AVG planes. They also established heavy flak positions close to the front line, where the low-flying American planes made such good targets.

Morale grew worse every day, as the Chinese and British armies retreated ever farther north. Stilwell wanted the enemy stopped. "Now they intend to hold the line," wrote R. T. Smith in his diary, "and want us to give them air support. Our twelve ships against the whole damn Jap Air Force. It seems mighty futile to all of us and we're wondering what's taking the U.S. so damn long to get something over here. At this rate our morale won't be very good fast! Phooey!"

Chennault did not like the morale missions either. He, too, thought they were a poor use of his planes, but he was caught in the middle. Now that he was back in the army, he had to take orders from his superior officer, Stilwell. He also had a contract to fulfill with Chiang Kai-shek calling for him to defend China against the Japanese. Thus, the morale missions had to continue and so did the escort duty. Accordingly, he scheduled a raid to support Blenheim bombers against Chiengmai, and that was what touched off the revolt. The last time the Flying Tigers went to Chiengmai, they lost Newkirk and McGarry. In favor of that earlier mission, however, was the fact that they had been able to surprise the enemy at dawn and get away fast. For the present mission, the British bombers did not even plan to take off until 7:00 A.M., putting them over the target well into the morning hours. Thus, there would be no chance to catch the enemy by surprise. The P-40s would be tied to the slower bombers, which would keep them over the target for a relatively long time.

Chennault's men refused to fly the mission and requested a personal meeting with him to air their gripes. On April 18, Chennault met with them in the beautiful lounge of the clubhouse. The pilots told him they felt they were being asked to sacrifice themselves on worthless missions in airplanes that were no longer fit for combat. The men were still willing to fight, to defend their airfields against Japanese attack, but until they got new planes, they were unwilling to undertake what they saw as useless offensive missions.

Chennault was angry. He reminded them that he was now a brigadier general in the United States Army—his promotion was a few days away, but he knew it was coming—and that he had to follow orders from Allied headquarters. Because of the worsening situation in Burma, the Flying Tigers would have to fly more, not fewer, morale missions, and to escort the Blenheims on the Chiengmai raid. They had no choice, he said.

This was not completely accurate. Chennault was in the army but his pilots were not. He had to carry out Stilwell's orders but they did not. They did have a choice. They could quit.

The arguments escalated and Chennault's temper rose. Finally, he challenged them and accused them of cowardice. "If you want to show the white feather," he said, "you can all quit."

The pilots were shocked. "Tossing in the 'white feather' phrase got under everybody's skin," recalled Buster Keeton. "My God—white feather!" said R. T. Smith. "After what guys like Tex Hill, Lawlor, Keeton, Older, and even I have shown we can do in the air, with all the odds against us. I came right out and said he knew damn well we were no cowards. The colonel said, 'By white feather, I mean insubordination.' I insisted it meant cowardice."

And so did every pilot there. It was pointless for Chennault to say that he had meant anything else. Clearly, he had gone too far.

"The pilots are bitter," wrote George Paxton in his diary. "They feel Chennault is bloodthirsty and will sacrifice the AVG to the last man. The situation is so hopeless. The demands made on him and the AVG are so great as to be absolutely impossible, except that Chennault will never admit impossibility. They are expecting us to fight the whole war out here. Chennault is desperate. He keeps telling us the most important thing is to beat the

Japs. That is more important than any of us personally, including himself."

After the meeting with Chennault, the pilots discussed the situation among themselves. They drew up a petition describing the inadequate condition of their aircraft and the absolute superiority of the Japanese Air Force, contending that the morale missions were not only dangerous but also unreasonable. The petition further stated that unless changes were made, they would resign. Of the 34 pilots of the Second and Third Squadrons present, 28 signed the petition. Olson gave it to Chennault, who immediately called a meeting for the following day.

This would be the showdown. If so many pilots quit, the AVG would fold, and if the First Squadron pilots at Kunming learned of the mass resignation, many of them would leave, too. Chennault would have no air force and a very doubtful future.

Although he was aware of this possibility, Chennault did not alter his attitude or his approach. He made no attempt to placate or appease his pilots. Such was not his style. He appeared as blunt and threatening as he had been the day before, feeling, perhaps, that the revolt represented disloyalty to him personally. He made it clear to the men that he was still their superior, and, by God, they had better obey his orders.

He told them he would not accept their resignations and that any further refusal to fly a scheduled mission or to attempt to resign would be considered desertion in the face of the enemy. As Keeton recalled it, Chennault said that if the pilots quit, they would be considered deserters. "He would send all our names to Washington."

Tall, serious Tex Hill rose to speak, and, more than anyone else present, saved the AVG that day. "We came to China as mercenaries," he said, "there are no bones about that, but now we have a different situation. Our country is at war. And these are our orders. This is what the Old Man says we got to do. We ought to do it."

He added that he didn't like the missions any more than anyone else, but the United States was fighting for its life and the pilots had to put all personal considerations behind them.

Hill volunteered to lead the mission to Chiengmai. Four others said they would go with him—Duke Hedman, Frank Schiel, R. J. "Catfish" Raines, and Ed Rector—and that effectively ended the pilots' revolt. Chennault tore up the petition.

Still, the men believed their stand had been worthwhile and that they had made their point about the foolhardy missions. "At least we showed [Chennault] what we thought of some of the missions and tactics employed," wrote R. T. Smith, "so he, and all of us, are forgetting the whole affair and carrying on as usual." But Chennault did not forget. He couldn't.

The escort mission to Chiengmai was scheduled for the following day, but the British bombers never showed up at the rendezvous point with Hill's flight. Luckily the raid did not take place; none of the Flying Tigers might have made it back. Two of the P-40s had oil trouble and a third had not been filled with sufficient fuel. They would not have been able to reach Chiengmai and return. Another ship had a burned-out generator—none of its guns would have been able to fire.

When Chennault returned to Kunming, he knew he had to do something about the morale missions. He shared his pilots' feeling that they were a waste. He wrote to Madame Chiang, describing how unproductive the missions were and how strongly they affected the pilots' morale. He asked her to convey his opinions to the Generalissimo and to secure his permission to abandon those missions and to let the AVG stick to what it did best—fight the Japanese planes and strafe the enemy supply routes. On April 23, he received the answer he hoped for. There would be no more such morale missions.

To boost the spirits of his men, Chennault sent a radiogram to Bissell asking for a message of encouragement to the AVG from President Roosevelt. Perhaps such an appeal would persuade the men to stay on and continue the fight as part of the army:

URGE IMMEDIATE APPEAL BY PRESIDENT ALL MEM-
BERS AVG REMAIN ON DUTY HERE WITH PROMISE
EARLY REINFORCEMENT. GROUP LITERALLY WORN
OUT NERVES MORALE SHOT. PILOTS QUITTING BE-

CAUSE OF PRESENT EMPLOYMENT OF LOW ALTITUDE
RECONNAISSANCE AND LACK OF SUPPORT FROM ANY
OTHER AIR UNIT.

Bissell reacted immediately to Chennault's request and in three
days a message from Roosevelt arrived at Kunming. It was everything Chennault wanted and it emphasized that reinforcements
would arrive for the military unit the Flying Tigers were slated to
become on July 4—the 23rd Fighter Group. Roosevelt, like
Bissell and other air corps leaders, assumed that the men of the
AVG would accept induction.

April 23, 1942

The outstanding gallantry and conspicuous daring
that the American Volunteer Group combined with
their unbelievable efficiency is a source of tremendous
pride throughout the whole of America. The fact that
they have labored under the shortages and difficulties
is keenly appreciated.

We are sending great numbers of new airplanes to
bring the 23rd Fighter Group up to full strength and to
maintain that strength for the coming critical periods.
There are reinforcements on the way, both ground and
flying personnel, and more are to come. The United
States is making a tremendous effort to get the necessary material into the hands of the men overseas. . . .

Leaves of absence should be given to AVG veterans
just as soon as replacements have absorbed your experience, training and tradition, for rest and recupera-
tion. It is planned that when replacements are ade-
quately trained AVG veterans will be recalled to the
States or other theaters of operations to import their
combat experience and training to personnel in newly
formed units.

Your president is greatly concerned that the 23rd
Group be fully supplied and kept in operation during
the critical phase of the operations now pending. He
has taken great pride in the worldwide acclaim given

the Group and places great hope in its future fighting as rapidly as it is re-equipped.

Franklin D. Roosevelt

Most of the men of the Flying Tigers were not impressed by Roosevelt's appeal. They wanted to go home. They had been in China too long.

Chennault had done his best to ease the plight of his men, but he was still angry. Frillman saw him when he returned to Kunming and remarked that "Chennault could look grim at the best of times, and for days after the mutiny his face was like a sprung trap." Even seven years later, when Chennault described the pilots' revolt in his memoirs, the anger was apparent.

Seven new P-40Es arrived on April 21. They were picked up in Karachi by a group of pilots led by Charlie Bond. They had left Kunming ten days earlier aboard a CNAC DC-3 in the company of an attractive blond woman wearing the insignia of a war correspondent. She had been interviewing members of the AVG.

Chaplain Frillman had run into her a few nights before when he was awakened by noisy laughter coming from the pilots' bar. He staggered into the middle of a terrific party, but among those present were some of the pilots who were scheduled to fly at dawn, only a few hours away. It was everyone's responsibility to see that pilots on dawn alert got to bed early the night before, so Frillman told the woman she would have to leave.

"But don't you know who she is?" one of the pilots said.

"I don't care if she's the Queen of England," Frillman said, "it's time to go." With that, the party broke up.

The next morning at breakfast, Frillman saw the woman sitting with Chennault. He called the chaplain over and introduced him to Clare Boothe Luce, co-owner, with her husband, of *Time* and *Life* magazines.

"We've met," she snapped. Her voice carried, Frillman recalled, "as heavy a frost as Stilwell's."

The CNAC flight stopped at Lashio, where the AVG pilots ran into an air corps officer who knew Bond and gave them an exciting bit of news. If they decided to quit the AVG, he said, Pan

American Airways would hire them on the spot for $750 per month. Bond and the others made a mental note of the offer. Like most of the men in the AVG, they were uncertain about their future.

Their next stop was Calcutta, where they visited Frank Swartz, the pilot who had been wounded in the air raid on Magwe. They did their best to cheer him, but the sight of Swartz and of a number of wounded RAF pilots, one of whom was wrapped in gauze from head to foot, depressed them. This could be the future for any of them. Swartz told them he was due to be returned to the States for plastic surgery, but he died while still in India.

Bond and his group had a wild time in Calcutta, acquiring a following of buxom chorus girls, lots of booze, and—a rarer treat—hamburgers and milkshakes for lunch. Their partying lasted all night, and they just made it to a BOAC flying boat for the last leg of their journey. One of the pilots arrived at the dock with a girl still clinging to his arm.

In Karachi the men found a large fleet of American planes— P-40Es, B-17s, and B-24s—more aircraft than they had seen since leaving home. It was good to see Americans in uniform, too. It meant that reinforcements might reach them in China before long. The base commander was British, and he soon dubbed the AVG pilots the "seven wild men," because they displayed no discipline on the ground or in the air. They were subordinate to no one, neither the RAF nor the high-ranking American officers, and the U.S. pilots stationed there envied them their freedom and free-wheeling style.

Bond and his men were impressed with the presence of the American air force, but not with its organization. "Hell," Bond said, "the USAAC is in a bigger mess than we are in the AVG." No one seemed to know what was going on.

It took four days to bring the planes back to China, laying over in New Delhi, buzzing the Taj Mahal, and roaring in over Calcutta at 500 feet, 1500 feet below the minimum altitude allowed. They stayed for two days, hunting for their chorus girls and managing to have an exciting time. Bond received a job offer from CNAC at $800 per month. They also met seven ground crewmen from Kunming who had quit and were on their way home. They painted a gloomy picture of the situation at Kunming and left Bond with the impression that large numbers of the AVG were leaving.

On April 20 they flew over the Hump at 12,000 feet to Loiwing, where Chennault—there to smooth over the pilots' revolt—greeted them and filled them in on the situation. The following day they flew on to Kunming where Bond was informed that he had been promoted to vice squadron commander of the First Squadron, Boyington's old job. Boyington had resigned that day. "Big news of the day," George Burgard noted in his diary, "was Boyington's resigning. This made most everybody happy."

Boyington had had a rough convalescence from the knee injuries he had received April 1, the day of Hodges's wedding. In the hospital, next to Kunming's Hostel Number 1, he had few visitors, and he had "a hell of a lot of time to indulge in feeling real sorry for myself." When he could no longer bear the inactivity, he got the doctor to put his knees in casts so he could fly again. Every day he would take up ships whose engines had been overhauled and fly them in slow circles over Kunming, getting them ready for others to take on combat missions.

Boyington's drinking grew worse, and before long he was getting into trouble. Skip Adair was ready to bring him to trial for breaking into the group's liquor supply. He was convinced that Boyington was responsible because he was the only man strong enough to twist the lock off the door with his bare hands. Boyington had an alibi, however, having spent most of the evening with Olga Greenlaw and some of the pilots.

Shortly thereafter, he went on a bender for six days and showed up for alert duty still under the influence. Bob Neale, the squadron commander, was irate and accused him of drinking while on duty. Boyington interrupted Neale's tirade to ask a question.

"Have you got the keys to your car?"

Neale, silenced for the moment, handed him the keys.

"Good-bye, fellows," Boyington said. "I am going over to the Adjutant's office and turn in my resignation. . . . Guess that's what you all want."

Boyington left Kunming on the next CNAC flight. He left a note for Olga Greenlaw, who was away from the base at the time.

"By the time you get here, I shall be gone. I have resigned because I think it was the best thing to do. 'For the good of the service' shall we say? I want you to know that I am not a coward, but I don't have to tell you that. Best of luck to you, and here's hoping we meet again."

"Another friend gone," Olga wrote later. "I felt sad and sorry for this boy who had bobbled his chances."

Japanese troops continued their push northward through Burma. The AVG at Loiwing flew almost daily strafing and bombing missions, pounding the enemy front lines, but nothing stopped the relentless drive. The American pilots could destroy a column of tanks and armored cars one day and find twice as many on the road the next day. "The Japanese have so much stuff and troops," Olson remarked, "that it is hard to stop them."

By April 25 the AVG was preparing to evacuate Loiwing. Trucks were being loaded with supplies—as they had been earlier at Mingadalon and Magwe—and were heading out on the Burma Road for the next post. Chennault ordered the Third Squadron, the Hell's Angels, to Mangshi, some eighty air miles away, adjacent to the Burma Road. The Second Squadron, the Panda Bears, would remain at Loiwing until the enemy got closer.

Olson's Third Squadron flew to Mangshi on the 28th. The new field was awful, with filthy accommodations in the middle of a malaria-infested area. Two ground crewmen got sick the first day, and everyone hoped they would not all have to stay there long. They didn't. In only four days, the AVG would be chased out of Mangshi, too.

As the end of April drew near, Chennault became concerned about how the Japanese Air Force would celebrate the Emperor's birthday on the 29th. He had been in the Far East long enough to know that April 29 was never a peaceful day. Surely some sort of victory would be attempted as a present for the Emperor. He also knew that the Japanese would expect him to be prepared for a major raid on the Emperor's birthday, so they might strike a day earlier. He believed the raid would come at Loiwing, his most vulnerable base.

Early on the morning of the 28th Chennault ordered a patrol to fly south into Burma to check out activity on enemy airfields. Every base they scouted was busy with preparations for what looked like a large operation. Chennault ordered all flyable P-40s off the field at Loiwing, sending them south to cover the likely bomber routes. But at 10:15 A.M. a force of 27 Japanese bombers came over undetected and bombed the field and the town. The runway was so heavily damaged that the AVG fighters had to land at Mangshi for refueling and rearming.

At the same time, Chennault received a report that Japanese fighters were strafing Lashio, the last Burmese town of any size that had not yet fallen into Japanese hands. Olson's Third Squadron was sent from Mangshi to intercept them, but they were gone by the time the AVG arrived. Shortly thereafter, Olson's group encountered 24 enemy fighters and shot down half of them, with only two P-40s downed and neither pilot injured.

The runway at Loiwing remained unusable until the following morning, but no vital facilities had been destroyed by the bombing. The CAMCO factory, with its store of spare parts and P-40s under repair, was untouched. It was not much of a birthday gift for the Emperor.

But what Japanese aircraft failed to accomplish, Japanese troops did. On April 29, Loiwing had to be evacuated. Enemy soldiers had raced through Lashio, only ninety miles away, and there was nothing to stop them from roaring up the Burma Road to Loiwing as fast as their tanks and armored vehicles could travel. Chinese resistance had collapsed into a disorganized retreat to the border. The men in Chennault's early-warning net had been killed in their isolated outposts or had fled for their lives.

The Americans burned everything at Loiwing—the clubhouse with the elegant lounge, the jukebox, the factory, and, sadly, 22 partially repaired or dismantled P-40s. By May 1, Japanese troops occupied the smoldering ruins. The war for Burma was over.

Mangshi was evacuated on May 1, and soon trucks and cars loaded with AVG ground personnel and supplies were strung all along the Burma Road, heading east toward Kunming. Olson's Third Squadron and Hill's Second Squadron flew in to Kunming, tired, dirty, unshaven, and disgruntled about being chased from one airfield to another.

The next morning Chennault sent eight planes to Paoshan on the Burma Road, 225 miles west of Kunming and only 80 miles from Mangshi. The pilots were to escort Chinese bombers in raids over Burma, trying to slow the Japanese advance. The field at Paoshan wasn't much, only a grass strip with no hard-surfaced runways, but it would do for a P-40. There was no longer any warning net in place to the west or south, so they would have to take their chances.

The pilots landed, refueled, and took off again as nine Chinese bombers flew over, heading south. Their mission was to bomb a bridge in Burma, but the Chinese flew over it and bombed the town of Lashio instead, hitting the railroad marshaling yards with one bomb, though the others went astray.

The Flying Tigers landed at Paoshan, and the pilots drove into the city to find their quarters in an old monastery. Paoshan was jammed with refugees, the streets so full of people that the pilots had to fire their pistols in the air so they could clear a path for their vehicles. The next day the Chinese canceled their bombing raid because of bad weather, so the Americans occupied themselves with a cribbage tournament, a reconnaissance flight over Loiwing, and the downing of an enemy observation plane that had floated lazily up into Bob Neale's gunsight.

May 4 was different. The pilots were lounging in the alert shack when Neale yelled for them to get to their planes, but it was too late. A formation of twenty-five Japanese bombers was overhead at 18,000 feet. Neale shot off his pistol to warn the others, then everyone took cover in the nearest ditch. Charlie Bond made it to his plane and started the engine.

"I sat there in my cockpit with my hand on the throttle. I paused a second. Hell, I can make it!" Concerned about getting airborne before the bombs dropped around him, he forgot to raise his flaps and barely cleared a pile of rocks at the edge of the field. He found that he was not climbing fast enough, checked his instruments, then realized that the landing gear was down.

Bond headed for the bombers and discovered they had by-passed the field and were making a run over the center of the city.

He scanned the sky for enemy fighters but did not see any. He didn't see any other P-40s either. He roared down on the Japanese formation in three passes, concentrating on one plane that finally caught fire and dropped to the ground. He turned on another and squeezed the trigger. Nothing happened. He was out of ammunition. All those targets and Bond did not have a single bullet left.

He flew back over the city, which was covered with fire and smoke, and made for the field. As he was about to lower the flaps and landing gear he heard several explosions. Three Zeros were on his tail, pumping bullets into his ship. Some of them pierced the gas tank behind the cockpit, setting it on fire. Flames whipped around his legs. Being burned alive was every fighter pilot's nightmare. For an instant, he thought about giving up, but he reacted the way he had been trained, rolled a half-turn to the right, and dragged himself out of the cockpit until the airstream pulled him free.

He hit the ground in a Chinese cemetery. His scarf and flying suit were on fire. He found a stream to roll in, but pain quickly set in as blood flowed and blisters formed. Some Chinese civilians, taking refuge in the cemetery, had seen him fall, and using sign language, he persuaded them to telephone the airfield.

"The agony of my burns had me on the verge of passing out. I wanted to die to get out of the pain. I would lie down, get up, walk around, lie down, get up, hold my hand in the air to reduce the circulation and throbbing pain, cry out loud, and pray."

Doc Richards arrived from the field and surveyed the damage. Two bullets had creased Bond's scalp, and his eyelashes and eyebrows were gone. The left side of his face, his shoulder blades, the middle of his back, and his left hand were burned and blistered. He had also sustained an open wound in his neck.

While the doctor was helping Bond into the jeep, Bob Neale and some others arrived to report that another pilot, Benny Foshee, had been hit by shrapnel. A Chinese doctor insisted on amputating one of Foshee's legs, but Foshee refused. He wanted Doc Richards. It was an eight-mile trip through the bombed city to reach the monastery, and by the time they got there, Foshee had died from loss of blood.

The devastation they saw in Paoshan was massive. The streets were littered with bodies, or parts of bodies, and the wooden buildings had been reduced to piles of charred debris. The men choked on the odor of burning flesh, and the screams of the wounded filled the air.

Back in Kunming, another pilot died. John Blackburn was killed when his ship spun into a lake while on routine gunnery practice. "Things for us not so good today," wrote Olson in his diary.

Chennault wanted revenge for the attack on Paoshan. At dawn the next day he sent nine airplanes to Yunnanyi, midway between Kunming and Paoshan. At 9:45, his radioman intercepted a Japanese message saying that one formation of bombers had taken off from Mingadalon while another was preparing to leave from Chiengmai. Estimating their speed and range, Chennault knew they could not reach Kunming, but they could converge on Paoshan. He radioed his nine pilots at Yunnanyi to patrol the Paoshan area and to expect the enemy at 12:30. The bombers flew in at a much lower altitude than the circling P-40s and hit the field at 12:30, but this day the AVG radios were working so the planes could be called in. The AVG shot down eight planes before turning toward a second wave of bombers escorted by fighters. The second wave turned tail when they saw the Flying Tigers coming toward them.

Chennault and his men could still beat back the enemy in the air, but on the ground the Japanese could not be stopped. On May 5, the day of the AVG victory over the ruins of Paoshan, a Japanese armored column penetrated seventy-five miles inside China. The enemy was on the Burma Road, and there was no organized army in the way. If they got onto the Plateau of Paoshan, they could race unimpeded to Kunming. If Kunming fell, China would be lost, cut off from all Allied aid. Not even flights over the Hump could help if Kunming was captured, for there was no other central point of distribution that planes from India could reach or from which the airlifted supplies could be sent to China's armies.

Only two things stood in the way of a rapid and complete Japanese victory: the mile-deep Salween River gorge and Chennault's AVG. On May 5, the Japanese reached the western edge of the gorge, pushing the fleeing Chinese soldiers and civilians ahead of them along the Burma Road. "The panic that followed was unimaginable," wrote Paul Frillman, after hearing the stories of those who survived the rout. "Terrified drivers rammed one another off the road, or took too many chances trying to get ahead and went over the brink with carloads of people. Many vehicles that had stalled or broken down were mobbed by passengers rushing up from cars trapped behind. They were pushed off into space, complete with any people who had been too slow to get off."

The lucky ones made it across the Hweitung suspension bridge, hanging above the dirty brown waters of the Salween River, and started up the road torn out of the cliff on the other side. Japanese artillery opened fire across the gorge killing people by the hundreds. The Chinese blew up the bridge just before the Japanese reached it, sealing the fate of thousands of refugees who had not yet been able to cross. Japanese armored vehicles ran up the center of the road, through the columns of refugees, leaving them trapped.

Bob Neale, on a reconnaissance flight, was the first to see what was happening. He would never forget the mass of humanity jammed on the narrow road hewn out of the rock. The ledge was packed with refugees as well as Japanese vehicles and troops. From the top of the gorge to the bottom, thirty-five hairpin turns twisted back and forth, twenty miles of road to travel the one vertical mile to the river and the destroyed bridge. The next day, as more enemy troops arrived, the traffic was bumper-to-bumper as the Japanese waited for their engineers to bring pontoons to build a new bridge. By the following day, or the day after, they were expected to be across the river and on their way to Kunming.

After the war it was learned that the Japanese had not planned to push toward Kunming at that time. Instead, they planned to invade India. Furthermore, the Japanese lacked air cover. The Salween Gorge was out of range of their fighter bases in Burma and East China. However, had they been able to cross the Salween with ease and discover the lack of resistance between the river and

Kunming, they might well have taken advantage of the opportunity to knock China out of the war.

Only the AVG now stood between the Japanese and apparent victory. The Chinese troops who had escaped before the bridge was blown up were too disorganized and demoralized to offer any but the most feeble resistance. There was no time for a new army to be sent to the Salween to establish defensive positions. Chennault was sure that his pilots could stop the Japanese, but he also knew the Chinese refugees trapped with them would die. He was faced with a grim decision, whether to sacrifice some to save so many more, and it was not a decision he could make on his own. He could not take responsibility for the fate of so many of the Chinese people, so he sent a radiogram to Madame Chiang on May 6, describing the situation and asking the Generalissimo to authorize air attacks on the road. He received his answer the same day: destroy the enemy.

If not for the arrival of the new P-40Es equipped with bomb racks under their wings, the AVG would have had a difficult time in the battle of Salween Gorge. For months, Chennault and his armorers had been trying to make dive bombers out of the older model P-40s but without success. They had tried to fashion homemade bomb racks, had practiced dropping empty liquor bottles filled with gasoline, and had dropped bombs made of lead pipes with a .50-caliber machine-gun bullet in the nose through the flare chute, but nothing worked. The newer P-40Es came equipped with wing racks that could carry six 35-pound fragmentation bombs, and Sgt. Roy Hoffman, Chennault's chief armorer, developed belly racks for the planes that could carry the Russian 570-pound bombs, which the Chinese had in large quantity. Now Chennault had his dive bombers.

He also had experienced ex-Navy dive bomber pilots who were eager to show off their skills against such a tempting target. Four of them volunteered to fly the P-40Es—Tex Hill, Tom Jones, Ed Rector, and Frank Lawlor. Four other ships, P-40Bs, went along as top cover, flown by Oley Olson, R. T. Smith, Erik Shilling, and Tom Haywood. They attacked on May 7.

When they arrived over the target, they saw that Japanese engineers were taking pontoons out of trucks and setting them on the riverbank. The rest of the 20-mile column of troops waited quietly, "trapped in the open like flies on flypaper, a sheer precipice on one side of the narrow road and a rock wall on the other."

Tex Hill led his four dive bombers toward the top of the road leading into the gorge, and they dropped the big Russian bombs. Vehicles disintegrated in fiery explosions. Portions of the cliff face broke free, closing sections of the road and preventing the retreat of the enemy. Hill's flight then dropped their fragmentation bombs and strafed the enemy column with their six .50-caliber guns, destroying almost everything in their path. When their ammunition had been exhausted, Olson's group bore down on the flaming column to continue the strafing.

The planes refueled at Yunnanyi, and the P-40Es were loaded with more fragmentation bombs. This time they also took on incendiaries. At the gorge, the Japanese panicked when they saw the AVG returning, but there was no escape. They were cut down by the hundreds amidst burning gasoline, exploding ammunition, and flaming armored cars and trucks. Smoke rose thousands of feet into the air to mark the site of the massacre.

Chennault pressed the attack for four days, sending every aircraft he had in relays against the forces in the Salween Gorge. The Chinese Air Force loaned the AVG a flight of Curtiss Hawk-3s, biplanes that carried a single bomb and could rake the enemy with a lone .30-caliber machine gun. The Chinese also provided a flight of Russian SB-3 bombers, but they were in such poor mechanical condition that they could carry out only one mission.

The AVG devastated not only the enemy in the gorge but also the columns of trucks and tanks to the west. They burned out every town for miles along the Japanese side of the Burma Road, thus destroying any place the enemy could use as a supply depot. After four days of these concentrated attacks, Chennault reported to Madame Chiang that the only traffic along the road was heading back into Burma.

The Japanese never crossed the Salween Gorge. The AVG continued to attack their positions periodically until the monsoon season began in early June. Because of the constant threat of air attacks, the Japanese were never able to assemble sufficient men and materiel to attempt a river crossing. The stalemate lasted two years, until in 1944 some soldiers finally did cross the Salween. By then, however, these were Chinese troops and they were heading for Burma.

The victory at the Salween alone would have been sufficient to justify the Flying Tigers' existence. If not for the handful of tired American pilots and their maverick leader, the Japanese would have crossed the river and threatened China. The men of the AVG may not have looked like much to Bissell and to the other USAAC officers gathering in China, they may have been unruly and undisciplined, but they could improvise and work miracles with castoff equipment and limited supplies. They didn't salute, but they would fight beyond the point of exhaustion. Their four days over the Salween may have been their finest.

Not content with striking the enemy at the Salween River, Chennault wanted to hit them deep in their own territory. Following a suggestion made by one of his pilots, Tom Jones, he sent his men on a raid against the Japanese airfields at Hanoi. The mission would also show the enemy how long a reach the AVG had. Jones, known as an "eager beaver," had been a navy dive bomber pilot, along with Jack Newkirk, before joining the AVG.

Jones had had a run of bad luck. He contracted malaria his first week in Burma during a tiger hunt he had organized. While the other men were getting combat experience, he was confined to the hospital. In April, when he was well enough to fly again, he shot down two enemy planes but was then downed and wounded himself. This time he got out of the hospital in time to take part in the Salween raids, for which Chennault promoted him to flight leader.

Unlike most of the pilots, Jones was keen on strafing and bombing missions, and during his hospital stays he had concocted plans for several daring raids. He persuaded Chennault that he could attack the field at Hanoi, 400 miles from Kunming, and Chennault told him he would approve the raid if Jones found enough volunteers to go with him. That was not so easy. Not only was Hanoi far beyond the range of a P-40, but it was also 100 miles inside enemy territory and heavily defended. The flight would be over dangerous terrain and through difficult weather.

Few of the pilots would even consider the mission, but after much cajoling and pleading, Jones persuaded five pilots to join him—Lewis Bishop, Frank Schiel, Chauncey Laughlin, Jim Howard, and John Donovan. Donovan had a premonition that he would be killed, but he didn't back out. He had come close to death the month before when his plane had been caught by a couple of Zeros. "Right then I realized just how careless I had become. I had been fighting in this war just long enough to become indifferent . . . instead of 'staying on the ball' as one has to all the time." He went to see Chaplain Frillman and wrote out his will, then composed a telegram for his parents in the event of his death. He left the message and the money to pay for it with a friend:

DEAR FOLKS. YOU MUST NOT FEEL BADLY ABOUT MY DEATH THE SMALL PART THAT I HAVE PLAYED IN THE WAR THOUGH IT HAS COST ME MY LIFE I AM GLAD TO GIVE THAT. LIFE HAS MEANT MUCH TO ME BUT NOT SO MUCH THAT I AM TOO DISTRESSED AT LEAVING AND NEITHER MUST YOU BE. I HAD ONLY A FEW THINGS PLANNED FOR THE FUTURE ONE OF THE MOST IMPORTANT WAS A NICE HOME. MOMMA WILL PLEASE ME MUCH IF SHE WILL LIVE IN A MORE COMFORTABLE HOME WITH MANY FLOWERS AND TREES. I AM HAPPY AND SO MUST SHE BE LOVE TO ALL. JOHN JUNIOR.

The pilots left Kunming on the afternoon of May 12 and flew to a former Chinese training field at Mengtz, close to the border. There they refueled and loaded their planes with bombs for the 100-mile flight to the Gia Lam airbase at Hanoi. One plane developed engine trouble and had to turn back, but the remaining five reached the field just as the sun was setting.

Japanese fighters and bombers were lined up on the runway along with a twin-engine transport that had flown in a group of high-ranking Japanese officers for a conference. Jones led his flight to the west so they could attack with the sun behind them and caught the enemy by surprise. The AVG roared over the field strafing and littering their fragmentation bombs among the parked aircraft. Japanese antiaircraft gunners recovered quickly and began to fire on the attackers before they started their climb away from the field. Donovan's plane was hit. A large chunk was torn from the fuselage, and it crashed in a fiery explosion.

By the time the four P-40s made their next pass, the smoke from the wreckage of Donovan's plane was mingling with that of burning Japanese aircraft. The AVG pilots destroyed the transport plane and ten additional airplanes and damaged as many as fifteen more, and left a string of craters the length of the runway. With bombs and ammunition gone, Jones led his flight north at full speed to escape about a dozen Type 97 fighters that had taken off during the raid. The Japanese planes could not catch them, however, and they returned safely to Kunming.

Jones was delighted with the success of his raid, and he began planning other missions and practicing his dive-bombing skills. Four days after the Hanoi raid, he and Jim Howard were diving on the practice range. As Jones went into his dive, his plane began to corkscrew out of control. He could not pull out in time and was killed instantly. Not a single piece of his ship was left intact.

The next day, May 17, Lewis Bishop, another ex-navy flyer, with five enemy planes to his credit, led another raid on Hanoi. They surprised the enemy, shot up the field, and got away without taking a hit. As they were heading home, Bishop decided to strafe some trains at a juncture called Lao Cai, north of Hanoi. He radioed the new target to his pilots. Apparently, the Japanese picked up the transmission because they were waiting for them. The antiaircraft fire was heavy as Bishop led his flight down to the target. He took a number of hits, and managed to get his crippled plane as far as the Chinese border before bailing out. The other pilots watched him float down over friendly territory and were horrified to see a strong north wind blow him back over Indochina. He was captured and spent three years as a prisoner-of-war. The AVG ranks were thinning, and there were still seven weeks to go before their contracts expired.

At Kunming, daily life between missions went on normally in the absence of any raids on the field. Chaplain Frillman found it peaceful enough to be concerned about the food the men were getting. All the canned goods ordered in Washington had survived Mingadalon and the trek up the Burma Road. They had not been stolen or sold, unlike so many of their supplies, and Frillman persuaded the Chinese cooks to use the canned bacon and ham, the pancake and biscuit mixes, and the dried fruits. The food from home helped liven up breakfast and dessert but did little for their main meals.

The cooks held steadfast to their belief that Westerners should eat only Western-style cooking, but they did not know how to prepare such food well. They would over-boil or over-fry the food. Frillman noticed that the cooks never ate it themselves. When he suggested that they prepare Chinese food for the AVG, he was told he was criticizing Chinese hospitality by implying that the people running the hostels were not cultured enough to understand the ways of Western food. Frillman had been in China long enough to know that it was useless to persist.

He was also concerned about the health and activity of the men, and he promoted an extensive program of sports and games. Baseball, volleyball, and tennis were played with great enthusiasm, accompanied by loud shouts and cheers. Chennault no longer played baseball with his boys in the afternoon, the way he did in the early days. Occasionally, however, he did come out to pitch, but the games were "more like ritual than sport," Frillman wrote. "While everyone loyally tried to keep on calling him 'the Old Man,' we couldn't forget that he was a General now."

Certainly no one could forget that Chennault was a general on the night of May 21, when the AVG assembled in the auditorium of Yunnan University in Kunming. Chennault and Clayton Bissell were there to talk about the future of the AVG. Chennault had warned Bissell that he might not be well received but that didn't stop him. Bissell was desperate to persuade the AVG personnel to accept induction into the army. He knew that replacement pilots and crews would not be available by July 4, the date of the disbanding of the AVG, so it was imperative that the AVG pilots and ground crew stay on. Without them, China would have no air force for a time, and Bissell would receive the blame.

Chennault had his own reasons for wanting his men to stay. If they did not, his own career would be in jeopardy. He would need to be at least as persuasive as Bissell, but he thought he had an advantage. After all, these were his men. They had been through so much together. Surely, out of loyalty to him, enough of them would stay on to constitute an effective fighting force.

Chennault spoke first and gave a straightforward presentation about how the men would benefit financially by accepting induction. He reviewed the terms of their CAMCO contracts and told them that if they accepted reserve commissions in the air corps, they would continue to collect their much higher AVG salaries until July 4. They would also receive pay for accrued leave, which no one had taken, plus $500 in travel pay, the amount CAMCO was obligated to pay them for their return trips home. In addition, each man would receive a lump sum equal to the difference between his AVG salary and the pay rate of his air corps rank, amounting to several hundred dollars per man. The men thought these terms seemed generous.

Then Clayton Bissell rose to speak, and his tone and manner turned an amiable meeting into an angry confrontation. Brusque and threatening, Bissell told the men of the AVG that if they did not accept induction, none of them would be able to get a job with CNAC, Pan American, or any other airline in the Far East. The men knew that wasn't true. Some of them already had commitments for airline jobs.

Bissell did not stop there. If the men chose to return to the States, he said, there was little chance of getting any kind of job that would protect them from being drafted into the army. Then, perhaps sensing that he was not succeeding, Bissell became more direct and said the men would be inducted as soon as they reached the States. As Keeton recalled it, Bissell said "the State Department would take our passports and the draft board would grab us. . . . Instead of keeping us here, he changed a few minds to the contrary. . . . Almost everybody was burned up about the talk by the great General Bissell."

If there had been any chance of inducting a large number of the AVG into the army, Bissell killed it that night. Most of the men did want to go home, but some might have been persuaded to stay if the attempt had been less bullying. "All the fellows feel that

Bissell is jamming the Army down our throats," wrote Charlie Bond. "I think his talk hurt more than helped his cause."

The pilots gathered in the bar after the meeting. "We cussed a lot," Bond reported, "and then discussed every aspect of what we had heard and what we should do. . . . I think most everyone had made up his mind to go back to the States and take the chance of being drafted."

The AVG would go out of existence on July 4 and few of its members would remain in China to serve in its replacement unit. The men Chennault had worked so hard to recruit, train, and keep supplied were slipping away. Chaplain Frillman observed that Chennault "must have felt that after the one great year he was sliding back into the frustration which dogged so much of his career. In the mess hall his manner became perfunctory, his jokes mechanical. In working hours at the airfield he looked even more like a man 'eating bitterness,' as the Chinese had it."

T W E L V E

EVERYONE IS COUNTING THE DAYS

Another pilot died the day after the meeting with Bissell. It happened during a bombing mission over the Salween Gorge. The pilots were supposed to hit enemy machine-gun nests, but they were too high to see them. Bob Little dropped down to 500 feet. Suddenly, one of his wings disintegrated, perhaps from antiaircraft fire or from a faulty bomb he was carrying. No one knows. His ship went into a spin, too low for him to bail out, if, indeed, he had survived the explosion. The rest of the flight dropped their bombs, strafed the target, and left.

The Greenlaws were in Delhi when they learned about Little's death. Olga broke down in tears. Harvey tried to comfort her, reminding her that he had told her not to get too attached to the boys.

"I told you many of these boys would die," he said, "many would go and never return. I tried to warn you, dear, to keep you from feeling the pain I felt when I was in the army—when a lot of my best friends went away and never came back. . . . Come on, Olga, you've got to be a good soldier."

"I didn't want to be a good soldier," Olga wrote later. "I

couldn't harden myself and forget. I kept remembering and thinking . . . about those boys—and what a lousy, rotten business this all was—this war—this great adventure."

Bob Neale and Little had been like brothers, and Neale took the death very hard. The following day, May 22, Neale refused to go on another bombing and strafing mission. It was suicide, he told Chennault, to send men on those kinds of raids in broken-down, worn-out airplanes. They were losing too many men, and Neale said he would not lead his First Squadron on any more offensive missions. From now on, the Adams and Eves would undertake only defensive missions.

Chennault was furious, but all the pilots in Neale's squadron stood by his decision. There was nothing Chennault could do. He could not afford to lose the entire squadron by dishonorably discharging the lot of them. The star on his shoulder gave him no power over civilians, and he knew most of his men were too tired, too angry, and too frustrated to follow him out of loyalty anymore.

But there was still a war to fight and missions to plan, and he hoped that when the shock of the recent deaths wore off, Neale and his pilots would change their minds about flying low-level missions. Three days later Chennault scheduled a mission to bomb a small town near the Salween where intelligence sources reported a concentration of several hundred Japanese troops. Eight pilots agreed to go. Six made it to the target.

Two of the planes had engine trouble. One of these, flown by Buster Keeton, lost power, got caught in a rainstorm over a 12,000-foot mountain range, and almost cracked up on landing back at Kunming. Later, Keeton and George Paxton talked about what was happening to the group. Keeton wrote, "I told him until those foolish bombing missions started coming off everything was okay, but everybody had gone to pot. We are here in a fighter doing every kind of work but fighting and the damn U.S. army sitting on their ????? in India not doing a thing. George [said] that the whole army was fighting amongst themselves and worse than the British when it came to doing something. They have the men and the equipment right there in India and won't send them over here to help out. It's a damn crime."

As May turned into June and the AVG began its last full month as a fighting unit, the mood of the group was reflected by one of the pilots: "Everyone is counting the days until July 4th." Physically, the men were at their lowest point. In terms of equipment, only half of their ninety-nine original aircraft were intact, and none of these would have been declared operational back in the States.

The AVG had received up to twenty newer model P-40Es—and they were more than welcome—but many more were needed, along with spare parts and other supplies. The AVG was getting no more than a trickle of the necessary equipment. The pilots who had gone to India to ferry back the new planes brought tales of abundant aircraft and supplies and crews, and the luxurious living available to the new Tenth Air Force. A pilot who had stayed at the Imperial Hotel in New Delhi, the finest hotel in all of Asia and headquarters of the Tenth Air Force, told Olga Greenlaw about the "air-conditioning, wonderful service, [and] millions of beautiful secretaries. That's the way to fight the war!" Scores of new planes, manned by scores of fresh crews, were now in India, and there they stayed—in case the Japanese decided to invade. Meanwhile, the AVG was lucky to get a few tires and spark plugs with which to carry on its daily war.

In June 1942, with his men counting the days until they could go home, Chennault was facing his toughest challenge yet from the Japanese. The enemy air force was threatening the remaining free portion of China from three directions. The main element was based in Burma and Indochina, the force Chennault had fought to a standstill for six months. The Japanese were building new airfields west of the Salween and were moving up troop reinforcements in their attempt to capture Kunming.

The second element of Japanese air power was based around Hankow, 800 miles northwest of Kunming. Their target—and that of the troops moving steadily up the Yangtze River—was Chungking, the capital of China.

The third air and land force was southeast of Hankow, in Chekiang Province, and its goal was to capture the air bases Chennault had built years before. Doolittle had planned to use some of these airfields, and they were the closest bases to Japan still in Allied hands. These were the fields from which Chennault had intended to bomb Tokyo, long before there was an AVG or an attack on Pearl Harbor.

Chennault's handful of planes and pilots had to defend against all these forces over vast distances and some of the worst terrain and flying weather in the world. He had chosen to fight only the enemy in Burma and Indochina—with his limited number of planes, it made little sense to divide his forces—but now the other threats were becoming more serious. He decided to take the offensive on the two new fronts, leaving only a small number of planes at Kunming. The move was audacious, certainly unorthodox, and definitely risky, though it was a carefully calculated risk. Chennault was a gambler, but not a reckless one.

"Imagine leaving only seven to ten planes here now with the Japs still boiling on the Salween front," one of his pilots said in admiration. "He plays for high stakes. It is the last thing the Japs expect. It even surprised us. If it works it will really be something. He certainly has guts."

One advantage Chennault counted on was the element of surprise. If he could reach the enemy bases at Hankow and those in Chekiang Province undetected, he could inflict heavy damage. The bases had not been attacked for almost two years, and Chennault believed the Japanese would be feeling complacent and might be lax about their early-warning detection and defensive measures. What did they have to fear from the AVG 800 miles away in Kunming?

Another advantage was that the Japanese air forces in these two new target areas were smaller and less experienced than the group in Burma and Indochina. Their planes were older models. The areas were used as training grounds for Japanese air crews to gain experience by bombing undefended targets.

Chennault was eager to undertake his new campaign, but the weather closed in over Kunming for the first few days of June, preventing him from transferring his P-40s to their new bases. Impatiently, he watched both the lowering sky and the calendar. Time was running out for his AVG. He had only one month in which to carry out his bold strategy.

The weather kept the P-40s grounded, but not the DC-3s of the CNAC. On June 3, one of them took seven of Chennault's pilots to Chungking to meet with Clayton Bissell and the other members of the army's regular commission examining board. The group of pilots included Charlie Bond, George Burgard, Charlie Sawyer, and Pete Wright, and they were applying for regular commissions. All wanted careers in the air force after the war, and they knew that their chances were none too good with reserve commissions only. For the army, here was a chance to induct at least seven experienced combat pilots on July 4.

Three of the pilots were disqualified immediately for physical reasons, including hearing problems and venereal disease. The others were required to take a written examination containing, Burgard recalled, "a bunch of foolish questions which had no bearing on fighting a war." They were asked to name some of the countries in South America, to tell what aluminum was made of, to explain the Monroe Doctrine, and to say who owned Samoa.

When Bond handed in his papers, he asked General Bissell what his chances were of getting a regular commission. None at all, Bissell told him, because of the date of his graduation from flying school. He was too old.

None of the seven AVG pilots received a regular commission, and they returned to Kunming disappointed and angry at the way Bissell and the board had treated them. The army wanted the AVG pilots to accept induction but would not help them become permanent members of the service. The men were good enough to fight for the United States in China but not good enough to serve with the regular army after the war.

At about the same time, Chennault sent a telegram to Pan American Airways, asking them not to hire anyone from the AVG until after they returned to the States. The reason for this request, he said, was that President Roosevelt had asked that the AVG pilots stay in China as long as possible. If Pan Am offered to hire the pilots on the spot—for higher pay and an absence of military discipline—they would be more likely to resign from the AVG and to refuse military induction. Chennault's attitude disappointed his pilots. When one of them accidentally saw a copy of the cable, he wrote, "I can't understand the Colonel. One time he is all for us and the next time he is the opposite. Everybody re-maining here has done their part, why can't he continue to help them?"

On June 5, the weather improved, and Chennault moved AVG headquarters and the First and Second Squadrons to Peishihyi Field, 30 miles from Chungking. The field was grass, but the hostel was new, much like the one at Kunming. There was one important difference—the food was more like the American cooking the men wanted. The city was an hour-and-a-half away, over a winding, unpaved road. When the men went to explore it, they found considerable bomb damage. For three years, when the monsoon season ended, the Japanese had bombed the city daily, facing only minimal opposition from the Chinese Air Force. For a time, Chungking was the most heavily bombed city in the world, yet commerce and the ordinary business of life continued. The men had money to spend but were surprised at how expensive everything was. Bond wanted to have a uniform made from some gabardine Burgard had brought back from India. The tailoring alone cost him $200 American. A Parker fountain pen sold for $85.

They had little time for shopping anyway. For three days Chennault kept them flying in formation low over Chungking and the neighboring towns to show the war-weary Chinese people that the Flying Tigers were there to defend them. More important, Chennault wanted the Japanese to know they were there.

A friend of Paul Frillman's described to him the reaction of the Chinese to the AVG's presence. "When the air began to tremble with a smooth new thunder, he looked out in time to see six P-40s in perfect V formation rounding the tip of the peninsula, just above the masts of the junks.

"They came up the Kialing [River], then climbed steeply and in pairs erupted all over the sky in a stunning display of acrobatic flying. Up and down the steep slopes, blue-coated crowds flowed into the staircase streets or out on flat roofs, waving and shouting, loud with exultation. The planes performed for an hour or more, and the human roar went on through every moment. The people of Chungking had every reason to cheer, for they were never bombed again."

When Chennault had firmly demonstrated the presence of his flyers to both friend and enemy, he quietly sent most of them away. Four planes remained in Chungking with instructions to show themselves in daily flights over the city. From the air, another dozen P-40s could be seen scattered around the perimeter of Peishihyi Field, but these were dummies built of paper and bamboo. On June 11, Chennault took the rest of his planes—four P-40E models and eight P-40Bs—to Kweilin in south central China, 350 miles from Chungking.

Kweilin, along with the fields at Lingling and Hengyang, formed a line of bases in east China built by Chennault before the war. From any of these fields he could strike at Hankow in the north or Canton in the south, as well as at Nanking and Shanghai. They were valuable sites for carrying the war to the enemy.

At Kweilin, Bob Neale was in immediate tactical command. Chennault decided which missions to undertake, and Neale determined how best to carry them out. Pilot Matt Kuykendall got lost on the flight from Kunming and crash-landed not far from Kweilin. He managed to reach it on foot two days later, but his plane could not be recovered.

The field at Kweilin was one of the best in China. The 6000-foot runway had a crushed rock surface substantial enough to take bombers as heavy as the B-17, the plane Chennault had designed it for. The field was surrounded by mountains, and the operations office was located in a huge cave at the base of one of these mountains. There it was safe from air raids and provided a clear view of the field and the lush valley beyond.

The AVG hostel was located five miles away. Built of camphor wood, it was comfortably outfitted with American furniture, hot showers, and a pool table. The men agreed that it was the nicest place they had stayed and that the countryside was the prettiest in all China. Both the airfield and the city, however, showed signs of war. They had been the target of bombing raids for more than two years. The people of Kweilin had gotten used to taking shelter in the caves in the foothills to watch the almost daily air attacks.

The morning after their arrival, the men of the AVG arose at 3:00 A.M. to prepare for their planned interception of the enemy. The air-raid warning net was functioning efficiently in the area, and at 5:25 the pilots scrambled in response to word that Japanese planes were on the way. Neale calculated the course and speed of the attackers and ordered his pilots to circle west of the field in three layers—his own flight of four planes at 18,000 feet, Bond's four ships at 15,000 feet, and Burgard's three as top cover at 20,000 feet. They all circled for about 35 minutes when they got the call from radioman Ralph Sasser.

"Come in, boys," he said, "the weather is fine."

The P-40s dove for the field as the enemy ships passed over it. There were twenty-one of them—five twin-engine Mitsubishi bombers, eleven Nakajima Type 97 fighters, and five twin-engine fighters of a type none of the Americans had seen before. They looked something like the German Messerschmitt 110s that the pilots had seen in newsreels of the fighting in Europe.

Bond's flight zoomed through the fighters to attack the bombers, which immediately lost interest in their target and tried to flee. Dick Rossi shot down one, and Bob Prescott and John Dean set two others on fire. Charlie Bond stuck on the tail of another bomber, pouring fire into the rear gunner's position, but five of his machine guns quit. He pulled away from the enemy's return fire to try to recharge his guns. Smoke poured from the instrument panel as the yellow coolant overheat light glared at him—his cooling system had been hit.

Bond dropped altitude and found that he had company, two Japanese fighters on his tail. He went into a maximum dive, heading for the ground, and one of the Type 97s pulled away. He leveled off at 1000 feet, but the second 97 stayed with him. "I was beginning to feel that my number was up this time," he said. His oil pressure dropped to zero, and smoke continued to curl from behind the instrument panel.

The Japanese pilot turned away, apparently convinced the American was finished. Bond began to climb, hoping to gain enough altitude to reach the field, but the engine quit on him. Still too low to bail out and too far from the field to try a dead-stick landing, he braced himself to come down in the rice paddies. He hit one paddy, bounced out of it and over a dike, and crashed into the next field. His head snapped forward and his forehead struck the gunsight, but he was alive, and he quickly clambered out of his smoking ship. Bond scanned the sky to see if any enemy planes were around to strafe him, then noticed several Chinese farmers going about their work in the rice paddies as though nothing unusual had happened. They didn't even look up.

Meanwhile, Neale's flight of four planes and Burgard's three were tangling with the Japanese fighters. In their first pass they shot down three of the Type 97s and one of the new twin-engine ships. Neale and Burgard got into a running dogfight with two of the fighters. Neale's got away, but Burgard shot down his quarry after chasing it for seventy-five miles.

When the battle was over, the Japanese had lost eleven of their twenty-one planes plus two probables. The AVG lost two— Bond's and Al Wright's. Wright had crash-landed and wrenched his back, but both he and Bond returned to Kweilin safely. Bond's injuries turned out to be only a cut forehead. Chennault chided him about his bad luck, and said with a grin that he hoped this would be the last of it. When the pilots in Kunming heard that Bond had been shot down for the second time, one of them said, "I wonder if old Charlie's got any other hobbies?"

The AVG's victory over the Japanese at Kweilin was seen by the local population as a miracle. This was the first time they had seen Japanese planes turned away and shot down. They quickly made their gratitude known to the Flying Tigers. The children followed the Americans around, idolizing them, and the adults laid plans for a celebration.

The pilots were curious about the enemy's new twin-engine fighter, and they did not have to wait long to learn more about it. The crew of a plane that Burgard had shot down was holding off some Chinese soldiers with a machine gun, but by noon Japanese planes had bombed and strafed the wreckage. Obviously they did not want the Americans to get ahold of the plane.

A week later, Chinese soldiers brought one of the Japanese crewmen to Kweilin. He was a twenty-six-year-old gunner who had been a chicken farmer before the war. The AVG men gave him water and cigarettes, and he told them all about the new airplane. It was called the Kawasaki Toryi, the Ki-45, and had indeed been patterned after the Messerschmitt 110. It had radial air-cooled engines instead of the German in-line liquid-cooled model, and bore two 13-mm cannon in the wings and an 18-mm cannon in the nose.

The Americans who had flown head-on attacks against the plane over Kweilin turned pale when they learned about the firepower, but the Japanese gunner told them that Japanese pilots were having a great deal of trouble keeping the guns firing in the air. He also told them his outfit had heard a lot about the Flying Tigers. The pilots let him look over one of the P-40E models, and he seemed especially interested in the six .50-caliber machine guns. They introduced him to George Burgard, but the Japanese turned away, refusing to meet the man who had shot him down.

The enemy did not return to Kweilin for quite a while. On June 14, Chennault left for Chungking for a conference with Gen. Lewis Brereton, commander of the Tenth Air Force. He was reluctant to leave Kweilin—it was the closest he had been to the front line in a long time. "The Old Man was pissed off at having to do it," Burgard noted. "He wanted to stay here and see the show as well as run it personally."

The Americans had time to explore Kweilin, and they found it to be the most attractive and cleanest Chinese city they had seen. It boasted everything they wanted in the way of shops, restaurants, bars, and, of course, women. The ground crewmen quickly became experts on the city's red-light district, and on the night of the 17th, dared some of the pilots to come along with them. As they entered the area, they got the impression they were about to parade down a narrow street where large numbers of Chinese women had assembled to cheer them. After all, the citizens of Kweilin had been effusive in their gratitude toward the Flying Tigers, and this looked like another such demonstration. Women and girls, ranging in age from about ten to over forty, stood shoulder-to-shoulder all along the street.

The ground crewman who had volunteered to be their "tour guide" motioned for them to follow him down the street. That was when the pilots realized that all the women were prostitutes. They giggled and chattered loudly as they reached out and grabbed at the Americans. Sometimes two or three women got hold of a man and tried to pull him in different directions. Shirts were ripped, buttons torn off, and belts wrenched from bush jackets.

Farther down the street, Chinese pimps took the men in tow and led them to a pleasantly furnished room behind a grocery store. It reminded them of a typical living room back home. The pilots were served tea, and then a stunning, elegant woman was ushered into the room. She wore a long, black, form-fitting gown, and her black hair was styled in pageboy fashion. She explained in good English that she was interested in being purchased for a long-term relationship. For $50 American, she would serve dinner, sing and dance, and stay with a man for the night, continuing the relationship as long as she was paid enough to maintain her position as a high-class professional prostitute. The Americans were reluctant to indicate any interest, and they headed back toward the hostel, talking all the while of what they had seen.

On June 20, the city of Kweilin formally honored the AVG at an elaborate banquet. Bourbon and Scotch were poured liberally—even the Chinese drank some, though they usually did not—and the Americans were given lavishly embroidered clothes showing eagles pouncing on the red sun of Japan. The pilots were introduced with much applause and bowing. The men felt the effects of the party the next morning, so it was fortunate that the Japanese were still avoiding Kweilin.

To thank the Chinese people for the banquet, nine pilots staged an air show. Nearly all the city's 300,000 residents turned out to watch. Thus the days passed happily for the pilots, and they counted them off. Only twelve more to go. All they had to do was stay alive for fewer than two weeks and they would be on their way home.

The pilots who had been left at Kunming were also counting the days, though for them the time seemed to pass more slowly. There had been no activity for sixteen days and the boredom was mounting. Whereas the AVG personnel at the new airfields had places to explore and sights to see, the group at Kunming had seen everything the city had to offer.

The only break in the monotony occurred on June 6, shortly after the others left, when they assembled in the largest hangar for an awards ceremony. Eight of the pilots were to receive medals from the Chinese—the Chinese Banner of the Clouds, Fifth Class, the highest decoration in the Chinese Air Force, and the Chinese Ten Star Wing Medal. Medallions were also awarded to those who served in the Rangoon fighting.

After the ceremony Chennault ordered a flight of P-40s to assemble over the city and then head north toward Chungking. As soon as they were out of sight, they were to double back and return to the field at a low altitude, just above the trees. Chennault wanted the Japanese spies in Kunming to think that all AVG forces had departed and that the city was without an air defense. Maybe this would lure the enemy into raiding Kunming, where Olson's Third Squadron would be waiting.

The pilots remained on alert duty every day for the rest of the month, but the Japanese did not come. Occasionally the air-raid alarm sounded and the pilots scrambled, but it was always a false alarm.

Army air corps pilots began to arrive at Kunming, the first of those who would replace the AVG. The Hell's Angels checked them out in the P-40, trained them in gunnery and tactics, and tried to teach them all they had learned about how to fight the Japanese and stay alive. The replacements were mostly young second lieutenants fresh out of flying school, too few to take over the AVG's job, and too inexperienced to serve as flight leaders or squadron commanders. The army would need to move a lot faster if it expected to carry on the AVG's combat record after July 4.

Throughout the month of June, the diary entries of the Kunming group were the same. "Alert duty all day, nothing new . . . continued alert duty, no activity." Sometimes an army transport plane would stop for refueling on the way to or from India, carrying smartly dressed staff officers with briefcases. Chennault fumed about their presence. They were still taking up space that could be used for vital supplies.

June also brought several crashes, though none involved any personal injuries. While dispersing P-40s to an auxiliary field, the flight leader tried, for some unknown reason, to land downwind. He touched down too fast and had to ground-loop the ship to keep from running off the end of the runway. The three other pilots in his flight followed their leader in, and two of them ended up in a pile at the end of the runway. "Three airplanes damaged while landing," noted Squadron Leader Olson, "the record here so far."

With so little to occupy them, many of the men focused on their departure and the problems they expected to face on their travels to the United States. "I don't think the Army will give us much help," Buster Keeton said, "as it is very easy to see they hate our guts tremendously. For no reason in the world other than jealousy." By June 21, the concern about getting home had increased. "The Army commander here stated that the Army would help us as far as Dinjan [a stop on the ferry route between Kunming and Karachi], but from there we would be on our own. A lot different status than when the Colonel gave us his last talk. Said they would help us all the way to the States." Keeton suspected that those who had been given dishonorable discharges earlier had gotten a better deal. At least they had been able to get home easily. Did the army plan to punish those who refused induction by denying them transportation after July 4? That thought was increasingly on the men's minds as the end of the AVG drew near.

The army made one last appeal to the Flying Tigers. On June 20, the official induction board, which the men called the "draft board," left Kunming aboard a DC-3 to visit the AVG bases. Chennault accompanied them. Kweilin was their first stop, and they met with each pilot and ground crewman. The board was composed of an air corps colonel and a naval officer, who was openly hostile to men who had formerly served in the navy.

When Charlie Bond was interviewed, he was asked about his plans. He said he would gladly stay if he were given a regular commission in the air corps. The air corps colonel on the board said there was nothing he could do, but he persisted in trying to persuade Bond to stay. He mentioned the possibility that Bond's ship might be torpedoed on its way to the United States. Bond said that after what he had been through, that possibility did not bother him.

The induction board signed up a few ground crewmen at Kweilin but not a single pilot. Bob Neale, who had been an ensign in the navy, was offered the rank of lieutenant colonel. Others who had been ensigns or second lieutenants were offered ranks as majors and captains, but no one was tempted. The board also had limited success at the other AVG bases, and they returned to Kunming on the 25th to make a final pitch. "Induction board met," Keeton wrote, "but without much results. A few radiomen, one mechanic, and no pilots are going to stay. Feel sorry for [General Chennault], but it was expected all along." Out of 250 men in the AVG, only five pilots and twenty-two ground crewmen accepted induction in the Army Air Corps.

Tex Hill was one of the pilots who agreed to stay. "I saw the Old Man in Chungking," he told Ed Rector. "He told me everybody's going home, but someone with knowhow has to stay to activate the new units. He wanted me to talk to you and some of the other fellows."

"I'm planning to go home," Rector said.

"So was I," Hill said, "but if all of us leave, this whole thing will fold up."

"I see he's sold you," Rector said. He said he would stay, too. Charlie Sawyer, Frank Schiel, and Gil Bright also agreed.

Tex Hill was right. Without more pilots, the whole thing would fold. The air war in China would come to a halt because the army was far from ready to assume the air operations the AVG had been conducting. The army's situation was so desperate that the induction board sent a radiogram to Stilwell, requesting that the deadline for induction of the AVG into the army be extended until October. The radiogram urged that the Flying Tigers' contracts to operate as civilians be extended until that date, "otherwise our operations are in serious jeopardy."

But it was too late. Back home, in the United States, the army had generated so much publicity about how the famous Flying Tigers were to become part of the Army Air Corps that it would be too embarrassing to admit failure. As Chennault noted, "the Chinese were not unique in their efforts to save face."

While the draft board was making its rounds, some of the AVG pilots were back in combat. Ed Rector took a flight of P-40s to the field at Hengyang, 200 miles northeast of Kweilin, to carry the war closer to the enemy. Early on the morning of June 22, he led a raid against Japanese ships on the Yangtze River, sinking three small transports and a gunboat.

When Japanese Air Force headquarters in Hankow learned of the attack, they sent 14 fighters to destroy the new AVG presence at Hengyang. For two years, Hengyang, like Kweilin and Chungking, had been a favorite target of the Japanese. They never met any opposition there. This time they went up against Rector's six P-40s. The AVG shot down four enemy planes without sustaining any losses, although pilot Van Shapard had a close call. He became separated from the others during the air battle and was chased by five Zeros.

Too low to dive away from them, he radioed the field and explained his problem. There were no clouds for him to hide in so he suggested he fly as low as possible over the field so that the ground crew could shoot at the Zeros with their tommy guns. Shapard left his microphone open as he approached the field. He began to sing an old Negro spiritual—something he was noted for doing—and came down over the runway with his rich baritone voice booming out and five enemy aircraft on his tail. The ground crew opened fire. Although they didn't hit anything, the Japanese gave up the chase.

The following day Chennault sent reinforcements from Kweilin to Hengyang, since the action seemed to be there. He ordered Charlie Bond to take a flight of seven ships but to be sure the Japanese spies in Kweilin did not know he was leaving. Bond led his planes in a wide circle to the south, giving the appearance of a routine patrol, and they reached Hengyang just before dusk, ready to hit the enemy when they came in the morning.

The pilots got up at 3:00 A.M. to prepare for the expected Japanese raid, but the weather was so bad the Japanese reconnaissance planes could not find the field. Next day the weather was worse. The AVG pilots did not even leave the hostel to go to the field. They sat around playing cards and listening to their one American phonograph record, "Moon over Burma."

They had planned to stay in Hengyang for just one day and had brought only their toothbrushes. By the second day, they would have given a lot for a change of clothing. And by the third, when the weather remained bad, they were fed up with life at Hengyang. "The food is getting worse with each passing day," Burgard noted, "and our clothes are getting smellier and dirtier at a rapid rate. It looks as though we are wasting our time here." But they were trapped until the weather improved.

Although none of his pilots was seeing any action at the moment, Chennault was fighting a different kind of war. The induction board had abandoned the attempt to get more AVG personnel to stay on after July 4, but Chennault had not. He was not ready to accept the idea that the outfit he had so carefully nurtured was breaking apart, so he made one final plea to his men. He argued, he implored, he even threatened. He told them the fight for China was all that mattered and that they should put aside their feelings about Bissell and the army brass and stay until they finished the job. But a few of the pilots reminded Chennault of how difficult it was to operate under army regulations and red tape, and of how there would always be someone like Bissell giving orders. At that, the Old Man exploded.

"Don't any of you try to tell me about red tape or difficulties or this man Bissell," Chennault said. "I've been literally wound up in it for twenty-three years, and I've been bedeviled with this Bissell for just about as long. I've been working this way since you were born. I know all the troubles we'll have, and more, too. But that doesn't count. All that counts is getting the Japanese out of China and winning this war. That's our job, that's our sacred duty. But let's fight the Japs, not among ourselves."

It was no use. Most of the men had had enough of China and of being at the tail end of a long and miserly supply line. And they did not have the same personal commitment to China as Chennault. They were not going to shirk their duty to fight for their country in time of war, after a leave, but they would not necessarily do the fighting in the Far East.

Paul Frillman, who had also turned down a commission so he could go home, wrote that the Flying Tigers "had been out of step with our complacent, isolationist country the year before, when we volunteered. Now we were out of step again, when the conventional thing was to rush to the colors. We all had more money than ever before, and wanted some leave to enjoy ourselves and see our families before enlisting for the duration."

Some of the men were not waiting for July 4. On June 28, 15 clerks and mechanics left Kunming. "They were certainly a happy bunch of men," Buster Keeton noted. Two days later, a group of 16, including some pilots, arrived in Kunming from Chungking with their discharge papers.

By June 30, Chennault and the air corps were frantic. There was no hope that the army would be prepared to take over in a few days. Chennault flew to Hengyang to discuss a new proposal with Bob Neale, his First Squadron commander. "The Old Man arrived at noon and tossed a bombshell." Neale called a meeting of the pilots and asked how many of them would be willing to extend their contracts for two weeks to allow the air corps more time to prepare.

He went on to explain that the Japanese had threatened to exterminate the new air corps unit when the AVG pulled out. Unless enough of the AVG pilots and ground crew stayed on to man the forward bases, the Japanese could easily make good on their threat. The clear implication was that the fate of the air corps outfit was in their hands. If the air corps were wiped out, the AVG would be responsible.

"I was mad as hell," Charlie Bond wrote. "I knew my conscience wouldn't let me do anything about it but say yes. I blame it all on the U.S. Army. They knew we were supposed to be disbanded on the fourth. Why the hell didn't they lay their plans accordingly and get their replacements in here? How can I say no under the circumstances?"

Chennault's last-minute appeal resulted in 19 pilots and 36 ground crewmen remaining for the additional two-week period.

Neale agreed to serve as commander of the combined army and AVG units during that time.* The terms of their agreement called for the AVG pilots to fly defensive missions only—against Japanese air attacks on Chinese cities—but all of them volunteered for offensive raids as well during their extra weeks of duty. They undertook strafing, dive bombing, and escort missions. Arnold Shamblin's plane was hit in a bombing raid against Nanchang, and he was captured. In the same raid, Johnny Petach's ship exploded over the target when antiaircraft fire blew up the bombs under his wings. His wife, the nurse Emma Foster Petach, had stayed on in China so they could go home together. She was pregnant when Johnny was killed. She named their daughter Joan Claire; the Claire was for Claire Chennault.

Toward the end of June, six B-25 Mitchell bombers were sent from the Tenth Air Force in India to Kunming, to help Chennault. Finally, after so many months of pleading, he had been given some bombers. On June 29 he ordered them to Hengyang, escorted by a flight of ten P-40s. The force thus assembled was the largest the AVG had been able to mount since the war began— seventeen P-40s and six twin-engine bombers.

Chennault wanted to attack Hankow right away, but the weather kept his planes grounded until the afternoon of July 1. He sent the B-25s and six P-40s north to hit the enemy airfield at Hankow, but only four of the bombers reached the target. One sustained a broken brake line and was scrubbed, and another became mired in the mud at the end of the runway. En route, the bombers twice got lost, but Ed Rector, leading the escort mission, brought them back on course. When they dropped their bombs, they missed the target completely, destroying instead a village on the Yangtze. By

---

*In addition to Bond and Neale, the AVG pilots staying on for two weeks were Bob Layher, Hank Geselbracht, Freeman Ricketts, Pete Wright, Al Wright, Joe Rosbert, Al Probst, George Paxton, Jim Howard, Bill Bartling, Bob Raines, Ed Loane, Arnold Shamblin, Van Shapard, Harry Bolster, Lester Hall, and Johnny Petach. Bolster, Shamblin, Loane, Shapard, and Al Wright had joined the AVG only a few weeks earlier, having previously served as flight instructors for the Chinese Air Force.

the time they passed over the Japanese airfield at Hankow, which was full of planes, they had no bombs left.

The following day the bombers went after the Hankow docks, which they did manage to hit, sinking supply boats and destroying equipment that was about to be sent to Japanese troops farther up the river. On July 3, the bombers and their fighter escort returned to Hankow and hit the airfield. Japanese Type 97s intercepted them but the B-25s easily pulled away. The P-40s shot down one enemy plane. Antiaircraft fire hit Harry Bolster's ship, but he bailed out and made it safely back to Chinese lines.

That afternoon, the air-raid warning net reported that a single enemy plane was headed toward the AVG field at Hengyang. The one plane turned out to be seven Zeros. Heavy cloud cover had confused the spotters, and the Flying Tigers learned the truth only when the Zeros were a short distance away. All but one P-40 got off the ground in time. The Japanese pilots strafed the field, setting the lone P-40 afire, and fled under cover of low-lying clouds.

The Fourth of July was a gloomy, chilly, dismal day at the AVG bases in China. The group was spread over hundreds of miles from Kunming and Chungking in the west to Hengyang and Lingling in the east. The men who had left early were already in India or beyond, and others planned to leave that day. In Dinjan, on the ferry route from Kunming to Karachi, George Burgard and a few other pilots were waiting for transport. "This was really a quiet Fourth for us. Much less exciting than we have been planning it to be ever since we learned that it was to be Independence Day for the AVG."

Some pilots from Kunming passed through Dinjan on a CNAC transport, but they continued on to Karachi after refueling. Later that night, Burgard and his group got word that they had seats on a flight the following day. It was a long way from Karachi back home, but at least they would soon be on their way.

In Kunming, a group including Buster Keeton—some of whom boasted hangovers from the previous night's party given for them by the Chinese—arrived at the airfield early to try to get on a plane bound for India. They waited most of the day, but no

CNAC transports were flying because of bad weather. They had to wait two more days.

The AVG group in the east, those staying on for the two additional weeks, spent July 4 on alert. The field at Lingling was hit by two salvos of bombs in the early hours. Some of the bombs exploded just outside the barracks, shaking the pilots out of their bunks.

At dawn, the warning net around Hengyang reported 12 enemy aircraft from Hankow heading for the AVG airfield. Bob Neale was already in the air, having left Lingling at 5:30 with a flight of four P-40s bound for Hengyang. He spotted the Type 97s and led the attack, and the Flying Tigers shot down six of them. This was the last air-to-air combat for the American Volunteer Group. The wornout pilots in their wornout planes had won one final victory against the odds.

Claire Chennault spent his last day as commander of the Flying Tigers in his office at the edge of the field at Peishihyi, outside of Chungking. He wrote a gloomy letter to Lauchlin Currie, stating that he had known as early as December 1941 that "the AVG was doomed and that the entire program we had mapped out and worked so hard to put through was likewise doomed. It was most disheartening after all the work had been done in spite of difficulties and obstructions. It is common knowledge that I opposed induction until the final decision was made early in April. My opposition was based upon my firm belief that the War Department had no real intention of replacing the AVG with a first-class pursuit group. Today, upon the eve of the demobilization of the AVG and three months after guarantees were given, my belief is fully justified. . . .

"I accepted recall to active duty in April in the hope of obtaining better coordination and more support. I regret this action now and believe that I should have returned to the U.S. and told the story of China to the public."

Jack Belden, a correspondent for Time-Life, who had been covering the activities of the AVG, stopped by the office to find out how Chennault was feeling on the day his consolation prize air force was breaking up. Chennault needed no prompting from Belden to reveal his thoughts.

"You know," he said, "I have had the greatest opportunity an air officer of any nation ever had. To collect and train a group like this with complete freedom of action caused me supreme enjoyment. Not only was I able to satisfy my desire to prove my methods sound, but I was able to contribute to the common cause.

"My only regret is that I was forced to use the AVG piecemeal. My original plan was to throw my entire force into each battle and wipe out entire formations of Japanese. Due to the smallness of our fields and other military necessities, we were never able to muster full strength at any one place. The Japanese never encountered the AVG as a whole but only small fractions of our group.

"We were very lucky. But individual courage and the willingness to carry the battle to the enemy against any odds were the real secret of our success.

"The AVG is the world's finest trained bunch of fighting airmen. I regret their disbandment. Now I only look forward to meeting the enemy."

Chennault would never fight the same kind of war again, a war on his own terms, a war of his own design, a war bearing the unmistakable and exclusive imprint of his own personality. All that was behind him, and an uncertain war and an uncertain future lay ahead. He was back to fighting his oldest enemy—his own superiors—as well as the Japanese.

The Generalissimo and Madame Chiang planned a farewell barbecue party for the AVG at the Chungking home of the president of China, Lin Sen. Chennault and most of the other AVG men at Peishihyi attended, but a few chose not to go. The weather was rainy, hot, and steamy, and Chaplain Frillman said he did not feel like getting into his full-dress uniform, even for the final gathering of the group he had served. He had found too many of Madame's gatherings to be a "curious mixture of Chinese opulence, Methodist austerity and YMCA heartiness." He thought they were embarrassing.

Frillman spent the evening dressed comfortably in shorts,

drinking beer in the AVG offices at the airfield, where some of the staff were recording the group's final tally. The statistics they gathered were awesome and seemed wholly out of proportion to the size and condition of the relatively tiny force.

The AVG was credited with destroying 297 Japanese airplanes, with another 150 or more listed as probably destroyed. The precise figure remains unknown because many planes had gone down at sea or in the jungles and mountains. Vast quantities of enemy supplies had been destroyed and more than 1000 Japanese killed.

The AVG, along with the RAF, had kept the vital port of Rangoon and the equally important Burma Road open for more than two months. By their actions at the Salween Gorge, the AVG had saved China from probable total defeat at the hands of the Japanese. Furthermore, the AVG had kept enemy bombers away from Chungking for a considerable time, and their presence in Kunming had saved that city from countless bombing raids. The effect of the Flying Tigers on the morale of both the Chinese and American people was incalculable. This handful of men had shown that the Japanese were not invincible—they could be stopped. For a time, the Flying Tigers provided the only victories against the Japanese anywhere in the Far East.

And the cost? Considering the conditions under which they fought and the equipment with which they waged war, their casualties were light. Twenty-three lives were lost: four pilots were killed in aerial combat; six died on strafing and bombing missions when their ships were hit by ground fire; three died in enemy air raids; and ten were killed in flying accidents. In addition, four pilots had been captured. Twelve P-40s were shot down in combat and sixty-one destroyed on the ground, including the twenty-two ships burned by the AVG when they evacuated Loiwing.

The financial cost also seems modest, considering the gains. The total cost of the year's operation came to $8 million, of which $3 million went for salaries and other personnel expenses. Chennault was disturbed that the total exceeded his original estimate, and he apologized to T. V. Soong. The Chinese finance minister said that "the AVG was the soundest investment China ever made. I am ashamed that you should even consider the cost."

For modern warfare, it was a bargain. When the army took over from the civilians, the cost relative to the gain skyrocketed.

Madame Chiang's barbecue was canceled because of the rain, and the party was moved indoors. Chennault was presented with an oil painting of himself with the Chiangs. Madame gave a speech, referring to the AVG, as she had on previous occasions, as the "flying angels" of China. But even on their last night, she could not resist commenting on their unorthodox behavior. "Flying angels, some of them a little naughty at times, naughty angels, but still our flying angels."

By AVG standards, it wasn't much of a party, and there was no chance to misbehave. The men drank nonalcoholic punch, played a game of musical chairs, and left at 11:00. The maverick war was over.

T H I R T E E N

IT WAS CLEARLY
TIME TO GO

The army took its revenge on the AVG members who did not accept induction by refusing to help them get home. "The Army is out to get us," said Buster Keeton while stranded in Karachi, "and it looks as though they will." Those who left before July 4 were able to catch rides on army planes from Karachi to the United States, but the rest were left to fend for themselves, even those who had volunteered for an extra two weeks of duty.

Frank Schiel, who had accepted induction, informed Chennault that Washington had sent orders to all U.S. Army Air Transport Command officers in India and Africa to give no priority to former AVG members. "Really I cannot understand this," Schiel wrote. "We didn't come over here for patriotic reasons but it worked out that we did our country a great service. Is there going to be no recognition, no compensation for all this?"

Not only did the army refuse to fly former AVG personnel on its planes, but it also put pressure on Pan American Airways, which was under contract to the army, to do the same. Charlie Bond heard from a friend in Karachi—a pilot for Pan Am—

that the army would not allow him to take ex-Flying Tigers as passengers.

By mid-July, 150 former AVG pilots, ground crewmen, and staff were stuck in Karachi. With all air transportation closed to them, the only way out was by ship, and there were not many of those headed for the States. What was worse, the army would not permit the men to stay at the military hotel at the airport and even tried to prevent them from talking to army personnel.

Many of the men had already sent most of their money home. Wartime Karachi was expensive, and daily living costs were consuming the remainder of their funds very quickly. After nearly three weeks of waiting, the American consulate was able to arrange their passage on the SS *Mariposa*, a passenger ship of the American President Lines. The fare was $150 for a double bunk cabin or $600 for first class. Most of the men chose third class, and they spent thirty-five days aboard ship, arriving in New York in the middle of September.

As on the voyage out, many of their fellow passengers were missionaries. Keeton noted that the "AVG has their poker games on one side of the ship and the missionaries have their singing and praying on the other side."

Of the five AVG pilots who accepted military induction, Tex Hill and Ed Rector finished the war with the rank of colonel. Charlie Sawyer made colonel after the war. Gil Bright left the air force a few years after the war ended. Frank Schiel was killed on December 8, 1942.

Eighteen former Flying Tiger pilots stayed in the Far East to fly for CNAC. Five ground crewmen also stayed on. The pay was good but the job was dangerous—flying supplies over the Hump. Three pilots were killed in crashes: Einar Michelson, Al Wright, and John Dean.

Most of those who returned to the United States reenlisted, joining that branch of the military they had served in before the AVG. A few of the pilots—Bob Neale, George Burgard, Jim Cross, and Buster Keeton—joined Pan American Airways.

Harvey Greenlaw went to work for Grumman Aircraft, and he and Olga were divorced in 1945.

Jim Howard served in the European theater and received the Medal of Honor for an aerial battle with 30 enemy fighters over Germany. He retired from the air force reserve as a brigadier general. Charlie Bond finally won his regular commission in 1948 and retired twenty years later as a major general in command of a tactical air force, the same rank and position held by Chennault during the war. At his retirement ceremony, Bond wrote, he "felt that the Old Man, wherever he was, would be happy to know that one of his men had followed closely in his footsteps. . . . I feel I owe him thanks as much as I do my other air force contemporaries."

A few of Chennault's ground crew came back to China to serve with him. Radioman Robert M. Smith spent the war as a communications officer. Walter Dolan, who had been Bond's crew chief, served in Chennault's Fourteenth Air Force, as did John Williams, who had been in charge of the air-raid warning net for the AVG.

Eight ground crewmen became pilots after they returned to the United States in 1942. Former radioman Carson Roberts flew C-47s over the Hump and was killed in North Africa. Bill Sykes, another radioman for Chennault, died in a flying accident in 1943. R. L. Richardson also earned his wings; he retired as a colonel.

In all, 15 former AVG personnel were killed in the war, including three CNAC pilots. Some thirty-five who survived the war remained in the service until retirement.

Paul Frillman was one of those who returned to China during the war but not as a chaplain. Doubtful about continuing in that capacity, he became one of Chennault's field intelligence officers. Most of these men were former missionaries who had lived in China before the war and knew the language. Shortly before the Japanese surrender, Chennault received word that a new type of Japanese fighter plane had been shot down in a region of China then under Communist control. Chennault wanted to send Frillman there to obtain information about the downed plane. At the time, however, Frillman was on leave, so he sent another field intelligence officer in his place. That man was shot and killed by Communist soldiers. His name was John Birch.

Chennault remained in China for three more years, until July 8, 1945, when he was forced out one month before the Japanese surrender he had fought so long and hard to bring about. These were years of continuing hardship and frustration. His first command after the AVG was dissolved was a motley, makeshift, and make-do organization called the China Air Task Force (CATF). Chennault wrote that the CATF was "patched together in the midst of combat from whatever happened to be available in China during the gloomy summer of 1942. That was precious little. As the stepchild of the Tenth Army Air Force in distant Delhi, the CATF had to fight, scream, and scrape for every man, plane, spark plug, and gallon of gas." The CATF consisted of the 23rd Fighter Group and the 11th Bombardment Squadron.

The new 23rd Fighter Group, to which Roosevelt had promised to send great numbers of planes and men, had 29 flyable P-40s, all veterans of service with the AVG. It would not be until December 1943 that the last of the P-40Bs, assembled in Rangoon so long ago, was officially retired. Chennault borrowed ten P-43s—the much disliked forerunner of the P-47—from the Chinese Air Force, but these planes were antiquated death traps. They had no armor plating or self-sealing gas tanks.

Months later, Chennault received some P-40Ks. Although these were a newer model, they were not new planes. They had already flown hundreds of hours in training and combat missions.

The 23rd was commanded by Col. Robert L. Scott, a fighter pilot who would win national prominence with his book on his experiences in China—*God Is My Co-Pilot*—which was made into a popular wartime movie.

The other part of Chennault's CATF command, the 11th Bombardment Squadron, was led by Col. Caleb V. Haynes and consisted initially of seven B-25s. With that handful of bombers and fighters, Chennault fought the Japanese on a 5000-mile front, juggling his meager forces by shuttling them from one airfield to another throughout unoccupied China. Kweilin was his main center of operations.

It was war on a shoestring again, with the army supplying twelve inexperienced pilots and twenty clerks and mechanics when the CATF took over from the AVG. The equipment Chennault used in the early months of operation of the CATF was left over from the Flying Tigers. The army was even unable to supply uniforms, and only a trickle of supplies was being ferried over the Hump.

Virtually everything the men needed had to be found locally or done without. There was no coffee, so they had to drink tea. No food supplies were coming in, so they existed on rice, bean sprouts, chicken, eggs, and pork as prepared by Chinese cooks—an unaccustomed diet for American stomachs used to beef and potatoes. There were not enough American-made bullets and bombs, so the CATF used machine-gun ammunition manufactured in eleven different countries and bombs made in France, the Soviet Union, and China. There were not enough aluminum belly tanks for the P-40s, so the Chinese fabricated them out of bamboo and fish glue.

There just wasn't enough of anything. The fields in eastern China where the men were based had no hangars or shelters for the airplanes. Mechanics wilted in the hot sun and chilled during the cold rains that followed, without enough clothing to cover them or keep them warm. They had few tools with which to work. Even simple items such as pliers were hard to find. At Hengyang, the 75th Squadron of the 23rd Fighter Group, commanded by Tex Hill, had only two sets of hand tools, and these were left over from the AVG. Hill's administrative staff included a sergeant and a mechanic, who set up office with one pencil, some rice paper, and an old typewriter borrowed from a missionary. At Kweilin, the 76th Squadron, led by Ed Rector, ran for a year with one man doing duty as adjutant and executive officer as well as intelligence, personnel, supply, and mess officer.

The living conditions at fields like Hengyang, Kweilin, and Lingling were awful. They had no comforts such as the AVG had enjoyed at Kunming or Loiwing. The barracks were primitive, crowded, and full of bedbugs, and the men were often sick from the unchanging diet. For one entire week, the bombers were forced to suspend operations because all the flying personnel had contracted dysentery. At Lingling, one of the cooks fried fish in tung oil, normally used to make paints and lacquers. All the men were violently ill for days. None of the bases had a flight surgeon, so the sick and wounded were cared for by medical missionaries.

Morale problems in the CATF were often severe, particularly during the early months. Small items that would have boosted morale—such as mail, razor blades, warm clothing, and cigarettes—were lacking for long periods. Chennault blamed Bissell for that and also for the delays in awarding promotions and decorations to his men. Bissell had stopped all promotions for six months until he could develop an official table of organization, without which, he insisted, no unit of the United States Army could function. Further, he consistently disapproved decorations proposed by Chennault while urging approval of medals for men in the Tenth Air Force in India.

The friction between Chennault and Bissell inevitably worsened. Bissell sent an inspector to report on Chennault's operation, and the officer strongly criticized the CATF because the men were unshaven, had muddy shoes, didn't salute, and were not in proper uniforms. Of course they did not have proper uniforms—the army hadn't provided any—but the excuse meant nothing to Bissell.

The CATF was one of the strangest groups in the history of the Army Air Force and the smallest to be commanded by a general officer. "It certainly was the raggedest," Chennault said. "Its paperwork was poor, and salutes were scarce, but when the signals were called for combat, it never missed a play." In the eight months of its existence, the China Air Task Force shot down 149 planes, with another 85 listed as probably destroyed, all at a cost of 16 P-40s. Its bombers dropped more than 300 tons of bombs on enemy targets with the loss of only one B-25. The CATF provided a further demonstration that even a small outfit that lacked proper supplies could beat back the Japanese—if that outfit were well led.

On March 10, 1943, after being grounded for a month because of lack of gasoline, the CATF was disbanded and replaced by the Fourteenth Air Force. Chennault, who had been promoted to the rank of major general a week before, was to lead it. More important to Chennault, however, was that the Fourteenth was separate from Bissell's command. Chennault now had the makings of a real air force, although it began on a small scale with the men and equipment from the CATF.

Chennault later received newer fighter planes—P-51Cs—which flew 150 miles per hour faster than any P-40. He also got the big four-engine B-24 Liberator bombers, as well as a full complement of staff officers. Unfortunately, he was so used to running an air operation by himself that he did not always take advantage of his staff's expertise. He tended to remain his own chief of intelligence and director of operations. Consequently, the Fourteenth Air Force, like Chennault's CATF and AVG earlier, became known for its poor staff work.

Other characteristics of the AVG and the CATF were inherited by the Fourteenth Air Force. In all three outfits, Chennault's men tended to ignore the formalities and trappings of military life. Uniforms were often not regulation, salutes were not the snappiest—when given at all—and paperwork scarcely more than perfunctory. The men of the Fourteenth were never good parade ground soldiers, and they were also noted for persistent feelings of insecurity. They realized they were at the end of a long and low-priority supply line. At a moment's notice, materiel designated for the Fourteenth Air Force could be diverted elsewhere. Perhaps in part because of this lingering insecurity, and because they sensed and reflected the attitude of their commanding officer, many of the men showed strong and bitter feelings toward Bissell, Stilwell, and others in authority. Like Chennault, they tended to be bad subordinates.

The Fourteenth eventually grew from 100 aircraft and 250 men to 1000 planes and 20,000 men, and they compiled a combat record of which any commander could be proud. The outfit destroyed some 2600 Japanese planes, with another 1500 probables, at a cost of 500 of its own aircraft. It is estimated that the actions of the Fourteenth killed nearly 67,000 Japanese troops, destroyed some 600 bridges, and sank 44 naval vessels. After the war, the commander of the Japanese armies in central China, Lt. Gen. Takahashi, said that as much as seventy-five percent of his opposition came from Chennault's men. If it had not been for the Fourteenth Air Force, Takahashi wrote, "we could have gone anywhere we wished."

Although Chennault now had a bigger air force, he was still plagued by the same problem—a lack of adequate supplies. And the bigger his force grew, the more supplies were needed. Everything had to be brought in over the Hump in C-47 transports, and then sent by truck and barge hundreds of miles from Kunming to the airfields in the east. Even with his two-star rank, Chennault found himself expending as much energy and anger in battles for supplies as he did fighting the Japanese.

Keeping the military supplied in China during the war seemed to many to be an impossible task. By July 1943, the Air Transport Command was flying in 4300 tons of supplies every month, but at tremendous cost. The transports burned one gallon of gasoline for every gallon they delivered. Eighteen tons of materiel were required for every ton of bombs Chennault dropped on the Japanese. Each transport plane could deliver only five tons at a time, if, indeed, it reached China safely. By the time the war was over, the Air Transport Command had lost 468 planes, an average of thirteen a month. (The monthly tonnage delivered increased to 13,000 by January 1944, and to 70,000 by May 1945, but this was still not sufficient to satisfy the military's needs.)

The 4300 tons being delivered each month in 1943 included several hundred tons of paper money to keep up with China's inflation rate, and China's four-million-man army and its war industry needed more supplies than the airlift could provide. In addition, Stilwell required far more than 4300 tons per month to carry on the training and equipping of the Chinese armies. And Chennault needed more than his share of 4300 tons a month to keep his planes flying. In an interview with Theodore White,

Chennault said, "I lie awake at night, dreaming gasoline. My stomach is getting nervous. I used 40,000 gallons this past ten days, and I got only 17,000 gallons in."

Thus, there was never enough to satisfy the demands of Chiang Kai-shek or Stilwell or Chennault. Priorities had to be established, and no matter which way the cake was cut, someone was going to go hungry. The man holding the knife in this case was Stilwell.

Chennault believed his outfit was suffering the most from the distribution of supplies. This was especially galling because he was convinced that if his air force were properly equipped, he could knock Japan out of the war. He proposed to accomplish this by cutting off the flow of Japan's war materiel that was being shipped through the South China Sea. All he needed was a sufficient number of planes and absolute authority—that is, to replace Stilwell as supreme commander of the China theater. As long as Stilwell remained in charge, he would continue to send supplies to the Chinese armies. To Chennault, this was a waste. He believed that air power alone could win the war.

Chennault's plans were overly ambitious and highly simplistic, but no more so than the claims of other air force leaders like Eaker, Spaatz, and Arnold, who were saying that air power could win the war in Europe without having to invade the continent. Chennault was not alone in believing in the supremacy of the airplane as a weapon of war.

The Chinese expressed a great deal of support for Chennault's ideas. If Chennault could defeat the Japanese by air power alone, then Chiang would not have to commit his army fully to the war, nor would he have to accept Stilwell's reforms and thus perhaps lose control of the army. He could continue to focus on the threat from the Communists within his own country, rather than on that of the Japanese. It would be an easy victory. Madame Chiang told Chennault that "if we destroy 15 Nippon planes every day, soon there will be no more left." Also, the Chiangs did not like Stilwell and would much rather see their loyal friend Chennault in command.

To no one's surprise, Stilwell did not favor the idea of being replaced by Chennault, and he disliked the plan for the conduct of the air war as much as he disliked the man who proposed it. But there were sound military objections as well as personal ones. Stilwell was alarmed by what he foresaw as the outcome of Chennault's proposed air strikes. If they were as effective as Chennault claimed, the Japanese would no doubt react with a concentrated drive to overrun Chennault's air bases in the east, from which the air strikes had come. And Stilwell knew that the Japanese would be successful because Chinese armies in the area could not hold. The air bases would be lost, the already weak Chinese armies would be routed and demoralized, and more Chinese territory would fall into enemy hands.

To Stilwell, the only way to defeat the Japanese was to continue to build up the Chinese armies until they could take the offensive and recapture lost territory, beginning with Burma. To accomplish this land strategy, Stilwell reasoned that *he* needed the bulk of the supplies airlifted over the Hump. To the Chinese leaders, and later to Roosevelt, Stilwell's strategy appeared to be slow, plodding, and costly, while Chennault's ideas offered a bold, daring, and quick victory. But Stilwell was correct about the vulnerability of Chennault's airfields. By the time those in power were convinced of that, it was too late.

Chennault used everything at his disposal to promote his plan to end the war. In the fall of 1942, Wendell Willkie, who had lost the 1940 presidential election to Roosevelt, was sent by the president on a fact-finding tour. When this popular politician reached China, he met with Chennault, who presented his case with such eagerness and conviction—for two hours—that Willkie asked him to draft a letter that he would personally carry to the president.

On October 8, 1942, Chennault produced what historian Barbara Tuchman called "one of the extraordinary documents of the war . . . the self-annunciation of a military messiah." Chennault wrote that he could defeat Japan with an air force of such small size that it would be considered ridiculous in any other theater of the war. With a force of only 105 modern fighters, 30 medium bombers, and 12 heavy bombers, Chennault proposed to bring about the downfall of Japan, perhaps within six months and certainly no longer than one year, if he were appointed American commander in China.

The military task, he indicated with confidence, was simple, but it had been complicated by those who had no understanding of the nature of air warfare. (He meant Stilwell and Bissell, of course.) Chennault then pointed out that once he had destroyed the Japanese Air Force, then the U.S. Navy could operate in Asian waters freely, and General MacArthur could push his forces forward in the southwest Pacific.

He compared his plan to that of Sherman in the Civil War, cutting Lee's lines of supply and communication. Chennault would sever the Japanese supply lines to the southwest Pacific, cutting off their imports of oil, rubber, and other vital natural resources.

In addition, he would "guarantee to destroy the principal industrial centers of Japan," so the enemy would be unable to supply its troops with war materiel. This would make it easy for the Chinese Army, the U.S. Navy, and MacArthur's troops to advance on Japan with light losses.

The plan was breathtaking in its clarity and confidence and in the scope of its touted results. But it was unrealistic to expect to defeat the Japanese in six months with a total of 147 aircraft. As Chennault himself later witnessed, the defeat of Japan required three years of heavy fighting and more than 20,000 combat planes. By 1945, hundreds of B-29s were being committed to single raids on Japan, more planes for each bombing raid than Chennault said he needed to end the war.

It was also highly unrealistic of Chennault to expect to receive 147 planes in 1942, given the U.S. commitments to its allies and to other theaters of war, and its general unpreparedness at the time. General Arnold dismissed the plan with the comment that Chennault was not "realistic about the logistics of his operation." General Marshall called it "nonsense; not bad strategy, just nonsense."

To President Roosevelt, the plan was more appealing, partly because of Chennault's success with the AVG in beating back the Japanese with only a handful of airplanes. Roosevelt did not believe that Chennault could, as he promised, defeat Japan within a year, but he thought that Chennault could certainly keep the pressure on the Japanese and therefore it would be worthwhile to continue to support him. At the least, providing Chennault with additional resources might help to keep China in the war, which would force Japan to maintain massive numbers of troops and planes there instead of unleashing them against American forces elsewhere in the Pacific.

After writing the letter for Willkie to take to the president, Chennault—and Chiang—kept up the pressure on Washington to oust Stilwell and give more supplies to Chennault. Joe Alsop, Chennault's aide, wrote to his old friend Harry Hopkins, Roosevelt's trusted advisor, arguing that the situation in China was fast approaching disaster. The only hope lay with Chennault. In March 1943, Alsop wrote a twenty-one-page letter blasting Stilwell as incompetent, ignorant of the benefits of air power, and antagonistic to the Chinese leaders.

The U.S. Navy also came to Chennault's aid. They had a long tradition of service in China and resented the supremacy of the army that had developed there since the war began. The naval attaché in Chungking, Marine Corps Col. James M. McHugh, a friend of Chiang's since the 1930s, urged Secretary of the Navy Knox to press for the ouster of Stilwell and Bissell and for their replacement by Chennault. McHugh believed that Chennault was the only military leader in China who could defeat the Japanese. Another naval officer in China, Cdr. Milton Miles, told the Navy Department that "if Chennault were given complete authority with no one but Washington to report to, he'd clean the place out."

Knox forwarded McHugh's report to Secretary of War Stimson, who passed it on to General Marshall. Marshall was irate. Even if Marshall had agreed with McHugh, he would still have been furious with Chennault for bypassing military channels, as Chennault had also done with the Willkie letter and the entreaties of Alsop. But Roosevelt saw McHugh's comments and read them with a great deal of interest.

Chennault was clearly getting his message across to the president. The battle lines had been drawn, and it began to look as though Chennault would be the winner. He had powerful friends with direct access to the president, while Stilwell, as was proper, honored the chain of command and reported, soberly and pessimistically, only to General Marshall.

In the spring of 1943, Chiang Kai-shek urged President Roosevelt to call Chennault to Washington so that he could hear the air leader's arguments in person. The president agreed. Marshall insisted that Roosevelt also bring Stilwell home so that both parties could be heard, and Roosevelt finally agreed to do so. The stage was set for a bitter confrontation, to be held within the White House itself.

On April 20, Chennault received word that Stilwell would be arriving at Chennault's headquarters in Kunming later that day. When he met the plane, Stilwell asked, "Where are your bags? Aren't you ready to go?"

"Go where?" Chennault said.

Stilwell led him away from the group of officers in attendance and explained that they had been ordered to Washington. He implied that the trip was the result of Chennault's machinations. Stilwell said he was on his way to India and had stopped only to pick up Chennault. Chennault asked permission to confer with Chiang Kai-shek first, and Stilwell agreed. They would meet in Karachi two days later and fly from there, aboard a C-87, the transport version of the B-24, to the States.

Aboard the transport, Chennault wrote out a new, more detailed plan for his air war in China. He used his briefcase as a desk and wrote in longhand with a leaky fountain pen. The proposal was essentially the same as he had presented in the letter to Wendell Willkie, but he increased the number of planes he thought were necessary to win the war. Now he asked for 150 fighters, 70 medium bombers, and 35 heavy bombers, plus 7000 tons of airlifted supplies every month.

Chennault arrived in Washington without a staff or even a proper uniform. Unable to obtain one since his induction, he wore a combination of a prewar olive drab tunic, a gray wool shirt, and a black tie. Some people wondered which army he was serving in. For a staff, he found Lt. Col. Harold Morgan, who had been with the Eleventh Bombardment Squadron in China. Morgan lacked a top-secret security clearance, however, and so was not allowed to attend the high-level meetings. Stilwell, as was his right, had brought his full staff from China.

Being back in Washington for a month was a heady experience for Chennault. He was a hero, lionized in the press, sought after by politicians, entertained lavishly by society leaders. The capital city was a brighter place when one was wearing two stars, and Chennault was greatly amused by the deference shown him by some of his one-time opponents.

Many important meetings were being held that month, as the visit of Chennault and Stilwell coincided with the Trident conference, a high-level British-American discussion of the future conduct of the war. Winston Churchill attended, along with the British joint chiefs of staff and more than 100 advisors. The war in China was only one of the topics to be dealt with, and it was far from a major one in the context of the global war.

Chennault and Stilwell participated in many of these meetings, although Chennault was frequently seated so far from the discussion leaders that it was hard, because of his hearing problem, for him to catch what was going on. More crucial, however, was the time he and Stilwell spent with Roosevelt. They all met for the first time on April 30, and it did not go well for Stilwell. He had prepared thoroughly, and he laid out his arguments for the recapture of Burma so that there would then be a land route into China. He pointed out how easily the Japanese could capture Chennault's air bases in east China if Chennault were to launch his proposed attacks.

"Nobody," Stilwell wrote, "was interested in the humdrum work of building a ground force but me. Chennault promised to drive the Japs right out of China in six months, so why not give him the stuff to do it? It was the shortcut to victory." But it was not only Stilwell's plan that sounded uninspiring to Roosevelt, it was Stilwell himself, who sat slumped in his chair mumbling about how China would not fight. General Marshall was distressed—he knew how persuasive Stilwell could be in a briefing—but that day Stilwell gave such a poor performance that

Roosevelt asked Marshall if the man were seriously ill. Marshall defended his commander as best he could, but he was nonetheless disappointed by the presentation.

Several explanations for Stilwell's behavior have been offered. First, he was incapable of arguing for a program if it appeared that he was also promoting himself. Second, he disliked Roosevelt intensely and knew that the feeling was, to some extent, reciprocated. And third, he sensed that Roosevelt was already favorably impressed by Chennault's slick and optimistic plan for winning the war.

Stilwell was correct. Roosevelt was very pleased with Chennault and his plan. Chennault later wrote that Roosevelt recognized the strategic importance of attacking Japanese shipping in the South China Sea and asked him if his planes could sink a million tons of enemy shipping in a year. Chennault told him they could destroy even more if they got 10,000 tons of supplies every month. At that, the president banged his fist on his desk and laughed.

"If you can sink a million tons," he said, "we'll break their back."

At a later meeting, Roosevelt asked Stilwell and Chennault for their opinions of Chiang Kai-shek. "A vacillating, tricky, undependable old scoundrel who never keeps his word," said Stilwell. Chennault had a different view. "I think the Generalissimo is one of the two or three greatest military and political leaders in the world today. He has never broken a commitment or promise to me." It would be another year before Roosevelt came to agree with Stilwell's assessment of Chiang, but at the moment, in the spring of 1943, Chennault's evaluation was the more acceptable to the president.

Chennault carried the day with his promise of a quick and easy victory. On May 2, Roosevelt told Marshall that nothing must interfere with Chennault's air offensive. Chennault was to receive the bulk of the supplies flown in over the Hump, and Stilwell's land war was to take second place. Chennault was not given overall command of the China theater, but his stature increased in Roosevelt's view while that of Stilwell receded. Roosevelt considered for a time recalling Stilwell, but Marshall and Stimson dissuaded him.

Shortly before Chennault was due to leave Washington, the president sent for him to ask if he felt he had gotten everything he needed. Chennault assured Roosevelt that if he received all the supplies he had been promised, his air force would accomplish its mission. Roosevelt asked an aide to bring maps of the China coast, and he and Chennault reviewed the plan for the aerial offensive. Roosevelt asked a great many detailed questions, and Chennault later said that he had rarely had such an interested audience.

When Chennault finished the briefing, Roosevelt said, "Now I want you to write me from time to time and let me know how things are getting along."

"Do you mean you want me to write to you personally?" Chennault said.

"Yes, I do," the president said.

Chennault's political victory was complete.

He began his air offensive in the fall of 1943, and the results were disastrous. As soon as the Japanese began to feel the effects of the air strikes, their armies in east China moved (as predicted) on Chennault's air bases. The defending Chinese armies quickly disintegrated in the face of the enemy and fled to the west, often with their leaders in the vanguard in convoys of trucks loaded with their families and their personal possessions.

All Chennault's bases in the east were captured. Lingling fell in September and Kweilin in November. Millions of dollars of supplies and equipment were destroyed by the Americans before evacuating Kweilin, which was then the main base for the Fourteenth Air Force. Journalist Theodore White watched the spectacle. "What followed that night was a wild and wonderful thunderpopping, flame-streaked, explosion-rocked orgy of destruction that is the most scarlet-and-brilliant night of my memory."

Not only were valuable supplies lost, but also the airfields from which Chennault had planned to carry the war to Japanese shipping and, eventually, to the Japanese homeland itself. He blamed Stilwell for not supplying the Chinese armies in the east with sufficient war materiel, but, in truth, lend-lease had supplied them so generously that the Chinese commanders had sold off huge quantities of goods on the black market. If anything revealed the political and military corruption so endemic in China, it was this rout in the east in late 1943 and early 1944.

Chennault's planes hammered the Japanese troops, but they could not stop the offensive. For a time it appeared that all of China would be lost. Chennault complained that his forces were hopelessly inadequate, and he badgered Stilwell and Washington for more planes and supplies. Stilwell considered this to be an attempt to "duck the consequences of having sold the wrong bill of goods." Chennault had assured Chiang that his air force alone could stop the Japanese. When Chennault found that he could not do it, Stilwell accused him of "trying to prepare an out for himself by claiming that with a little more, which we won't give him, he can still do it."

Stilwell did not accept Chennault's protestations and neither did Stimson, Marshall, and others in the War Department. They concluded that Chennault's air offensive to end the war had failed and was not worth the cost. In their view, the commitment of such a large number of transport planes to supply Chennault had hurt the war effort in Europe, where Patton's army had been halted because it could not be properly supplied. Roosevelt became convinced that Stilwell had been correct, and because of the devastating military losses in China, he also lost confidence in Chiang Kai-shek.

The United States showed its displeasure with the Chinese leader by cutting off additional economic aid. Secretary of the Treasury Morgenthau discovered evidence of the massive embezzlement of American funds by Chiang and his family. He called them crooks, vowed never to give them "another nickel," and suggested that they "go jump in the Yangtze." The enthusiasm with which Washington had courted China in 1941 and 1942 turned to distrust and disgust.

General Marshall warned the president that the only way to save China from total military collapse was for Chiang to turn over his armies to Stilwell, the one American the Generalissimo hated more than any other. On July 6, 1944, Roosevelt cabled

Chiang, suggesting just that. Chiang agreed, in principle, to Roosevelt's request but stalled for time.

On September 15, Chiang astounded everyone with a message to Roosevelt announcing that he would never give up his armies to Stilwell. His timing was perfect. Roosevelt was preoccupied with more urgent problems and was unwilling to force a showdown that might lead to China's pulling out of the war. Also, by that time the war in the Pacific was going well. MacArthur was about to invade the Philippines, bases in the Marianas were being prepared for planned B-29 raids on Japan, and Stalin had agreed to declare war on Japan after Germany surrendered. Hence, while it was important that China continue to fight, it was no longer such a vital part of the overall war. The joint chiefs of staff were no longer interested in supporting the war in China and it was not worth the trouble to insist that Stilwell prevail over Chiang.

On October 18, 1944, Stilwell was replaced by Maj. Gen. Albert C. Wedemeyer, who had been chief of staff to Lord Louis Mountbatten in Ceylon. Wedemeyer would be Chiang's senior American military advisor. A separate India–Burma command would be headed by Lt. Gen. Daniel Sultan, who had served as Stilwell's deputy commander.

Although Stilwell was ordered to leave immediately, he took the time to write what Tuchman described as a "very decent" letter to Chennault, "taking pride in his achievements and acknowledging the admiration in which he was held by the Chinese." For his part, however, Chennault remained bitter toward Stilwell and could neither forget nor forgive. In his postwar memoirs Chennault noted that Stilwell left "a legacy that is still costing both the United States and China heavily. During his regime he bled China white and squandered most of the American resources available in the CBI theater on a military campaign of minor value while the fundamental problem of preserving China as a base of military operations and a strong postwar ally was subverted to his personal quest for supreme command."

Chennault did not go to Stilwell's headquarters to see him off. Instead, the departure ceremony featured T. V. Soong, who was about to become China's prime minister, and China's minister of war, whose dismissal Stilwell had frequently demanded. Stilwell listened to the flowery words of farewell, suffered through the exquisite courtesies, then turned to his aide.

"What the hell are we waiting for?"

Stilwell was gone.* Chennault would be next.

Chennault had made powerful enemies in Washington, and he was more vulnerable to their attacks since the failure of his air offensive against the Japanese. There was no question that some high-ranking military and civilian leaders wanted to recall him. This was proving difficult, however, partly because Chennault was such a popular and heroic figure in the United States. Books had been written and movies made about Chennault and the Flying Tigers. He had achieved something of the status of a national idol.

Even the failure of his recent air offensive had been offset by his substantial past and continuing achievements. Although his Fourteenth Air Force had not ended the war, they had killed many of the enemy and were forcing the Japanese to maintain an air force in China, one that otherwise would be used against Americans elsewhere in the Pacific. In addition, Chennault was still in the president's favor. Roosevelt admired Chennault's fighting spirit, of which he was frequently reminded in letters from Joe Alsop.

There was one point on which Chennault's detractors believed he might be vulnerable. This involved not strategic or tactical issues, but moral and legal ones, that is, Chennault's alleged involvement in smuggling and black market activities. If it could be shown that he was guilty of profiting illegally from his position, that would be more than ample reason for his dismissal. In the winter of 1944–1945, two investigations were launched, one civilian and the other military.

During this time, General Wedemeyer, who had replaced Stilwell, received a visitor from Washington, a special agent of the U.S. Secret Service. "He reported directly to me in great confidence that he had been sent to investigate Chennault and a mem-

---

*Stilwell was given a desk job in Washington, compiling the history of the CBI theater, and in June 1945 was assigned command of the Tenth Army, which was expected to lead the anticipated attack on Japan. He died in October 1946.

ber of his staff who were alleged to be smuggling—bringing in contraband in the cargo planes that were operating between Burma–India and Kunming, China. I gave this Secret Service man every assistance, and he reported just before returning to the United States that he had not obtained evidence to confirm the allegation."

Why was the Secret Service, a civilian agency and a branch of the Treasury Department, investigating the activities of an American army general serving overseas? Morgenthau, the secretary of the treasury, had never been an enemy of Chennault, and it is doubtful that Roosevelt would have concerned himself with such a matter at that stage of the war. If he had, he would surely have asked General Marshall to investigate through the army's Criminal Investigation Division (CID), whose job it was to deal with illegal activities such as smuggling.

As it was, the CID had already conducted an investigation of Chennault at the direction of Hap Arnold, who was concerned about Chennault's alleged financial dealings in China. Indeed, this was a major reason for Arnold's distrust and dislike of Chennault. And the matter of the bordellos resurfaced, first at Kweilin and later at Kunming. A CID report on the Kweilin bordello and on smuggling operations there in 1943 had been given to Stilwell, who wrote in his secret black book: "Officers pimping. Hauling whores in our planes. Sent for Chennault. He *knew*."

The CID investigated the Kunming establishments again later in the war. "Of course there were houses where pilots could hire a prostitute in Kunming," recalled General Wedemeyer, "and those houses, as General Chennault explained to me, had been operating there for some time, with his Fourteenth Air Force flight surgeon exercising some supervision concerning sanitation and disease control." It was a continuation of the practice Chennault had begun earlier in the war of setting up safe brothels for his men so that venereal disease would not exact such a high toll. These were not profit-making ventures but were designed to increase the combat efficiency of the outfit. Clergymen in the States, and the Women's Christian Temperance Union, had voiced periodic complaints, but Chennault was unconcerned about these attacks.

Far more serious was the CID's investigation of smuggling activities that implicated Chennault, at least indirectly. On December 21, 1944, the CBI *Roundup,* a news release of theater activities published in New Delhi, contained an article entitled "Hump Smuggling Ring Exposed by Army." The story received wide publicity in American newspapers and magazines over the following months and was discussed on worldwide broadcasts of the "Army Hour" radio program.

The article described the exposure of a major smuggling ring that had been operating over the Hump since 1942. Profits were estimated to be in excess of $4 million. "There is under charges a total of 87 major cases, with profits of more than $5000 each and 213 minor cases with profits of less than $5000. . . . The principal groups of smugglers that have been identified were members of the U.S. Army; American Volunteer Group, the famed 'Flying Tigers'; China National Airways personnel; Red Cross members; technical representatives of U.S. aircraft manufacturers; and British, Indian, and Chinese civilians."

Chennault responded to the *Roundup* article with a letter to General Sultan, commander of American forces in Burma and India. He pointed out on March 17, 1945, that he had read the relevant court-martial orders and failed to find "any foundation of the statements appearing in the press releases that many members of the Armed Forces have been tried by General Court-Martial for these offenses." If, Chennault continued, the CID had cleared up 87 major cases and 213 minor ones, then one would certainly expect to find records of courts-martial and other disciplinary actions.

He also objected to the mention of AVG personnel as being guilty of smuggling, noting that the AVG, as a civilian operation, was not subject to military law. Furthermore, even if they were bound by military law, the investigation of any alleged offenses committed in 1942 would be barred under the Statute of Limitations, Articles of War 39. Thus, Chennault concluded there were no legal grounds for releasing information that damaged the reputation of the AVG. "The nature of the press releases leads me to believe that the entire matter has been exaggerated to the detriment of the members of the AVG and to me as their leader."

He asked General Sultan to take "corrective action," but the harm had already been done. The AVG, the Fourteenth Air Force, and Chennault became linked, for many people, with smuggling and black market activities.

Chennault was aware that some of the people questioned by the CID had been asked specifically about his own possible involvement in smuggling operations. No connection with smuggling ever surfaced, but in at least one instance, Chennault was accused by CID agents of adultery, which, even if true, was not illegal. Chennault suspected that the CID was out to get anything they could on him, and he ordered the Office of the Inspector General to investigate them.

One of the suspects in the smuggling operations who had been interrogated by the CID was an old friend of Chennault's, Harry Sutter, a Swiss national who was employed by the Chinese Air Force as an instructor. When questioned later by the Office of the Inspector General, Sutter revealed how intensely the CID agents had tried to get him to smear Chennault's name. In a statement dated March 15, 1945, and classified "Secret," Sutter said that in his questioning by CID agents, "Chennault's name was brought out several times. The first time they wanted to know what General Chennault's interest in me and my wife were. Secondly, did I know that General Chennault was the leader of the large-scale smuggling? Thirdly, what was the relationship between General Chennault and my wife? They also mentioned General Chennault's name in several affairs that have taken place prior to this investigation. . . . The process of questioning took place on three or four occasions. On each occasion the American CID tried very hard for me to admit that General Chennault was involved or implicated in the smuggling in China. They also brought out the occasion of the AVG's when they were in Burma and again tried to bring General Chennault's name into this matter."

Sutter said he had been threatened with a 14-year jail term if he did not "come clean." He also recalled "some insinuating things that were passed between the questions about the relations between General Chennault and my wife, whether I was very dumb or blind to know that there was not something taking place."

When Chennault learned of this he complained in writing to General Wedemeyer, asking him to take steps "to end the embarrassment to me. Such extreme measures as Courts-Martial proceedings against the CID officials concerned, or even against me, would be welcome as an expedient to terminate this situation."

The CID did not continue their probe. If someone were trying to force Chennault out of his command by linking him with smuggling or other illegal activities, he did not succeed. There was no evidence of wrongdoing on Chennault's part.

But there were other ways of bringing about the same result. If Chennault could not be relieved of command for illegal activities, perhaps his command could be altered in such a way that he would choose to resign on his own.

Franklin Roosevelt died about a month after the CID probes ended, and Chennault was left without a patron in high places. Marshall and Arnold acted quickly. In a blunt statement to Wedemeyer, Arnold called for Chennault's retirement as soon as possible.

"General Chennault has been in China for a long period of time fighting a defensive war with minimum resources," wrote General Arnold. "The meagerness of supplies and the resulting guerrilla type of warfare must change to a modern type of striking, offensive air power. I firmly believe that the quickest and most effective way to change air warfare in your Theater, employing modern offensive thought, tactics and techniques, is to change commanders. I would appreciate your concurrence in General Chennault's early withdrawal from the China Theater. He should take advantage of the retirement privileges now available to physically disqualified officers that make their pay not subject to income tax."

Had Chennault seen the message referring to him as physically disqualified, he would probably have challenged Arnold and his staff to an arm wrestling contest. He would also have been irate to learn of the stated reason for his retirement—a change from defensive to offensive aerial warfare in China. If any air commander believed in taking the offensive, of striking the enemy first—even if all he had to do it with was a half-dozen P-40s—it was Claire Chennault. And once his Fourteenth Air Force was finally equipped with modern planes, he had been on the offensive even more. This was the man who wanted to bomb Tokyo in 1940! Arnold had offered a poor excuse for dismissing Chennault. To accuse him of being unable to employ modern offensive thought, tactics, and techniques was to discredit all he had accomplished. It challenged the very nature of the man himself.

Arnold also intended to get the Fourteenth Air Force out of the way because it was too tied to Chennault and his ideas, too reflective of the maverick spirit of its leader. He wanted to replace it with the Tenth Air Force, now in India. Since Burma had been recaptured, there was little for the Tenth to do where it was. Moving it to China would put it in the front line. The commanding officer of the Tenth was Maj. Gen. George Stratemeyer, who had once served as Arnold's chief of staff. Chennault's Fourteenth was to be shunted to an area north of the Yangtze River, where there were few targets and fewer supplies; it was far from the distribution center at Kunming. Two veteran fighter groups and the two best medium bomber squadrons from the Fourteenth would become attached to Stratemeyer's force. Thus, the Fourteenth would no longer be large enough to constitute an air force. Instead, it would be the size of a wing, a considerable demotion for Chennault and one Arnold knew he would not tolerate.

As Chennault described it, the plan was to "let the Fourteenth die on the vine, subsisting on less than its familiar starvation diet with no important targets while the Tenth smashed to final victory." And so, Chennault added, "It was clearly time to go."

On July 8, 1945, eight years after he had first offered his services to China, Chennault wrote to Wedemeyer, requesting retirement for reasons of health.

"I approved his retirement," General Wedemeyer said, "and recommended that he be given a Distinguished Service Medal for his outstanding service as an intrepid and effective air commander of the Fourteenth Air Force during my period of command."

The wording of the citation, awarded in August 1945, belied Arnold's stated need for a more offensively oriented air leader in China.

"Although limited by the difficulties of supply, to the smallest air force in the United States Army, he exacted a heavy toll of enemy personnel, shipping, materiel and equipment. His force contributed beyond expectation to limiting Japanese air and ground activity and was a major factor in rendering impotent the enemy's air drive in China. . . . In the performance of his task, General Chennault evidenced tactical and strategic skill, foresight and professional attainments which reflect great honor upon himself and the military service."

Not bad for a beat-up old army captain the military hadn't wanted.

Chennault left China on August 8, angry and embittered. For eight years he had fought the Japanese, far longer than any other American. And just when victory was in sight, he was being prevented from sharing publicly in the glory. If anyone deserved to stand on the deck of the USS *Missouri* to witness the Japanese surrender on September 2, 1945, it was Claire Chennault. As it was, he heard about the surrender somewhere over Egypt, while he was flying home.

He took back with him the love and gratitude of the Chinese people and of the men who served with him. There had been tearful and touching farewells when he made the rounds of his airfields. In Chungking, some two million people jammed the streets, cheering as the Generalissimo's car took Chennault through the city. The narrow streets were so mobbed that the chauffeur finally cut off the engine and let the people push the car up the steep hills to a large open square that had been decorated for a farewell ceremony. The platform bore the Flying Tiger insignia, and an arch had been erected and covered with pine branches and flowers.

Chennault stood beneath the arch while the Chinese bestowed hundreds of gifts on him—jade, antiques, paintings, scrolls, and embroidered silks. Each of the grateful Chinese citizens even indulged in the barbaric Western custom of shaking hands, out of respect for Chennault. In the evening Chiang Kai-shek presided over a dinner for Chennault and presented him with the White Sun and Blue Sky, China's highest award. The Generalissimo apologized for Madame Chiang's absence—she was in Brazil— saying that she would be better able to express their feelings of gratitude.

At Kunming, Chennault loaded all the precious gifts, which he would later donate to Louisiana State University, aboard his C-47. Hundreds of Chinese lined the runway, shooting off firecrackers so that devils would be frightened out of the way. Among the crowd watching the plane take off was Anna Chan, who, as a fledgling reporter, had interviewed Chennault two years earlier. This lovely and charming young woman of twenty and the fifty-five-year-old Chennault were very much in love. When he kissed her good-bye, he had said, "I'll be back."

Chennault returned to China the following January, having retired from the army a second time. He had done some fishing back home in Louisiana and had undertaken a brief lecture tour. But after only a few months in the States, he headed across the Pacific to the country he had called home for eight years, and to Anna Chan.

He toured the war-ravaged country and conferred with the Chiangs and other leaders, and concluded that he had another job to do in China. The country needed an air transport system to help its economic recovery. The movement of goods into and out of China, and within its huge land mass, was at a standstill. Even sorely needed relief supplies sent by the United Nations were piling up in warehouses in the port cities, with no way to move them inland.

And so Claire Chennault started another air force, this one devoted to peaceful aims and to saving lives. He went back to the United States in May to seek financial support for an airline in China but found little help until he talked to Fiorello La Guardia, then director of the United Nations Relief and Rehabilitation Agency (UNRRA). The colorful former mayor of New York City awarded a sizable contract to Chennault and Whiting Willauer to establish the Civil Air Transport (CAT), an airline to distribute relief supplies throughout China. Willauer had been with China Defense Supplies during the AVG period and had later served in China as a lend-lease official. The treasurer of the Civil Air Transport would be James Brennan, a wartime supporter of Chennault's who had also been personal secretary to T. V. Soong. The attorney for CAT was Tommy "the Cork" Corcoran, who had served as the legal advisor for the AVG. The contract provided for the purchase of nineteen surplus C-46s and C-47s at reduced prices, and the loan of the money to pay for them.

Under Chennault's aggressive leadership, CAT became a phenomenal success. In the beginning it operated on a shoestring and under great adversity, conditions that seemed to bring out the best in Chennault, as they had in 1940. The airline began flying in January 1947, one month after Chennault married Anna Chan, and by April 1948 it was delivering two million ton-miles per month. Before long, CAT employed 1100 people, many of whom were pilots and ground crewmen from the Flying Tigers and the Fourteenth Air Force, who were glad to be back serving under the Old Man.

Chennault was not the only ex-AVG man to start an airline after the war. Bob Prescott, one of the original AVG pilots, founded the National Skyway Freight Company with eleven other wartime pilots and mechanics and fourteen Budd Conestoga twin-engine transport planes. Their initial contracts were with the California Fruit Growers Association to haul fruit from the West Coast to the East. Times were hard, and sometimes there was no cargo to haul. The airline several times came close to bankruptcy. But Prescott persevered and eventually his outfit became an international cargo airline, known today as the Flying Tiger Line.

By 1948 Chennault found himself in a war again, the civil war that erupted in China between the Communists, led by Mao Tse-tung, and the Nationalists under Chiang Kai-shek. Chennault's planes were called on to haul military supplies, often to beleaguered cities. Two years before the Western world marveled at the Berlin Airlift, Chennault had accomplished the same thing several times in China. His planes supplied raw cotton to the mills of Chengchow in northern China and flew out finished cotton goods. As a result, 20,000 people were able to keep their jobs in the cotton mills while the city was under siege.

When Chiang's armies were surrounded in Mukden, Manchuria, for six months, Chennault's planes brought in thousands of tons of food and supplies and took out hundreds of wounded troops. Mukden fell under the relentless onslaught of the Communist forces, and the CAT flew up to 50 missions a day to Nationalist troops in other parts of Manchuria, flying into hastily built fields that were often under artillery fire. In the end, nothing was able to stop the Communists, and Chiang's armies fell back to the Canton area.

Chennault came to consider the Communist takeover to be as great a threat to American interests in the Pacific as the Japanese drive a decade before. "The United States is losing the Pacific war," he said, and he predicted that if the Communists were not stopped in China, there would be a "ring of Red bases . . . stretched from Siberia to Saigon." He believed that China needed American aid and, in 1949, he was back in Washington working with T. V. Soong and Tommy Corcoran to lobby for $700 million in military aid for Chiang. Some critics of assistance to China pointed out that a portion of any military aid would inevitably benefit Chennault because it would go to his airline to pay for the transportation of supplies. The aid proposal was unsuccessful, and in July Chennault tried to persuade the U.S. Congress to finance another Flying Tigers, a new volunteer air force to save China. *Life* magazine referred to Chennault's proposal as the "last call" for China and reported that with such a force, Chennault could keep a portion of southern China free from Communist control. "A fighting American," *Life* wrote, "says that a third of its good earth . . . can be saved."

The Truman administration, however, was unwilling to become involved in China's civil war or to give any more aid to China. President Truman believed that the Chiangs and the Soongs were "all thieves, every last one of them." Washington was in no mood to make them richer.

Chennault was on his own this time. There would be no new AVG for China. By October 1949, the Communists had taken all of mainland China, and Chennault found that 73 of his airplanes, the bulk of his fleet, had been impounded on the airfield at Hong Kong. British courts declared that the planes belonged to the new government of China. It would take Chennault nearly three years of legal battles to regain control of his planes. It was a hollow victory, however, because the planes had sat unprotected in the heat and humidity, and were sacked by vandals and thieves. They were worth very little by the time he reacquired them.

During that period the CAT came close to bankruptcy. The outfit moved to Taiwan with Chiang's Nationalist government and slowly began to recover. When the United States entered the war in Korea in 1950, CAT planes were chartered to haul cargo and troops.

In 1954, the CAT became involved in the war in Indochina between the French and the Communist Viet Minh. When the French garrison at Dienbienphu was surrounded, Chennault's pilots, flying U.S. Air Force C-119 transports, flew many missions to drop supplies by parachute to the French. One of Chennault's pilots, James McGovern, was shot down and killed on one of these missions, along with his co-pilot, Wallace Buford, and several French cargo handlers. They may have been America's first casualties in the long war in Vietnam.

When the Viet Minh defeated the French, Chennault grew increasingly worried that the Communists would overrun all of Southeast Asia. He was ready to go to war to stop them, as he had gone to war against the Japanese, and his idea once again was to use a volunteer air force. He pushed for American support for an invasion of mainland China by Chiang's forces and those of Syngman Rhee, the president of South Korea, and he lobbied for a 470-man International Volunteer Group to be patterned after the Flying Tigers.

Chennault described his plan in articles in *Look* magazine and other publications, promising that he could have the volunteer group operational in 90 days. He said he already had a list of combat-experienced pilots and ground crew who were eager to join up. The project had the support of Admiral Radford, chairman of the joint chiefs of staff, and of a number of influential senators and congressmen.

Training sites were selected in Central America with the help of Chennault's partner in the CAT, Whiting Willauer, who was then the American ambassador to Honduras.* Chennault inspected

---

*Willauer was later responsible for much of the planning of the Bay of Pigs invasion. Willauer and Brennan sold the CAT to the Central Intelligence Agency. It became Air America and played a vital part in overt and covert operations in the Vietnam war and throughout Southeast Asia.

several of these sites, but when he returned to Washington he found that considerable opposition had developed in the State Department, the Defense Department, and the Nationalist Chinese Air Force, which apparently resented the implication that the Nationalists were not capable of defeating the Communists themselves. That was the end of Chennault's last chance to go to war.

Anna Chennault called 1956 "the year of the cough." Chennault had kept as physically fit as his busy work and travel schedule would permit, playing tennis and badminton, and baseball with the CAT's baseball team he organized. His only illnesses were the recurring bouts of bronchitis that had troubled him for years. Still, he did not change his habit of chain-smoking throughout the day and sometimes at night as well, when Anna would find him pacing the floor thinking about some problem. She urged him to smoke less, but he said that smoking was one of the few pleasures he could afford.

The Chennaults bought a house in Monroe, Louisiana, where they spent a month or two each year. He seemed to feel better away from the cold, damp climate of Taiwan. He proposed a driving trip across Canada, but on the way back he asked Anna to drive. That was when she realized just how ill he was. He checked into Walter Reed Army Hospital in Washington, where the doctors found a tumor on his left lung. It was malignant. A year or so later he was told he had no more than six months to live.

He continued to travel and to work, somehow dragging up amazing reserves of energy. When he went to New York for a board meeting of the CAT, he spent an afternoon with Paul Frillman, the AVG's chaplain, who now headed a public relations firm. Frillman accompanied him to a photographer's studio where his picture was to be taken for a cigarette advertisement. Chennault said he was doing it only to help pay his medical expenses.

"We went up to a loft," Frillman said, "where two skittish young photographers had assembled heaps of pseudo-Chinese junk, and stayed hours while they plunked the general up and down in arrangements of phony gongs, soapstone dragons, and other gimcracks.

"They mauled the ailing Tiger around as if he were a bundle of rags. 'Look there!' 'Look here!' 'Hold your hands this way!' 'Blow the smoke that way!' they would order, then they touched up his cheeks with theatrical makeup. I had never seen that hawk face so full of concentrated hate."

There were some happy moments, too. He took Anna to Europe for a delayed honeymoon and returned to Taiwan for the CAT's tenth anniversary. But he was too weak to cut the cake at the celebration. When the Chennaults arrived back in San Francisco on January 10, 1958, the reporters were waiting. One asked if it were true that he had cancer.

"Afraid I have," he said. "That's what the doctors tell me."

"What do you plan to do, General?"

"Do?" he said. "Why, I'm going to try to outlive it. If the Lord gives me enough time, I'll beat this one, too."

Claire Lee Chennault died on Sunday, July 27, 1958. When he was buried in Arlington Cemetery, it was with the three stars of a lieutenant general. Two days before Chennault's death, President Eisenhower had telephoned him at the Ochsner Foundation Hospital in New Orleans to tell him of the promotion. Chennault could not speak much by then—even breathing was difficult—but he was clearly pleased by the honor and grateful for the many congratulatory telegrams that poured in.

Many of the people who had served with him in China attended the funeral. His old Washington squadron was there—Corcoran, Willauer, T. V. Soong. Madame Chiang, Chennault's "princess," stood with them in the glaring sun to say her farewell. Joseph Alsop attended, along with AVG pilots Tex Hill and Ed Rector. Among the military officers were an air force colonel and a major, Chennault's sons, carrying on the family name in the service of their country. The well-known generals of World War II also came to pay their respects—Nathan Twining, Curtis LeMay, Albert Wedemeyer, George Kenney, Thomas White, Carl Spaatz, Bedell Smith.

Chennault had come a long way from the field in rural Louisiana where he saw his first airplane, a long way from retirement as a captain in 1937, a long way from a jungle airstrip in Burma where he whipped a group of adventurers like himself into one of the greatest fighter outfits in the history of aviation, a long way from the lonely flight back to the States in 1945, full of resentment at being deprived of attending the surrender of Japan.

He had fought hard for the tributes he finally received at Arlington, the respect, adulation, and love of those who had served with him, and the thanks of a grateful nation. Nothing had come easy for Chennault. But he had won.

ACKNOWLEDGMENTS

I am grateful to the many people who graciously gave of their time and recollections, their papers and diaries. I particularly wish to thank General A. C. Wedemeyer, General Bruce K. Holloway, General James H. Howard, and Joseph Alsop. Some others with whom I talked and corresponded preferred to express their views "off the record." I am also grateful to General Kelsie L. Reaves for putting me in touch with his West Point classmate, General Holloway, and for keeping me supplied with army magazines.

A complex and unexpected chain of events brought me into contact with several people from Chennault's early years, who were able to help me fashion a portrait of his character and the events in his life in the period before the Flying Tigers. For this I am grateful to my neighbor, Harry Hoover, for putting me in touch with Peggy McDonald (Mrs. Billy McDonald), who sent me on to Sebie Biggs Smith, who suggested I contact Ivaloo Watson (Mrs. Rolfe Watson). All these people were generous in supplying recollections, letters, cablegrams, photographs, and tape recordings.

The Chennault papers, on deposit at the Hoover Institution of War, Revolution and Peace at Stanford University, are a valuable source of data on the American Volunteer Group. The material includes correspondence, group orders, combat reports, and personnel records. The papers are also available on twelve reels of microfilm at the Manuscript Division of the Library of Congress.

A guide to the collection has been prepared by Robert Hessen: *General Claire Lee Chennault: A Guide to His Papers in the Hoover Institution Archives* (Stanford, Calif.: Hoover Institution Press, 1983).

The Larry Pistole collection of Flying Tigers memorabilia contains a number of diaries on deposit at Texas A&M University. I am grateful to Charles Schultz, University Archivist, and to Terry Anderson, for making available the diaries of George Burgard, John Donovan, Olga Greenlaw, Robert Keeton, Charles Mott, Arvid Olson, Robert M. Smith, and Pete Wright.

At the Office of Air Force History, Bernard Nalty, Susan Cober, and Roger Jernigan provided information from their extensive holdings, including interviews with R. A. Breitweiser, Bruce Holloway, and Laurence Kuter. I thank them for their time and expertise.

Jeri Nunn of Columbia University's Oral History Research Office made available the interviews from the Flying Tigers Association 1962 reunion. These include recollections of Anna Chennault, Tommy Corcoran, Tex Hill, Matt Kuykendall, Joe Jordon, Gale McAllister, Robert Neale, Charles Older, Robert Prescott, Doreen Davis Reynolds, Lewis Richards, Don Rodewald, Wilfred Schaper, Robert M. Smith, Tom Trumble, and Harvey Wirta. Additional material was found in the papers of Paul Frillman, Sebie Biggs Smith, Henry Wallace, and John Williams.

Larry Wilson and his staff at the National Air and Space Museum spent a great deal of time locating photographs and acquainting me with their laser videodisc system for storing photographs.

Colonel John R. Vance, an astute military historian, and a prisoner-of-war following the fall of Corregidor, read the manuscript. I am grateful, as always, for his insightful comments, particularly his assessment of combat air tactics and antiaircraft operations, which he prepared for the Army War College in the 1920s.

Captain Thomas B. Payne, a navy fighter pilot and survivor of the USS *Houston*, put me in touch with Elizabeth Ferguson, of the San Diego Aerospace Museum, and John Williams, historian of the Flying Tigers Association.

Popular periodicals consulted include *The New York Times,*

Time, Newsweek, Life, Collier's, Saturday Evening Post, and *China Monthly.* Military publications include *Flying, Army, Air Force Magazine, Airman, Strategy and Tactics, Aerospace Historian,* and the *Journal of the American Aviation Historical Society.*

Official military histories that provided background information are the Craven and Cate air force history and the Romanus and Sunderland China–Burma–India volume. In addition, every writer on this period is indebted to Barbara Tuchman, for her classic work on Stilwell; to Sterling Seagrave, for his analysis of the influence of the Soong family; and to Michael Schaller, for his evaluation of U.S.–China relations.

My thanks are also due to Anita Diamant, my agent, for her continued encouragement, and to Tom Dunne and his staff at St. Martin's Press.

I am especially grateful to my wife, Sydney Ellen, for her tireless contributions to this project. She tracked down people and papers, led me through the mazes of libraries and archives, and shared in the interviewing and the reading of seemingly endless feet of microfilmed records. She polished my prose, corrected historical inaccuracies, and undertook the proofreading and indexing. Without her help, the book would still be a messy sheaf of papers.

NOTES

CHAPTER 1

Alsop remarks from interview with author, May 1985. Tuchman quotation p. 278. Morgenthau conversations with Lord Lothian, Soong, Roosevelt, and Hull in *Morgenthau Diaries,* pp. 365–367. December 19 meeting of Roosevelt and his cabinet, and follow-up meeting on December 22, described in Langer and Gleason, *Undeclared War,* pp. 303–304; Schaller, *United States and China,* pp. 63–64; and Schaller, *U.S. Crusade in China,* pp. 74–75. Description of Corcoran in Seagrave, p. 366; quotations in Terkel, p. 319, and Nalty, pp. 33–34. Chennault quotations from *Way of a Fighter.* Morgenthau quotation on Currie in Schaller, *U.S. Crusade in China,* p. 55. Navy report on effects of oil embargo, and Ickes's reaction to it, discussed in Toland, *Rising Sun,* p. 108; Welles's and Hull's reactions in *Morgenthau Diaries,* pp. 377, 380. July 23, 1941, telegram from Currie to Chennault in Chennault papers. Information on organization and training of First American Volunteer Group and preparation for Second American Volunteer Group in Chennault papers.

CHAPTER 2

Descriptions of Chennault in Wedemeyer, p. 202; Curie, pp. 395–397; Copp, *A Few Great Captains,* pp. 105, 259, 321, 322; Boyington, p. 40; Greenlaw, pp. 95–96, 105, 181; Sevareid, p. 332; Tuchman, p. 474; Scott, *Flying Tiger,* pp. 27–28, 149; Scott, *Boring a Hole,* p. 127; White, pp. 138–139; and various oral histories and interviews with the author. Chennault quotations from *Way of a Fighter.* Frillman quotations pp. 19, 62–63. Chennault's uniform described in Greenlaw, p. 154. The influenza story in Nalty, p. 7. Chennault's letter to his father quoted in

Hotz, p. 54; the "Pop Chennault" quotation in Hotz, p. 58. Seagrave quotation on the Soong sisters, p. 8.

CHAPTER 3

Chennault quotations from *Way of a Fighter.* Westover quotation in Craven and Cate, pp. 64–65. Chennault quotation on aerial bombardment in Hotz, p. 69; Curry quotation on Chennault in Hotz, p. 60. The "sense of persecution" quotation in Tuchman, p. 277. Information on the "Three Men on the Flying Trapeze," Chennault's invitation to China, and the letter to the Montgomery *Advertiser* provided by Sebie Biggs Smith. Additional information from Mrs. Billy McDonald.

CHAPTER 4

Chennault quotations from *Way of a Fighter.* Information on the Japanese invasion of China in Stanley, especially pp. 26, 95, 106. The story of Donald in Selle. Stilwell quotation on Madame Chiang in Tuchman, p. 245; on Chiang, p. 475. White quotations pp. 74, 136–137. Description of Chiang in Seagrave, p. 157. Japanese bombing tonnage and aircraft losses in Caidin, *Ragged, Rugged Warriors,* pp. 59, 96; International Squadron in Caidin, pp. 72–73, 86–87. Smith quotations from letters and interviews with Sebie Biggs Smith. Neutrality laws discussed in Schaller, *U.S. Crusade in China,* p. 69, and Utley, p. 11. Chennault letter to newspaper in Hotz, pp. 82-83; Art Chen story in Hotz, p. 86. Greenlaw quotation p. 20. Okumiya quotation in Okumiya and Horikoshi, pp. 61–62. Rolfe Watson telegram courtesy of Mrs. Rolfe Watson.

CHAPTER 5

Chennault quotations from *Way of a Fighter.* Personal experiences and recollections of AVG personnel (e.g., Burgard, Donovan, Howard, Keeton, Mott), as attributed, from various letters, unpublished diaries, oral histories, and interviews; see also Cornelius and Short, pp. 104, 105, 114; Hotz, pp. 121, 144, 167, 212. Bond quotations and experiences in Bond and Anderson, pp. 20–26, 35, 47, 76, 97, 98, 152. Boyington quotations and experiences pp. 16, 20, 21, 102. Frillman quotations and experiences pp. 56–60, 68. R. M. Smith quotations and experiences pp. 16–20, 118–119. R. T. Smith quotations and experiences, p. 46. Greenlaw quotations pp. 30–31, 45, 46, 80, 118. "Most undisciplined outfit" quotation in Scott, *Flying Tiger,* p. 57. CAMCO contract, employment terms, AVG disciplinary actions, and various memoranda in Chennault papers.

CHAPTER 6

Chennault quotations from *Way of a Fighter.* Greenlaw quotations and experiences pp. 17, 32, 38–44, 61. Alsop remarks from interview with author. Howard remarks from interview with author. Boyington quotations pp. 40–43. Pentecost quotation in Nalty, p. 48. R. M. Smith quotations pp. 23–24. R. T. Smith quotations pp. 98, 121–122. Frillman quotations pp. 70–71, 85–86. Bond quotations in Bond and Anderson, pp. 44, 46, 51. Scott quotations in *Boring a Hole,* p. 129. Hill quotation in Cornelius and Short, p. 120. Currie quotation in Utley, p. 135. Recollections of Mott and Keeton from various unpublished diaries and oral histories. AVG training described in Hotz, pp. 112–115. Cables between Chennault and China Defense Supplies in Chennault papers; cables from Alsop on behalf of AVG in Chennault papers; uncensored newspaper stories on AVG in Chennault papers.

CHAPTER 7

Chennault quotations from *Way of a Fighter.* Bond quotations in Bond and Anderson, pp. 52–68. Frillman quotations pp. 88, 91. Greenlaw quotations pp. 71–72, 86–87, 89, 94. Boyington quotations pp. 49, 50. R. M. Smith quotations pp. 46–49. R. T. Smith quotations pp. 3, 160, 165. Recollections of Burgard, Keeton, Olson, and others from various unpublished diaries, oral histories, and interviews; see also Hotz, pp. 16–22, 37–44, 124. Knox remark to Soong quoted in Seagrave, p. 374. "Megwa fegur" quotation in Toland, *Flying Tigers,* p. 56. Cables between Chennault and China Defense Supplies in Chennault papers; general operational information on AVG in Chennault papers.

CHAPTER 8

Chennault quotations from *Way of a Fighter.* Cables and other correspondence between Chennault and CDS, and between Chennault and Pawley, in Chennault papers; general operational information on AVG in Chennault papers. "*Fei Weing*" and Radio Tokyo quotations in Hotz, pp. 22, 126. Bond quotations and experiences in Bond and Anderson, pp. 63–76, 83–99, 115. Boyington quotations and experiences, pp.

53-67, 146. Greenlaw quotations and experiences pp. 98, 114–123, 130. Recollections of Burgard, Keeton, Wright, and others from various unpublished diaries, oral histories, and interviews; see also Cornelius and Short, pp. 137–140; Hotz, pp. 128–130. Foster-Petach story in Hotz, p. 141. Mihalko story in Toland, *Flying Tigers,* p. 76. Churchill quotation in Hotz, p. 152.

CHAPTER 9

Chennault quotations from *Way of a Fighter.* Bond quotations and experiences in Bond and Anderson, pp. 91–108, 120–129. Frillman quotations and experiences pp. 114–133. Greenlaw quotations and experiences pp. 128–131, 154–155, 213; also unpublished diary. Boyington quotations and experiences pp. 73–80. Recollections of Burgard, Donovan, Keeton, and others from various unpublished diaries, oral histories, and interviews. Fox–Sandell conversation in Hotz, p. 158. Description of Rangoon in Whelan, pp. 137–138. Madame Chiang's remarks in *China Monthly,* April 1942. Cables and other correspondence between Chennault and CDS, and between Chennault and Madame Chiang, in Chennault papers.

CHAPTER 10

Chennault quotations from *Way of a Fighter.* White quotations p. 139. R. M. Smith quotations and experiences pp. 85, 106. Bond quotations and experiences in Bond and Anderson, pp. 132–150. Boyington quotations and experiences pp. 98–110. Frillman quotations pp. 127, 139. Greenlaw quotations pp. 252, 284. Recollections of Olson, Keeton, Burgard, and others from various unpublished diaries, oral histories, and interviews. Material on Stilwell from Tuchman and *Stilwell Papers.* Newkirk story in Hotz, p. 199. Brereton remarks in Nalty, p. 118. "Piss on you" story in Spector, p. 349. Cables between Chennault and Madame Chiang in Chennault papers; Chennault correspondence in Chennault papers; silver star story in Chennault papers.

CHAPTER 11

Chennault quotations from *Way of a Fighter.* R. T. Smith quotations and experiences pp. 282–285. Greenlaw quotations pp. 248–250, 283–284. Frillman quotations and experiences pp. 140–159. Bond quotations and experiences in Bond and Anderson, pp. 152–167, 177–179. Boyington quotation p. 110. Recollections of Keeton, Burgard, Olson, Donovan, and others from various unpublished diaries, oral histories, and interviews. Paxton quotation in Hotz, p. 216. Hill quotation in Cornelius and Short, p. 153. Cables in Chennault papers.

CHAPTER 12

Chennault quotations from *Way of a Fighter*. Bond quotations and experiences in Bond and Anderson, pp. 179–200. Greenlaw quotations pp. 236, 305. Frillman quotations and experiences pp. 158–163. R. T. Smith quotation p. 342. Recollections of Keeton, Burgard, Olson, and others from various unpublished diaries, oral histories, and interviews. Rector-Hill conversation in Toland, *Flying Tigers*, p. 119. Chennault remarks on Bissell quoted in Scott, *Flying Tiger*, p. 75. Chennault-Belden conversation in Hotz, p. 258. Chennault correspondence in Chennault papers.

CHAPTER 13

Chennault quotations from *Way of a Fighter*. Bond quotations in Bond and Anderson, pp. 209, 222. Robert M. Smith quotations pp. 109–110. Information and quotations on Stilwell from Tuchman, pp. 398, 431, 432, 482, 585–586, 643; see also Schaller, *U.S. Crusade in China*, pp. 136–137. Chennault conversation with White in White, p. 142; White's recollections of Kweilin p. 173. Recollections of Keeton and others in various unpublished diaries, oral histories, and interviews. Wedemeyer quotations p. 327 and letter to author. Navy Department support for Chennault in Schaller, *U.S. Crusade in China*, p. 134. Morgenthau quotation in Schaller, *United States and China*, p. 85. Arnold quotation in Coffey, *Hap*, p. 300. Arnold's letter on Chennault's retirement in Spence, p. 240. Anna Chennault's recollections from *The Education of Anna*. Chennault quotation on the Communists in Manchester, p. 634. Chennault's 1949 lobbying for a volunteer air force in Schaller, *United States and China*, p. 118, and *American Occupation*, p. 183. Information on CID investigations in Chennault papers; DSM citation in Chennault papers.

BIBLIOGRAPHY

Bond, C. R., Jr., and Anderson, T. H. *A Flying Tiger's Diary*. College Station: Texas A&M University Press, 1984.

Boyington, G. *Baa Baa Black Sheep*. New York: G. P. Putnam's Sons, 1958.

Brereton, L. *The Brereton Diaries*. New York: William Morrow, 1946.

Caidin, M. *Barnstorming*. New York: Duell, Sloan and Pearce, 1965.

Caidin, M. *The Ragged, Rugged Warriors*. New York: E. P. Dutton, 1966.

Chennault, A. *A Thousand Springs: The Biography of a Marriage*. New York: Paul S. Eriksson, 1962.

Chennault, A. *Chennault and the Flying Tigers*. New York: Paul S. Eriksson, 1963.

Chennault, A. *The Education of Anna*. New York: Times Books, 1980.

Chennault, C. L. *Way of a Fighter*. New York: G. P. Putnam's Sons, 1949.

Coffey, T. M. *Hap: Military Aviator*. New York: Viking Press, 1982.

Coffey, T. M. *Iron Eagle: The Turbulent Life of General Curtis LeMay*. New York: Crown Publishers, 1986.

Copp, D. S. *A Few Great Captains: The Men and Events That Shaped the Development of U.S. Air Power*. Garden City, N.Y.: Doubleday, 1980.

Copp. D. S. *Forged in Fire: Strategy and Decisions in the Air War over Europe, 1940–1945*. Garden City, N.Y.: Doubleday, 1982.

Cornelius, W., and Short, T. *Ding Hao: America's Air War in China, 1937–1945*. Gretna, La.: Pelican, 1980.

Craven, W. F., and Cate, J. L. *The Army Air Forces in World War II. Vol. 1. Plans and Early Operations, January 1939 to August 1942*.

[U.S. Office of Air Force History.] Chicago: University of Chicago Press, 1948.

Crozier, B. *The Man Who Lost China*. New York: Scribner's, 1976. (A biography of Chiang Kai-shek.)

Curie, E. *Journey among Warriors*. Garden City, N.Y.: Doubleday, 1943.

Dallek, R. *Franklin D. Roosevelt and American Foreign Policy, 1932– 1945*. New York: Oxford University Press, 1979.

Fairbank, J. K. *The United States and China*, 4th ed. Cambridge, Mass.: Harvard University Press, 1983.

Frillman, P., and Peck, G. *China: The Remembered Life*. Boston: Houghton Mifflin, 1968.

Greenlaw, O. S. *The Lady and the Tigers*. New York: E. P. Dutton, 1943.

Gunther, J. *Inside Asia*. New York: Harper, 1942.

Hotz, R. B. *With General Chennault: The Story of the Flying Tigers*. New York: Coward-McCann, 1943. Reprint, Washington, D.C.: Zenger, 1980.

Kimball, W. F., ed. *Churchill and Roosevelt: The Complete Correspondence. Vol. 2. Alliance Forged, November 1942–February 1944*. Princeton, N.J.: Princeton University Press, 1984.

Langer, W. L., and Gleason, S. E. *The Challenge to Isolation: 1937– 1940*. New York: Harper, 1952.

Langer, W. L., and Gleason, S. E. *The Undeclared War, 1940–1941*. New York: Harper, 1953.

Manchester, W. *American Caesar: Douglas MacArthur, 1880–1964*. Boston: Little, Brown, 1978.

Morgenthau, H. *From the Morgenthau Diaries: Years of Urgency, 1938–1941*. Edited by J. M. Blum. Boston: Houghton Mifflin, 1965.

Nalty, B. C. *Tigers over Asia*. New York: Elsevier-Dutton, 1978.

Okumiya, M., and Horikoshi, J. *Zero!* New York: E. P. Dutton, 1956.

Pilots Manual for Curtiss P-40. Appleton, Wisc.: Aviation Publications, n.d. (reprint).

Pistole, L. M. *The Pictorial History of the Flying Tigers*. Orange, Va.: Moss, 1981.

Pogue, F. C. *George C. Marshall. Vol. 2. Ordeal and Hope, 1939– 1942*. New York: Viking Press, 1965.

Romanus, C. F., and Sunderland, R. *United States Army in World War II: The China–Burma–India Theater. Stilwell's Mission to China*.

Washington, D.C.: Department of the Army, Office of the Chief of Military History, 1952.

Rosbert, C. J. *Flying Tiger Joe's Adventure Story Cookbook.* Franklin, N.C.: Grant Poplar Press, 1985.

Sakai, S. *Samurai!* New York: E. P. Dutton, 1957.

Schaller, M. *The U.S. Crusade in China: 1938–1945.* New York: Columbia University Press, 1979.

Schaller, M. *The United States and China in the Twentieth Century.* New York: Oxford University Press, 1979.

Schaller, M. *The American Occupation of Japan: The Origins of the Cold War in Asia.* New York: Oxford University Press, 1985.

Scott, P. D. *The War Conspiracy: The Secret Road to the Second Indochina War.* Indianapolis: Bobbs-Merrill, 1972.

Scott, R. L., Jr. *Flying Tiger: Chennault of China.* Garden City, N.Y.: Doubleday, 1959.

Scott, R. L., Jr. *Boring a Hole in the Sky.* New York: Random House, 1961.

Seagrave, S. *The Soong Dynasty.* New York: Harper & Row, 1985.

Selle, E. A. *Donald of China.* New York: Harper & Row, 1948.

Sevareid, E. *Not So Wild a Dream.* New York: Alfred A. Knopf, 1946.

Smith, R. M. *With Chennault in China: A Flying Tiger's Diary.* Blue Ridge Summit, Pa.: TAB Books, 1984.

Smith, R. T. *Tale of a Tiger.* Van Nuys, Calif.: Tiger Originals, 1986.

Spector, R. H. *Eagle Against the Sun: The American War with Japan.* New York: Free Press, 1985.

Spence, J. *To Change China: Western Advisers in China, 1620–1960.* Boston: Little, Brown, 1969.

Stanley, R. M. *Prelude to Pearl Harbor: War in China, 1937–41.* New York: Scribner's, 1982.

Stilwell, J. W. *The Stilwell Papers.* Edited by T. H. White. New York: William Sloane, 1948.

Terkel, S. *The Good War: An Oral History of World War Two.* New York: Pantheon, 1984.

Toland, J. *The Flying Tigers.* New York: Random House, 1963.

Toland, J. *The Rising Sun: The Decline and Fall of the Japanese Empire, 1936–1945.* New York: Random House, 1970.

Tuchman, B. W. *Stilwell and the American Experience in China, 1911–45.* New York: Macmillan, 1971.

Utley, J. G. *Going to War with Japan, 1937–1941.* Knoxville: University of Tennessee Press, 1985.

Wedemeyer, A. C. *Wedemeyer Reports!* New York: Devin-Adair, 1958.

Whelan, R. *The Flying Tigers: The Story of the American Volunteer Group*. Garden City, N.Y.: Doubleday, 1942.

White, T. H. *In Search of History: A Personal Adventure*. New York: Harper & Row, 1978.

White, T. H., and Jacoby, A. *Thunder Out of China*. New York: William Sloane, 1946.

Wings Over Asia: A Brief History of China National Aviation Corporation. China National Aviation Association Foundation, 1971 (pamphlet).

INDEX

INDEX